The War Against
the Amazons

The War Against the Amazons

Abby Wettan Kleinbaum

New Press

McGraw-Hill Book Company

New York   St. Louis   San Francisco   Bogotá
Guatemala Hamburg Lisbon Madrid Mexico Montreal Panama
Paris   San Juan   São Paulo   Tokyo   Toronto

1 2 3 4 5 6 7 8 9 DOCDOC 8 7 6 5 4 3 2

ISBN 0-07-035033-7

LIBRARY OF CONGRESS CATALOGING IN PUBLICATION DATA

Kleinbaum, Abby Wettan.
  The War against the Amazons.
  Bibliography: p.
  Includes index.
  1. Amazons. 2. Amazons in literature.
  3. Sex role. I. Title.
  HQ1139.K57   305.3   82–7781
  ISBN 0–07–035033–7

Book design by Victoria Wong

To the living memory of Joan Kelly.
She was the Amazon of us all.

Acknowledgments

I owe this book to my first History of Women students at Manhattan Community College back in the spring of 1972, who begged me to tell them if women had ever been powerful and set me in search of the Amazons. What I found instead of ferocious warriors was a male-created myth of extraordinary longevity and resilience. I set about an investigation of almost a decade, to see what men, and later, women, had been saying about themselves when they recounted Amazon legends. I have selected just a few of the myths from the enormous volume of literature and art dealing with Amazons in Western culture. My feminism and my training as a historian of ideas shaped the questions I brought to this material. A psychologist or an anthropologist would have written a different book.

In charting *The War Against the Amazons*, I benefited from the help, suggestions, and advice of many friends old and new, as well as perfect strangers who were willing to share their expertise. Throughout my work on this project I was helped enormously by being able to bounce ideas off my former mentor and dear friend, Joan Kelly. She read and criticized large portions of the manuscript. Other readers were Phyllis Stock, Scott Morton, Eleanor Riemer, Marilyn Arthur, Tamara Green, Francis Jennings, Gloria Levitas, Elizabeth A. R. Brown, and Louis Hammer. The Medieval Research group of the Institute for Research in History was kind enough to devote a meeting to critique the "Sword of Vengeance" chapter. I had the privilege, early in the project, of presenting some preliminary ideas at a meeting of the

New York metropolitan chapter of the Coordinating Committee for Women in the Historical Profession. I received helpful suggestions from Patricia Mainardi and Natalie Zemon Davis, and consulted by phone with Dietrich von Bothmer and William Fenton. I was also fortunate to have as a resource the cinema expertise of my colleague Roger Dooley, the photocopying machine so generously shared by my friends Tage and Betsy Anderson, and the record collection of my friend David Chertok, who may have the only viable recording of *By Jupiter* in New York. And finally, Bonnie Anderson read the entire manuscript and offered many useful insights and suggestions.

I enjoyed the research facilities of the New York Public Library where Sheila Curl of the Rare Book Room found some illustrations for me. I also worked at Columbia University, the City University of New York Graduate Center, SUNY Albany, and the New York State Education Department libraries. I am grateful to Debby Edel and Joan Nestle for permitting me to consult the Lesbian Feminist Archives. Over the past decade I have cherished the help and good spirits of my husband, my parents, and my mother-in-law, for listening, proofreading, and providing invaluable childcare, and indeed supplying very nearly the support one could hope to have from a true community of Amazons.

Contents

The War Against
the Amazons

Introduction

The Amazon is a dream that men created, an image of a superlative female that men constructed to flatter themselves. Although men never invoked the Amazon to praise women, they described her as strong, competent, brave, fierce, and lovely—and desirable too. Like her modern day incarnation, Wonder Woman, her strengths and talents have a supernatural quality. She is therefore a suitable opponent for the most virile of heroes, and a man who has never envisioned harming a woman can freely indulge in fantasies of murdering an Amazon. The conquest of an Amazon is an act of transcendence, a rejection of the ordinary, of death, of mediocrity—and a reach for immortality. If the Amazon excels in military prowess, then the skill of the hero who defeats her is even more extraordinary. If she is beautiful and pledged to virginity, then the sexual power of the hero who wins her heart and her bed is without measure. If she builds powerful armies, strong cities, great stores of riches, then these serve as trophies for her male conquerors. To win an Amazon, either through arms or through love or, even better, through both, is to be certified as a hero. Thus men told of battling Amazons to enhance their sense of their own worth and historical significance.

For nearly three millennia, generation after generation of men in the West, champions all, have enlisted in the war against the Amazons. The opponents are mythical, but the battles are nonetheless real. Abundant works of literature and art bear witness to the powerful hold that a struggle against Amazons has had on the Western imagination since the days of Homer. Though wounded, battered, defeated, and overcome by the javelins of classical heroes, by the moral indignation of the Fathers of the Church and numberless Christian defenders, by the fantastic spells and powers of Renaissance heroes, and by the boldness and greed of the early modern conquistadors, Amazons lived on to emerge again and again in Western culture. They survived the rationalization and the co-optation of Enlightenment philosophes, the exorcism of nineteenth-century social scientists, and the historical explanations of twentieth-century thinkers. Even as Western sensibility changed, as it shifted from pagan to Christian, from rational to romantic, from critical to emotional, the image of a struggle against Amazons has remained a vital motif. Whether they have been envisioned as a threat to the classical polis or to the Christian soul, or a challenge to the right order of civilization, the seemingly incorrigible Amazons must be opposed and overcome as a fresh contest in every age. Every battle has its own special character, since the weapons that men have raised have varied over the course of time. But the tradition that men certify themselves as heroes by defeating superlative *women* has remained immutable.

Over the centuries, as men honed their weapons and built their arsenals, few women have grasped Amazon images. The reason lies in the fact that Western culture has been a theater in which men paint their visions and tell their dreams. There have been a few exceptions: Christine de Pisan's Amazon accounts in the late Middle Ages; the armed women of eighteenth- and nineteenth-century revolutionary France; the modern skilled horsewoman; and most significantly, the twentieth-century community of gay women which has claimed the Amazon as its own. While men of the modern age have attempted the strategy of understanding and explaining Amazons through elaborate psychological and historical theories, increasing numbers of women have opted to join them: they feel irresistibly drawn to the idea of Amazons. Its core is the image of a free and autonomous community of women, women functioning without the aid, direction, instruction, or authority of men. The Amazon woman exhibits the highest degree of courage, strength, martial prowess, and competence; she founds cities and states, and rules nations. Through the Amazon idea there is a glimpse of women as builders of civilization.

But many women approach the Amazon with caution and insist on taking a long pause for reflection. The Amazon is, after all, a dream with a past, a vision originated by men. As surely as no spider's web was built for the glorification of flies, the Amazon idea was not designed to enhance women, but to serve the needs of its male creators. It is not difficult to understand why many women want to know exactly where the Amazon has been.

This book is an attempt to investigate the long war against the Amazons. Its data are not mythical women, but the artistic and literary artifacts of Western culture that document the long struggle against them. It is not a survey of dead Amazons, but of the high endeavors for which the imaginary women were sacrificed. It will reveal that in the characteristically human, and even commendable pursuit of excellence, men have often been marvelously silly.

The First Battle:
Greeks and Romans vs.
Amazons

Herodotus, the Father of History, begins one of his accounts with the casual reference, "in the war between the Greeks and the Amazons" (Bk. 4, 110).[1] He could safely assume that his audience knew all about the enmity between Greek and Amazon. The only additional information Herodotus's readers needed was *which* of the Greek-versus-Amazon conflicts he intended to serve as the starting point of his story, and he accomplished this by adding that his events begin after the Greek victory "at the River Thermodon." The classical reader would have immediately recognized this river in Asia Minor as the site of the Amazon capital Themiscyra where the great hero Heracles successfully accomplished one of his Labors. The ninth task in a series of a dozen extremely dangerous and almost impossible chores that Heracles was fated to carry out was the capture of the sacred girdle or sash of the Amazon queen. According to some versions of the legend, he took the Athenian hero Theseus with him to the Amazon state.

Herodotus himself told no details of the Greek victory; but later compilations of the story[2] say that after the battle, Heracles gave Queen Antiope her freedom in exchange for her armor and her girdle, but he gave her sister Hippolyta to Theseus, king of Athens, as a captive. Theseus is said to have married his Amazon and taken her with him to Athens, where she gave birth to Hippolytus, an extraordinarily handsome son.

But Herodotus's story concerned another result of the Greek victory. He wrote that the Greeks "sailed off in three ships with as many Amazons on board as they had succeeded in taking alive" (4. 110). Herodotus wrote that those three ships never reached Athens. The Amazons were able to overpower and murder their captors without great difficulty. But they had not the slightest knowledge of navigation. The women were aimlessly adrift, and were somehow carried by wind and wave to Lake Maoetis (Sea of Azov), in Scythian territory. The Amazons scrambled ashore right where their boats went aground and made their way inland until they came upon a herd of wild horses. Mounting the horses, they began to feel at home again, and they rode off "in search of loot" (4. 110).

If the tradition that made the Amazons Scythian women existed in Herodotus's day,[3] then he deliberately chose to ignore it, for he related that "the Scythians could not understand what was happening and were at a loss to know where the marauders had come from, as their dress, speech, and nationality were strange to them. Thinking, however, that they were young men, they fought in defense of their property, and discovered from the bodies which came into their possession after the battle that they were women" (4. 111). Herodotus wrote that this discovery led to a change in Scythian tactics. They sent some of their young men to camp within range of the Amazons, with orders to give ground if pursued, and then move near the women again. The motive behind this strange cat-and-mouse courtship was the Scythian desire "to get children by the Amazons" (4. 111).

For Herodotus, the assumption that Scythian men would be attracted to women addicted to plunder, slaughter, and treachery was a perfectly reasonable one. He discussed Scythian character at great length in Book 4 of his *Histories*. He reported that Scythians drank the blood of their enemies in cups fashioned out of the skulls of their hapless victims, wore cloaks made of the fine white hides they prepared from human scalps, and carried quivers made from the right hands of their enemies, with the fingernails remaining, perhaps as a decorative touch (4. 64–65). The Scythians were nomads, hunters, and horsemen, and they carried all their possessions on their wagons. They had no cities to burn, no monuments to destroy. They fought for love of war, booty, and conquest.

The Scythians were attracted to the women who suddenly appeared in their midst: "every day the two camps drew a little closer. Neither party had anything but their weapons and their horses, and both lived the same sort of life, hunting and plundering" (4. 112). Curiosity finally led to an intermingling of Scythians and Amazons, and from the first tentative friendships (developed through the use of sign language) there grew strong ties of love, "each man keeping as his wife the woman whose favor he had first enjoyed" (4. 114).

The Scythians told the women of their families and their property, and invited them to live among them as lawful wives. But Herodotus knew that the Amazons, as he envisioned them, could never live peacefully in a community of Scythian women. His Amazons answered the Scythians by citing their distaste for confinement on a nomad's wagon: "we are riders; our business is with the bow and the spear, and we know nothing of women's work: but in your country no woman has anything to do with such things—your women stay at home in their wagons occupied with feminine tasks, and never go out to hunt or for any other purpose. We could not possibly agree. . . ." (4. 114). Herodotus insisted that the Amazons were not totally uninterested in the Scythians' proposal. It was not marriage, but the prospect of having to behave as wives, that was abhorrent to them. They answered the men with a proposition of their own: "If . . . you wish to keep us for your wives and to behave as honorable men, go and get from your parents the share of property which is due to you, and let us go off and live by ourselves" (4. 114). The Scythians agreed to the Amazons' proposal, and each man claimed his share of his family's possessions. Then the entire group of newlyweds crossed the Tanais (Don), and traveled east for three days, and then north for three. And that, according to Herodotus, was the origin of the Sauromatian people.

This account explained for Herodotus and many of his contemporaries the differences they could observe among their northern neighbors. To understand the unfamiliar customs of the Sauromatian women, the Greeks had only to assume that these women "have kept to their old [Amazonian]

ways." These habits included "riding to the hunt on horseback sometimes with, sometimes without their menfolk, taking part in war, and wearing the same sort of clothes as
men . . ." (4. 117). The Amazonian heritage also accounted
for another remarkable Sauromatian custom: "they have a
marriage law which forbids a girl to marry until she has killed
an enemy in battle" (4. 117). Herodotus's observations appear
to be buttressed to some extent by the findings of Soviet
archaeologists. In investigating female burials in the Don
region, they have reported a relatively large percentage of
tombs containing weapons.[4] Herodotus's story also credited
the Amazons for inadvertently creating the Sauromatian
tongue: "the language of these people is Scythian, but it has
always been a corrupt form of it because the Amazons were
never able to speak it properly" (4. 117).

Thus Herodotus saw the formation of the Sauromatian
language and people as an incidental result of Heracles' and
Theseus's attack on the Amazon capital in Asia Minor. Herodotus also mentions the Amazons' supposed retaliation
against Athens, a mythical confrontation of great importance
in his day. In relating the events of the Persian Wars, he has
the Athenians vying with the Tegeans for the honor of oc-
cupying the left flank against the Persians in the combined
Greek effort against those very real foreign invaders. The
Athenians based their claim for this honor, Herodotus wrote,
by citing two victories against the Amazons: "at the River
Thermodon, and on the occasion of their inroad into Attica"
(9. 27).

Even though there may never have existed corroboration
of physical Amazon remains in Athens, the artistic and literary evidence of the Golden Age testify to the fact that an
Amazon attack on Athens, and a costly and hard-earned victory of Athenians over Amazons, was a major component of
classical consciousness in Athens as well as elsewhere in Greece.
The most complete surviving account of the Amazon siege of
Athens is the work of the biographer Plutarch written about
A.D. 100. His *Life of Theseus* relied heavily on the (now lost)
work of the fourth-century B.C. historian and glorifier of
Athens, Cleidemus. Cleidemus's book must have been very

full for Plutarch was able to render a battle description, replete with details on the dispositions of the right and left wings of the Amazonian as well as the Athenian armies.

Seven hundred years after the very real Persian conflagration, and fourteen hundred years after the supposed Amazon siege, the second-century Roman Pausanius wrote a travel guide for his contemporaries. It included a walking tour of Athens, and he described Amazon graves lining the side of a road leading from the citadel to the port of Piraeus. Modern scholars are unable to concur on what route Pausanius took on his tour, and the task of finding those graves, and many of the monuments both Pausanius and Plutarch described (the Amazonium, the Temple of the Furies, the Horcomosium), only taunts us with its futility. Athens has been a city rich in time and poor in space, and its many layers of history, enormous in weight, have crushed and obliterated the most distant past: any blood Amazons are supposed to have shed in Athens has blended with the dust and, like their bones, is gone.

Yet as Herodotus recorded, classical Athenians were very proud of the performance of their ancestors in this exploit, and Plutarch shared their view that the Amazon invasion "would seem to have been no trivial nor womanish enterprise" (*Thes.* 27. 1). Citing Hellanicus (a fifth-century b.c. author whose work does not survive), Plutarch claimed that the Amazons came to Athens with a formidable army, which made the entire journey from Themiscyra by land, crossing over the frozen Cimmerian Bosphorus, and marching through Thrace. Although Plutarch was skeptical about the ability of the women to make a journey of such length, he did not dispute the Amazon presence in Athens: "the fact that they encamped almost in the heart of the city is attested both by the names of the localities there and by the graves of those who fell in battle" (*Thes.* 27. 2).

Virtually all authors, whether they viewed the attack as myth or history, agreed that the Amazon motive was to avenge the theft of the girdle, the abduction of Princess Hippolyta, and the burning of Themiscyra by Theseus and/ or Heracles. There is a great deal of variation in the details

Phigaleia frieze from the Temple of Apollo, built by Ictinus, the architect of the Parthenon, late fifth century B.C. (*Courtesy Trustees of the British Museum*)

of their accounts. Plutarch suggested that the Amazons ventured alone, while both Justin (2. 4) and Diodorus (4. 28) have them joining forces with the Scythians. According to Diodorus, the Amazons returned with, and in effect dissolved into the Scythian people, while Justin depicted a falling out between Amazons and Scythians, with the Scythians abandoning the women before they gave battle to the Greeks.

According to Plutarch's story, the frightened Athenian king Theseus sacrificed to Fear, praying it would inflict the hearts of the Amazons. From the Delphic Oracle he received the advice to strike first, and so it was the Athenians who launched the first encounter. The various sources concur that the battle lasted several months, and that every foot of land taken or lost, captured or recovered, was paid for dearly with lives on both sides. Some related that Hippolyta, the Amazon wife or captive of Theseus, managed secretly to transport many wounded Amazons to Chalcis, where they recovered. According to Plutarch, those who did not survive were buried in a place in Chalcis called the Amazonium. A truce, in which Hippolyta may or may not have been instrumental in negotiating (Diodorus [4. 28] said she was already dead, killed by the Amazon Molpedia while she was fighting at Theseus's side), was finally worked out between Amazons and Athenians, and the Athenians built the Horcomosium, or Oath House, to commemorate the solemn promises exchanged.

The story of the attack on Athens by formidable warrior-women is an excellent example of how the Greeks, especially the Athenians, used the idea of combat with Amazons to enhance their own image and to reinforce their perception of themselves as historically significant. It was only because they had been so daring that the Amazons had chosen to attack them, and the Athenian victory was so great that, according to Plutarch and Pausanius, a major route to the acropolis of Athens was lined with Amazon tombs. After the Persians burned the citadel, and the finally victorious Athenians set about the task of rebuilding it, they adorned the major temple, the Parthenon, with relief sculptures depicting not combat with Persians, but combat with larger-than-life adversaries—centaurs, giants, and Amazons. Any plucky mortal could kill a Persian, but it takes a hero to triumph over an Amazon. To fight an Amazon was the greatest trial of male strength and courage, a challenge fit for a Heracles and a Theseus. All other conflicts paled before this struggle, and the legend that their ancestors of old had resisted the onslaught of these warrior-women was an everlasting source of civic pride for the Athenians.

It was the Athenian custom to hold a public funeral for all those who died defending their city. The concluding part of these ceremonies was a funeral oration, usually delivered by a speaker chosen for his distinction in public life. If in the unlikely event that Athenians held such a ceremony for those who supposedly fell fighting Amazons, that oration, like all literature that may have existed in the thirteenth century B.C., does not survive. But the deeds of the citizens who fought off the Amazon invaders are not unsung. The oldest extant funeral orations dating from the fifth century B.C., seven hundred years after the legendary attack, include praise for the earliest of Athenian heroes.

The funeral oration best known in classical times was the *Menexus* of Plato, which Plato ascribed to Socrates. According to Cicero (*Orator* 151) this speech was so popular it was read in public every year. Its theme was the strength and victories of the Athenians, from earliest times to Socrates' day. In praising his countrymen, Socrates (Plato) stated, "time would fail me to tell worthily of their defense of their country against . . . the Amazons and even earlier invaders."[5] The Amazons occupied a similar position in the fourth-century B.C. orations of Isocrates and Demosthenes.

Isocrates introduced the Amazon attack as historical fact in his *Panathenaicus* (193, 194,) giving as chief Amazon motives the recovery of Hippolyta and the taking of revenge against both Theseus and Hippolyta, since the women viewed Hippolyta's apparent love for Theseus and willingness to marry him and accompany him to Athens as a violation of Amazon law. So they set out to punish their errant princess and her newly adopted city. In his *Panegyricus* Isocrates emphasized that the Athenian response to the Amazon attack was swift and terrible: "for while Hellas was still insignificant, our territory was invaded . . . by the Amazons, the daughters of Ares [Mars]. . . . How great were the disasters which befell them is evident; for the tradition respecting them would not have persisted for so long a time if what was then done had not been without parallel. . . . We are told regarding the Amazons that of all who came not one returned again, while those who had remained at home were expelled from power because of their disaster here" (*Paneg.* 68). Thus the Athenians created a world safe from Amazons.

To Demosthenes also, the Athenian victory over attacking Amazons was a noble service for all Greeks: "they so prevailed over the invading host of Amazons as to expel them beyond the Phasis . . . [The Amazons were] invaders whom all those dwelling on our front to the westward neither withstood nor possessed the power to halt" (*Funeral Oration* 8).

For at least one fifth-century orator, the total destruction of Amazon power provided the occasion not only for pride in Athens, but also for the venting of misogyny. At the risk of denigrating his own ancestors, Lysias argued that the Amazons of old were really not all that formidable as opponents, but being the first people to mount horses and to use iron, they were able to take advantage of "the inexperience of their foes" (*Funeral Oration* 4). Using their great daring, the Amazons were able to strike terror in the hearts of their enemies and conquer all the nations around them: "they were accounted as men for their high courage, rather than as women for their sex" (*Funeral Oration* 4).

It was not until they invaded Athens, Lysias argued, that the Amazons confronted men of true courage. Lysias allowed the Amazons no motive for their attack on Athens: Theseus, and the abduction of an Amazon princess, are absent from his *Funeral Oration.* It was greed alone that led the Amazons to Athens, and to disaster: "having met with valiant men, they found their spirit now was like to their sex; . . . and by their perils rather than their bodies they were deemed to be women" (*Funeral Oration* 6). Athenians annihilated the Amazons, who "perished on the spot, and were punished for their folly, thus making our city's memory imperishable for its valour." But the Amazons "rendered their own country

nameless," for by "their unjust greed for others' land, [they]
justly lost their own" (*Funeral Oration* 6).

The convention of praising Athenians as being the first
people to dare to oppose the Amazons continued even into
Roman times, when Athens had long ceased to be a self-
ruling state, and Athenians were not citizens of Athens, but
subjects of Rome. The question of Athenian autonomy may
have become moot, but the issue of male dominance and the
proper ordering of sex roles was always relevant. Any story
of a clear male victory over Amazon attackers was too com-
fortably reassuring to die along with Athenian independence.

The second-century A.D. orator Aristides emphasized
that the Amazons were on the verge of complete control of
both Europe and Asia, until they confronted the Athenians:
"now from this point, as if a rope had broken, all snapped
back, and the Amazons' march of empire was undone. And
here too the city aided the whole race, and now it is doubtful
if Amazons ever existed" (*Panathenic Oration* 83–84). Only
because of the courage and the strength of the Athenians of
old are we permitted the luxury of doubting the existence
of Amazons.

In Athenian art, the Amazon theme played the same unify-
ing function as it did in oratory, with Amazonomachies (battles with Amazons) popular in reliefs, sculptures, and vase
paintings.

But the Athenians were not the first of the Greeks to em-
ploy Amazons in art. Heinrich Schliemann, the great amateur
archaeologist who discovered Troy, also made some spectacular finds on the Greek mainland, including the oldest known
Amazon representation. At Tiryns Schliemann found a fragment of a terra-cotta shield dating from the end of the eighth
or early seventh century B.C. depicting either Achilles or Heracles and an Amazon. Bronze reliefs depicting the same, and
dating from the late seventh and early sixth centuries, have
also been discovered.[6]

There are two waves of Amazon popularity in Athenian
art. The first is their sudden appearance in force on the vase
paintings of the mid-sixth century B.C.[7] The Amazons in
this group fight on foot and are equipped like Spartan sol-

diers. The scene is usually the battle at Themiscyra, and this group includes the only known representation of the Amazon capital in antiquity. The artist showed the gates of the city as crenellated battlements (somewhat evocative of medieval castles), with Amazons standing guard close by.[8]

The second wave of Amazons, however, are not defending their own city; they are attacking Athens. In the middle of the fifth century B.C. scantily clad Amazons on horseback fighting nude Greek footsoldiers are prominent on Athenian vases. Dietrich von Bothmer argues that these new Amazons are the result of the artistic influence of the various works adorning the newly constructed acropolis of Athens, which included Amazonomachies, by the painter Micon and the sculptor Phidias.[9] Under the leadership of the statesman and general Pericles, the Athenians summoned the best artistic talent available to replace the old citadel that had been destroyed during the Persian Wars. Amazons played an important role as subjects in these new creations.

On the now almost obliterated frieze on the west side of the Parthenon, Phidias sculpted in marble mounted long-haired Amazons in combat with nude Greeks. But when he carved the shield of Athena Parthenos he was unable to maintain his artistic detachment. So strong was his identification with the struggle against Amazons that, according to Plutarch, "when he wrought the battle of the Amazons on the shield of the goddess, he carved out a figure that suggested himself as a bald old man lifting on high a stone with both hands, and he also carved a very fine likeness of Pericles fighting an Amazon" (*Per.* 31). This bid for everlasting renown for himself and his patron helped to bring about his imprisonment and death. However, before his demise, Phidias executed relief carvings of Amazons on the throne and also on the footstool of the cult image of Zeus at Olympia. According to the first-century author Pliny the Elder (*HN* 31. 19), Phidias came in second in a contest held by the priests of Ephesus for the best bronze representation of an Amazon to stand in the Temple of Ephesus.

The first-century geographer Strabo (*Geog.* 2. 5.4) mentions but does not subscribe to the tradition that Amazons

founded the city of Ephesus. This same tradition would link
Amazons with the worship of Artemis, whose cult was cen-
tered at Ephesus. The second-century master of travelogue,
Pausanius, claimed that the Amazons had not founded, but
worshipped at Ephesus, first when fleeing from Dionysus in
the very distant past, then again when they were on the run
from Heracles, and finally when they were en route during
their Athenian campaign. Whether as founders or as wor-
shippers, the association of Amazons with the city of Ephesus
was a very ancient one, making the artistic competition plausible.[10] None of the original bronze entries survives, but three
types of Amazon statues are preserved in marble copies, including that of the reputed winner of the competition, Polyclitos, and those of Phidias and Cresilas.

All three surviving types depict an Amazon in a short tunic,
with one breast bared.[11] Whether Phidias's Amazons on the
Parthenon reliefs also bared one breast is difficult to tell,
because they are now so badly defaced even the sex of the
riders cannot be easily determined. But the fragments of
marble copies of his shield of Athena Parthenos also show
the Amazons with one breast exposed, and the other draped,
but fully articulated.[12] There was no Hellenic artistic or
literary tradition that Amazons removed or suppressed one
breast. Such stories begin to appear only in Hellenisitc or
Roman literature.[13] But the Hellenic artistic tradition
showing Amazons with one breast bared exerted an influence
on later literature. It became a convention, especially with
Roman authors, that Amazons ride into battle with a single
breast exposed. This was a symbol of their combat readiness
and a titillating detail for those hearing the accounts of the
struggle.

The painter Micon created frescoes of Amazons battling
on horseback, which adorned the Temple of Theseus[14] and
the Painted Stoa in the Athenian acropolis. The frescoes
themselves are gone and survive only in the scanty literary
descriptions of Aristophanes (Lys. 678–9), Pausanius (1. 15.2),
and Arrian (Anab. 7. 13.6). We are told that his Amazons
were mounted, and perhaps like those of the vase paintings
of this period, wore Oriental trousers and jerseys in the

Wounded Amazon. Marble copy of bronze original, thought to be by Polyclitos or Cresilas, fifth century B.C. *(Courtesy The Metropolitan Museum of Art, Gift of John D. Rockefeller, Jr., 1932)*

Battle of Greeks and Amazons. Fragment of frieze from the Mausoleum at Halicarnassus, ca. 350 B.C. (*Courtesy Trustees of the British Museum*)

Persian, Thracian, or Scythian style under armor, with a pointed Phrygian cap, lappets flying over the ears.

Elsewhere in Greece, Amazons adorned the Athenian treasury at Delphi, the frieze of the Temple of Apollo at Bassae, and the throne and footstool of the statue of Zeus at Olympia. The popularity of Amazonomachies in Greek art reflects a general trend in Greek culture, for Amazons appear frequently in the literature as well. They are not the dominant theme, but a significant one. Amazons receive mention in the medical writings of the Hippocratic corpus, in the histories of Herodotus, and the philosophy of Plato. Amazons also figured in the poetry of Pindar and the tragedies of Euripides and Aeschylus. The latter in particular depicted them as dangerous: as manless and man hating. In his *Suppliant Maidens* (287), Aeschylus called them "flesh devouring," an epithet that can be explained only by the Greek connection of Amazons and Scythians, and the Greeks' worst fears of the latter, as evidenced by Herodotus in Book 4 of his *Histories*.

The Greeks did not take Amazons only as a source of fear and heroic struggle. Amazons also figured in Greek comedy. The only surviving comic work, however, with any reference to Amazons is the *Lysistrata* of Aristophanes. Its plot involves the seizure of the acropolis of Athens by war-weary Greek women, and is an obvious parallel to the mythical Amazon siege of the same citadel. In addition, Edmonds's study of the fragments of Attic comedy turns up several titles among the old and middle comic plays that obviously dealt with and featured Amazons.[15]

There was little danger in poking fun at Amazons because in the doling out of ridicule the passage of time creates a comforting cushion of safety. The Athenians of the fifth century B.C. could assuredly regard Amazons, if they ever existed at all, as having expired centuries before their own time. Or could they? A story of Hellenistic origin would portray the case quite otherwise.

In the middle of the first century before Christ, Diodorus Siculus told of a bizarre incident that reputedly happened to Alexander the Great in 323 B.C. in Hyrcania, an ancient province of northern Persia. The story appears to have predated Diodorus's time. Four hundred years later, the Roman, Quintus Curtius, following many authors before him, added additional embellishments to the account.

It seems that Thalestris, an Amazon queen whom these authors depicted as coming from the region of Themiscyra, conceived a desire to have sexual relations with Alexander. According to Diodorus, she was an extraordinary woman, even for an Amazon: "remarkable for beauty and for bodily strength . . . admired by her country women for bravery" (17. 77.1).

The authors agree that the queen left the bulk of her army at the frontier of Hyrcania and went forward to meet Alexander with a smaller body of three hundred women. For Diodorus, they were "Amazons in full armor" (17. 77.1). Quintus Curtius made their costume a bit less modest: "the clothing of the Amazons does not wholly cover the body; for the left side is nude as far as the breast, then the other parts of the body are veiled. However, the fold of the robe, which they gather in a knot, does not reach below the knee" (6. 5.27).

Why did Thalestris deviate from the legendary old Amazonian custom of random mating? For Diodorus, the answer was obvious: "Alexander had shown himself the greatest of all men in his achievements, and she was superior to all women in strength and courage, so that presumably the offspring of such extraordinary parents could surpass all other mortals in excellence" (17. 77.2–3). Thus it was the desire to mate with the world's most outstanding man that drove Thalestris over hundreds of miles into Alexander's camp, a distance great enough to cause Strabo to remark, "of the numerous historians, those who care most for the truth do not make this assertion," adding that, "the stories that have been spread far and wide with a view to glorifying Alexander are not accepted by all; and their fabricators were men who cared for flattery, rather than truth" (2. 5.4–5).

Quintus Curtius insisted, however, that Thalestris did make the journey, only to find after gazing at Alexander and "carefully surveying his person" (6. 5.29), that you cannot judge a king's appearance by his reputation. For the body of Alexander "did not by any means correspond to the fame of his exploits." But Thalestris was a practical woman, and she was determined to accomplish her mission. She just closed her eyes and continued her wooing. She won him by the promise to give him any male offspring resulting from their union, since her only interest lay in a female child. A son, even of Alexander, could make no claim on her attention and energy. Quintus Curtius marveled at "the passion of the woman, being as she was more keen for love than the king" (6. 5.30). Both sources agree that "thirteen days were spent in satisfying her desires." For an Amazon and an Alexander, even love assumes a heroic dimension.

But there was no issue from their union, and Thalestris is said to have died without creating the woman, who following her father's example, would have made the world her own. What did result from the supposed encounter was a controversy among the authors of antiquity as to whether such a moment in history ever occurred. Strabo argued that distance alone would make such a journey of a Themiscyrean queen unlikely. Strabo is one of the few authors of antiquity who doubted not only Thalestris, but also the very existence of Amazons. He did, however, faithfully and meticulously record all the Amazon stories associated with the places he described in his *Geography*. He based his doubts on the character of these stories:

> our accounts of other peoples keep a distinction between the mythical and historical elements; for the things that are ancient and false and monstrous are called myths, but history wishes for the truth, whether ancient or recent, and contains no monstrous element, or else only rarely. But as regards the Amazons, the same stories are told now as in early times, though they are marvellous and beyond belief. For instance, who could believe that an army of women, or a city, or a tribe, could ever be organized without men, and not only be organized, but even make inroads upon the territory of other people, and not only overpower the people near them to the extent of advancing as far as what is now Ionia, but even send an expedition across the sea as far as Attica? For this is the same as saying that the men of those times were women, and the women were men. (2.5.3–4)

Strabo's questions and doubts do not appear to have been widely shared. In his *Alexander* 46, Plutarch presented a long list of authors who spoke either for the possibility or impossibility of such a visit. He decided for the latter, his translator argues, because the incident is "poorly attested, not because Amazons do not exist. Disbelief in Amazons as such is a modern phenomenon."[16]

For Plutarch, the clinching argument against the affair of Alexander and Thalestris was the testimony of one of Alexander's generals who was with the king throughout the Persian campaign. When Lysimachus first heard the story of Alexander's supposed tryst with the Amazon queen, he "smiled gently and said: 'And where was I at the time?' " Plutarch adds, however, that "our belief or disbelief of this story will neither increase nor diminish our admiration for Alexander" (45. 2).

Plutarch's views were still echoing a generation after his death in Arrian's *Anabasis of Alexander*: "I do not myself think that the race of Amazons survived so long [as the time of Alexander]. . . . And yet I do not think it credible that this race of women, often mentioned by good authorities, never existed at all. . . ." (7. 13.5).

But it was not through tales of the love life of Alexander, but through accounts of the battles of the Trojan War, that the West best remembered Amazons. There is hardly a telling of the Troy story that does not devote a chapter or at least a verse to Penthesilea, the Amazon queen who came to fight on the Trojan side. As Western thinkers became increasingly pro-Trojan, following the example of Vergil and his hero, Aeneas, accounts of Troy's demise and the bitter struggles in its defense, already popular in Homer's day, became increasingly more important.

Arctinus of Miletus composed his epic *Aethiopis*, the earliest of the Troy accounts, to tell the story of the war including the Amazon participation in that struggle, perhaps as early as the lifetime of Homer. Homer mentioned Amazons twice in the *Iliad* (3. 189; 6. 186) but he did not tell of their arrival at Troy. His work ends with the death of the Trojan hero Hector: Arctinus continued the story, telling of Memnon, king of Ethiopia, and Penthesilea, Queen of the Amazons, coming to the aid of the Trojans in the last year of their doomed struggle.

Like the works of the other cyclic poets with the exception of Homer, Arctinus's epic survives only in insignificant fragments, and it is through the very brief summary of the fifth-century A.D. philosopher Proclus that we learn what Arctinus said of Penthesilea: "the Amazon Penthesilea, the daughter of Ares and of the Thracian race, comes to aid the Trojans and after showing great prowess, is killed by Achilles and buried by the Trojans. Achilles then slays Thersites for abusing and reviling him for his supposed love for Penthesilea."[17] The *Aethiopis* must have been extant through much of the classical age, and the story of Penthesilea's participation at Troy appears to have been widely known.[18] Diodorus Siculus (2. 46.5–6) and Justin (2. 4), as well as other authors, told the story. But the fullest surviving account of the Amazons at Troy is a fourth century A.D. version by Quintus, a Greek citizen of Smyrna, one of the cities the Amazons are reputed to have founded.

It is not possible to prove that Arctinus's work was still extant in Quintus's day, but Quintus's long epic, at least in its discussion of Penthesilea, conforms itself to the surviving crude summary that we do possess of the *Aethiopis*. Modern scholars argue that Quintus Smyrnaeus's epic reflects a world view that is quite different from both the sensibility of Homer's day and from that of classical Greece. Arctinus's *Aethiopis*, for example, has the foul-mouthed Thersites accuse Achilles of falling in love with the Amazon he killed. In Quintus Smyrnaeus's poem, Achilles is without question overcome by the passion of love and the grief of remorse for the dying Amazon. Dietrich von Bothmer finds neither romance nor regret in the classical representations of Achilles and Penthesilea, only scenes of intense combat.[19] It is only in later works, especially in the sarcophagi of Roman times, that the Amazon dies in the arms of the hero. Yet, in spite of the romanticism and emotionalism of his work, Quintus of Smyrna was essentially telling a story that dated back to Homeric times.

Quintus's story has Penthesilea dash into battle, refusing
to heed the warning of Hector's widow Andromache about
Achilles' prowess. Although the author intended no humor,
it is hard not to smile at his description of the Amazon queen
dressed for battle readiness. It was the war god Mars himself
who supplied Penthesilea with her sumptuous armor, made
of gold, silver, and ivory. Her costume included greaves, a
coat of mail, a breastplate, a shield, and last but not least, a
magnificent plumed helmet. She was also armed to the teeth.
According to Quintus, her left hand held the band of her
shield as well as two large javelins, and she carried a huge
double-headed axe in her right hand. Quintus would have
us believe that the queen could not only move with this equip-
ment, but also give battle and even prevail over dozens of
Greek heroes whom she left in the dust in agony, lying on
the corpses of their horses or their companions.

When she spied Achilles and Ajax, she aimed a javelin at
Achilles. Quintus has it bounce off his shield. As the furious
Amazon aimed another javelin at Ajax, she commenced a
battle of words:

> With my blood is mingled war!
> No mortal man begat me, but the Lord
> Of War, insatiate of the battle-cry.
> Therefore my might is more than any man's.
>
> (I. 570–74)

But her javelin only brushed against Ajax's leg greave, and
he laughed in scorn, leaving what he thought was an easy
prey to Achilles. Achilles boasted of his killing of Hector, and
said that if Penthesilea were a daughter of Mars, he was a
son of Cronos, invincible in battle. As he spoke he hurled a
spear, which pierced her right breast. She dropped her axe,
her eyes dimmed, and her life began to slip away.

As she spied Achilles about to drag her from her horse,
Quintus has her muse over whether she should beg for her
life ("for O, I long to live") (I. 610) or fight on and attempt
to strike with her sword. But the hero gave her time for
neither, for Quintus's Achilles impaled the Amazon atop her
horse with one long death-dealing spear. Quintus portrays

the fall of the queen and her mount as causing panic to run through the Trojan camp. As the warriors raced for the safety of the Trojan walls, Achilles stood over Penthesilea's body, gloating:

> In dust lie there
> A prey to the teeth of dogs, to raven's beaks,
> Thou wretched thing . . . it was the darkness
>   shrouded Fates
> And thine own folly of soul that pricked
>   thee on
> to leave the works of woman and to fare
> To war, from which strong men shrink shuddering
>   back.
>
> (I. 642–54)

But Quintus's story turns abruptly from a rough-and-tumble adventure narrative to a love tragedy of the most soul-wrenching intensity. As his hero bends down to despoil the Amazon of her gorgeous armor, his sentiments change entirely: according to Quintus, the Amazon had not neglected her grooming and her makeup. In the dirt and gore, Quintus has Achilles spy " 'neath dainty pencilled brows, a lovely face, lovely in death" (I. 658–59). The Greeks thronged to marvel at her corpse. In death, in blood, in dust, she was the model of womanly perfection. If we take the word of Quintus, each Greek silently prayed, as he gazed upon her,

> that fair and sweet like her their wives would seem,
> laid on the bed of love, when home they won.
>
> (I. 668–70)

A most profound remorse seized the heart of Achilles,

> who might have borne her home, his queenly
>   bride,
> To chariot-glorious Pythia; for she was
> Flawless, a very daughter of the Gods
> Divinely tall, and most divinely fair.
>
> (I. 672–74)

According to Quintus, the god of war did not take this killing lightly, for Mars rushed down from Mount Ida, causing the earth to tremble and smoke. With thunder and storm, with wind and rain, he threw his divine tantrum, until Zeus sent two thunderbolts to put him back in place.

Quintus's work appeared after several centuries of literature bearing witness to a strong Roman interest in the events of the Trojan War. But most of these earlier works focused on the Trojan prince Aeneas, the legendary founder of Rome, rather than the Amazon allies of Troy.

Romans liked to remember that even Homer had praised Aeneas. Centuries after Homer, but before the time of Vergil, Romans were reading the Trojan dramas that Livius Andronicus translated from Greek in the third century B.C. They also enjoyed the poetry and drama on Trojan themes by Naevius and Ennius. In the second century B.C. Pacuvius and Accius wrote Trojan dramas, and a lost work of the scholar Varro, *De Familiis Trojanis*, traced the lineage of many Roman noble families back to Trojan heroes.[20] It was these writers who elaborated on Homer's sketch of Aeneas, and who served as probable sources for Vergil. In the *Iliad*, Homer predicted that Aeneas would survive the bloody conflict and go on to rule the Trojans in a new nation. It remained for Vergil to complete the story of Aeneas in the *Aeneid*.

Vergil had a perspective from which Amazons could be seen, for the first time, as fighting on the correct side. If Romans embraced Trojans, how much more so could they have cherished Amazons, who came to the aid of Troy. If the Greeks found Amazons so awesome and formidable as foes, then how glorious could they have been to Romans, as allies of their ancestors.

But the theme of Amazons as allies failed to capture the imagination of Vergil. Instead, he secured the stature of his hero by giving Aeneas an Amazon opponent to overcome, just as the Greek heroes had to do. The *Aeneid* opens after the fall of Troy, and thus Vergil does not recount the noble story of the Trojans and their friends to save the city. Although it plays a very minor role in his epic, Vergil is not entirely ungrateful for the effort the Amazons made on behalf of Troy. In Book I Aeneas arrives at Carthage as its

queen, Dido, is supervising the decoration of a newly constructed shrine dedicated to Juno. She chose an artistic theme
that would remain popular for the next three millennia: the
fall of Troy. One of the painted scenes showed

> Penthesilea in her fury leads
> the ranks of crescent-shielded Amazons.
> She flashed through her thousands; underneath
> her naked breast, a golden girdle; soldier-
> virgin and queen, daring to war with men.[21]
>
> (693–97)

There is one other mention of Penthesilea in the *Aeneid*,
which is not particularly complimentary:

> . . . when Penthesilea,
> Mars' daughter, in her chariot returns,
> a victor, and with shrill and shrieking clamor
> other woman troops run wild with half-moon shields.
>
> (871–74)

Here Vergil is comparing the Amazon who defended Troy
to an Amazon entirely of his own creation: Camilla.

Vergil was conscious that he was creating in his *Aeneid* a
national, patriotic epic for Rome. In fact, it was Augustus
himself, the first emperor and creator of the Roman imperial
form of government, who urged Vergil to complete his poem,
and who, in violation of Vergil's will, prevented the destruction of the unfinished manuscript after the poet's death. So,
like Dionysus, Bellerophon, Heracles, Theseus, and Achilles,
Aeneas received an Amazon opponent. Yet Vergil seems to
have ignored the tradition that had made the Amazons phys-
ically attractive and desirable. His Camilla has no sexuality—
she is a special ward of the goddess Artemis (Diana), and as
such "she cherished an endless love of her arms and of virginity" (768–69). Like the goddess herself, Camilla is irrev-
ocably chaste. Not that it mattered to Aeneas. Vergil's hero
has not the slightest desire to imitate Theseus and marry a
conquered Amazon. It was not the men of Tuscany but their
mothers who admired Camilla, and "wanted her, in vain, as
a daughter-in-law" (768–69).

Much of what the Greeks had found so frightening in the

idea of Amazons was their manlessness: Amazons were supposed to be creators and perpetuators of a female community, which except for reproduction, was entirely separate
from the world of men. Vergil's Camilla, however, lacks this
female community. She is reared not by a strong and powerful Amazon mother, but by her father, Metabus, the de-
posed and hunted king of the Volscians, a hermit and a
misanthrope, an outcast from all human society.

Fleeing from the Volscians, who were enraged with his
tyranny, Metabus took his infant daughter with him in exile.
She is named Camilla, after her mother Casmilla—reminis-
cent, of course, of Hippolytus named for his Amazon mother
Hippolyta. Although the Greeks had much to tell us about
Hippolyta, Vergil has nothing to say about Casmilla in the
Aeneid. Camilla's mother is only a name.

Hounded by pursuers close by his heels, Metabus arrived
at the Amasenus River. It was swollen and roaring, storm-
tossed and flooding. In spite of his great strength, Metabus
feared he would lose Camilla if he attempted to swim across
with her. So he used a piece of bark to secure her to an
enormous javelin, and then, after dedicating the child to
Artemis, he hurled the javelin across the foaming waters to
the safety of the opposite bank. Swimming across the river,
he recovered Camilla unharmed.

Metabus nurtured her, placing the udders of wild mares
into her tiny mouth. Inexperienced as he was, he seemed to
possess all the wisdom of the Amazons in the field of child
rearing:

> As she took her first steps, he placed a pointed
> lance head within her hand, and from that little
> girl's shoulder he made a bow and quiver hang.
>
> (756–58)

He modeled her dress after the lion skin of Heracles: "in
place of golden hairbands and long robes/a tiger skin hangs
from her head and down her back" (759–60).

When Aeneas and his Trojans gave battle to the Latins,
Camilla led the Volscian troops on the Latin side. There is

no question of her identity: she fights "like an Amazon, one breast laid bare for battle" (855), a custom dictated by Greek artistic tradition. On the battlefield, Camilla wreaks havoc. All around her, she leaves men in agony, vomiting blood and gore, biting the dust with clenched teeth and dull eyes. But ultimately, Camilla falls. She has her father's great physical strength, but her strength and her virginity did not spare her from a woman's vulnerability. On the field she spies the ornate and elaborate purple and golden armor of the Trojan warrior Chloreus, and her fate is sealed.

Though Metabus had deliberately kept Camilla away from gold and finery, he failed to make her immune to what Vergil saw as woman's greatest weakness. She could not take her eyes off the costume of Chloreus, though Vergil leaves the reader to decide if her motive was "to hang up the Trojan arms in the temple,/or just to dress herself in captive gold" (1035–36). All the training her father gave her, the wild mares' milk and raw meat diet of her infancy, her keenly tuned senses, her skill at hunting, were to no avail. Her attention was distracted, and she acted only out of determination to win Chloreus's arms.

On the other hand, her killer, an Etruscan named Arruns, prayed to Apollo to give him the honor of striking down Camilla. His request was for renown and not for wealth: "I do not ask for spoils, nor for a trophy; I want no booty from the beaten virgin" (1050–51). Vergil makes his death wish for Camilla seem far nobler than hers for Chloreus. All Arruns wanted to do was to "fell the brutal plague" (1054) and then return to his city in glory. In the mind of Arruns, Camilla did not deserve an honorable death. Any death he could deal to her would be in the service of humanity. To Arruns's misfortune, Vergil has the winds scatter the second half of his wish so Apollo does not hear it.

Out of the cover of ambush, Arruns hurled his swift lance at Camilla. With her eyes fixed on the gold of Chloreus, she was virtually the only Volscian not to hear the missile's terrible hissing sound, until it had plunged deep into her breast. Thrilled, yet astonished by his success, Arruns never completed his escape. The goddess Artemis sent Opis, one of her

nymphs, to emerge and deal Arruns the same death he gave
Camilla.

And where was Aeneas? It was enough for Vergil that the
reputation of his hero's arms should have brought to him all
those renowned enemies. It was not necessary for him to give
direct battle to Camilla, nor does Camilla merit death by a
hero's hand. Just as many readers have found Aeneas somewhat wanting as a hero (his Homeric "piety" being one of
the dullest of virtues), Camilla, with her equally unexciting
virtue of virginity, is neither a heroine nor an Amazon of
outstanding quality.

However, not every Roman associated Amazons with virginity. In his *Art of Love*, the first-century poet Ovid compared
himself to the divine metalsmith Vulcan: he was arming the
lover who "by my steel shall lay low the Amazon" (6.744). A
master in the battle of the sexes, Ovid was proud of the
"armor" he presented to the novice: "Penthesilea must fall
before your steel" (*Rem. Am.* 676).

For Seneca, too, the struggle against an Amazon was sexual. Amazons were virgins, but extremely sensuous ones, whose
resolve was likely to yield before the strength and presence
of a true hero. Witness a choral remark in his *Hercules Furens:*
"there she (Hippolyta) who rules o'er tribes unwed, with a
golden girdle about her loins, stripped the glorious spoil from
her body, her shield and the bands of her snow-white breast,
on bended knee looking up to her victor (Heracles) . . ." (540–
46). However, in his *Hippolytus,* or *Phaedra,* Seneca has the
nurse account for Hippolytus's ability to resist Phaedra's advances by noting, "thou wouldst know him of Amazon breed"
(232). Seneca's character presented the idea that an Amazonian heritage gives a person the strength to sacrifice sexuality. But in trying to convince Hippolytus to accept Phaedra,
the same nurse argued, "look at thy mother's kingdom; those
warlike women feel the yoke of Venus" (575).

Roman interest in Amazons was never completely detached from their interest in Troy, and when Amazons appear in Roman literature, they are often a by-product of
Roman treatment of Trojan themes. Ovid's poetry abounds
in references to Greeks and Trojans who participated in the

Trojan War, and many of Seneca's plays deal with Trojan subjects. His contemporary, Dio Chrysostom, in his *Trojan Discourses*, retold the Troy story so much from the Trojan point of view that he tried to eliminate source information from Homer, on the (mistaken) idea that Homer favored the Greeks.

Though Dio Chrysostom's *Discourses* may have been written purely as a Sophist stunt to prove that you can argue anything if you argue well, they are important because they summarize an anti-Homeric tradition that dates back far in classical times, to the writings of Xenophon and Plato.[22] One of Dio Chrysostom's most serious charges against Homer is that Homer did not pay enough attention to the really important events, like the battle against the Amazons. In picking and choosing events and incidents, "Homer selected the more unimportant and trivial things and left to others the greatest and most impressive" (11. 33). In particular, "why did he not mention the expeditions of the Amazons and the battle between Achilles and the Amazon, which is said to have been so splendid and so strange?" (11. 31).

After accusing Homer of deliberate distortions, Dio Chrysostom advances a few of his own: Memnon the Ethiopian was a nephew of Priam (11. 1), Helen was never abducted and the Trojans did not cause the war (11. 47), Memnon and the Amazons came when Priam and Hector were winning the war, and the Greek force was all but destroyed (11. 114). Finally, the Greeks never won the war, but slipped away from Troy under a truce. Troy was never captured; her walls were partly dismantled to allow the Greek gift of the horse to be admitted: "hence the ridiculous story of the capture of the city" (11. 123).

It is difficult to understand Chrysostom's motive in asserting these variations on the epic cycle, other than to cast doubt and aspersions on Homer. But why change a story that Homer did not tell? Chrysostom appears to be the earliest source for the tradition that became popular in medieval literature: that it was Neoptolemus, or Pyrrhus, the son of Achilles, who killed Penthesilea, not Achilles himself. This hardly changes matters for Penthesilea, since both father and son were considered great heroes, and the finality of her death is the same in either case.

For all his embellishments on the Troy legends, Dio Chrysostom showed himself to be far less creative than a long succession of Roman rulers who envisioned themselves as engaged in the battle against the Amazons. In some cases these rulers saw themselves as fighting along with the Amazons. Caesar was the first ruler to call himself an Amazon, although he did so only in jest.

Suetonius reports that Caesar was so exhilarated when he received command of all of Gaul, he bragged "that having gained his heart's desire to the grief and lamentation of his opponents, he would therefore from that time, mount of their heads" (1. 22). To this reference to fellatio, one detractor responded with the insult, "this would be no easy matter for any woman." Caesar's response was to accept graciously the feminine designation, without giving up his boast of power. He proudly noted that "the Amazons in days of old held sway over a great part of Asia" (1. 22). And if military and sexual prowess are the same, as Caesar suggested, Amazons can mount.

The emperor Nero (reigned A.D. 54–68), touched perhaps by madness and certainly by a vivid poetic imagination, took up an opportunity that Vergil had ignored: glorifying Amazons as allies. He was perhaps the first Roman to focus on fighting alongside Amazons, as opposed to the Greek and sometime Roman obsession of fighting against them. Of course, the reality of Amazon supporters was not possible, since even if they ever had existed and some of them still survived, nobody had the slightest idea of where to find them. But Nero, master of theatrical art, was content with the illusion of Amazon supporters. According to Suetonius, when Nero was preparing his campaign to suppress an uprising in Gaul, one of his first cares was "to have the hair of his concubines whom he planned to take with him trimmed man-fashion, and to equip them with Amazonian axes and shields" (6. 44).

The reign of Commodus, more than a hundred years after Nero, marked the close of the Golden Age of Rome. The mad emperor Commodus did not want posterity to remember him as a friend of Troy and an ally of Amazons: he wanted to be remembered as an Amazon, an aspiration neither Vergil nor Nero had the boldness to conceive.

Dio Cassius, Commodus's contemporary, explains what the title "Amazonius" signified to Commodus: " 'Amazonius' and 'Exsuperatorius' he applied constantly to himself, to indicate that in every respect he surpassed all mankind superlatively" (83. 15.3–5). The use of the title Amazonius was also a means for Commodus to identify himself with Heracles, for as Harold Mattingly notes, Heracles triumphed over Amazons, and bore the title Amazonius. Commodus issued coins celebrating himself as the "Roman Heracles," as well as a medallion in A.D. 192 with himself on one side and an Amazon on the other.[23] Some scholars have argued that the Amazon on this medallion portrays Commodus's concubine, Marcia,[24] but it is clear that Commodus's association with Amazons was designed not to glorify Marcia, but himself. According to the Scriptores Historiae Augustae (*Comm.* 2. 8–9), when Commodus dressed Marcia as an Amazon, he, too, donned an Amazon costume, and even wished to enter the arena of Rome so attired.

To flatter Commodus, the Roman Senate renamed the month of December, Amazonius. And when Commodus participated in public games, he required the senators to shout, "Victor thou art, and victor thou shalt be, from time everlasting Amazonian, thou art victor" (S.H.A. *Comm.* 2. 8–9).

The actual identification of emperors and Amazons does not appear to have outlived the reign of Commodus. In the late third century Romans returned to the theme of battling Amazons. The emperor Aurelian proudly displayed captured Gothic women who were taken among the Goths with "a placard [which declared them] to be of the race of Amazons" (S.H.A. *Aurel.* 34. 1). Hence a laurel wreath for Aurelian, and, for the everlasting glory of mankind, another hero.

Amazons in Roman culture were more than an aberration of a few mad emperors and their zealous flatterers. Amazons enjoyed a widespread and deeply rooted popularity. In fact,

in the second and third centuries, Amazons were frequently
selected by wealthy Romans to adorn their sarcophagi and
other funerary monuments, usually in the form of Amazonomachies.

According to Carl Robert, the oldest of the Amazon sarcophagi dates from the late fourth or early third century B.C.
On this, as well as the others that have been discovered in Greece, the theme is an Amazonomachy, probably
of the Amazon attack on the Athens of Theseus. But most
of the Amazon sarcophagi were found in Rome or elsewhere
in Italy, and are of a later date.[25] The largest group is from
the second and third century A.D. They portray the Trojan
struggle between Achilles and Penthesilea, often including a
scene showing Achilles holding the dying Penthesilea. Adolf
Klügman noted the "wildness" and "liveliness" of these battle
scenes: "nowhere does one see so many slaughtered horses,
so many Amazons pulled down by the hair, or by the helmet,
as on these reliefs."[26]

Renaissance and Baroque artists studied these sarcophagi
carefully, and greatly admired their presentation of the struggle and action of fierce combat. Carl Robert argues that Rubens's famous seventeenth-century painting *The Battle of the
Amazons* (see coverleaf) is closely modeled on his sarcophagus
number 79.[27] A comparison of the two works, divided as they
are by fourteen hundred years, and fashioned of completely
different media, makes this assertion undeniable.

For many scholars it has been easier to explain the influence these sarcophagi exerted on later art and culture than
to explain the motive behind their creation. What has fighting
against Amazons to do with death? For some, these monuments are a disturbing factor, data which do not fit their
notion of the dignity and rationalism of the Roman world.[28]
Yet it is indisputable that a significant number of Romans
chose the theme of battling Amazons as the statement in
which they wanted to leave their remains.

The distinction of presenting the most absurd explanation
for this Roman "foible" belongs to the German-Swiss sociologist of the mid-nineteenth century, J. J. Bachofen. He
presents a convoluted theory in which live Amazons repre-

Achilles and Penthesilea sarcophagus, Roman second century A.D.
(*Courtesy Alinari/Editorial Photocolor Archives*)

Combat of Greeks and Amazons. Sarcophagus from Salonica, ca.
second century B.C. (*The Louvre, courtesy Cliché des Musées Nationaux*)

sent "dark, sterile, man-hating," but dying Amazons represent the fulfillment of the true feminine sublimity, which is recognized only in motherhood and death.[29]

Missing in Bachofen's theory, as well as in others that have been advanced since his day,[30] is the recognition that the Romans sought to identify not with dying Amazons but with the heroes who killed them. The warrior-women in the classical world represented the timeless and the transcendent, and it was the task of true heroes to overcome them, either through military valor or sexual prowess, or perhaps both. These were simply two different paths to the same victory. Between Greek and Amazon, and Roman and Amazon, the normal condition was war.

Notes

1. Herodotus, *The Histories,* trans. Aubrey de Selincourt (London: Penguin Books, 1959). All citations from Herodotus are from this edition.
2. Diodorus Siculus 4.16 and Justin 2.4. Citations from Justin are from *The History of the World,* trans. G. Turnbull (London: S. Birt & Dod, 1746). Unless otherwise stated, Greek and Latin sources are cited in Loeb Classical Library editions (London and Cambridge, Mass., William Heinemann and Harvard University Press).
3. Arctinus has the Amazons come from "the Thracian race," *The Aethiopis,* in *Hesiod and the Homerica,* Loeb Classical Library. Aeschylus has the Amazons descend from the Caucasus, *PV* 723–5.
4. See T. Sulimirski, *The Sarmatians, Ancient Peoples and Places* series, ed. Glyn Daniel, vol. LXXIII (New York: Praeger, 1970), pp. 35–60.
5. *Menexus,* 239b, from *The Dialogues of Plato,* trans. B. Jowett (Oxford: Clarendon Press, 1953), I, 686.
6. See Dietrich von Bothmer, *Amazons in Greek Art* (Oxford: Clarendon Press, 1957), pp. 1–5.
7. Ibid., p. 6.
8. Ibid., p. 14, pl. x.
9. Ibid., p. 163.
10. The stories of these earliest Amazons appear to be of Hellen-

istic origin. The best literary account is in Diodorus Siculus, 3. 52–72, which places them in Libya and depicts them as first opposing, then fighting along with Dionysus.

11. See Vagn Poulsen, *Die Amazone des Kresilas* (Bremen: Walter Dorn, 1957) for plates showing the three types of Amazon figures.

12. Bothmer, *Amazons in Greek Art,* pp. 208, 209–214, pl. lxxxviii.

13. Justin, a third-century author whose work is thought to be a Latin epitome of an earlier Greek work by Pompeius Trogus, derived the word *Amazon* from the women's supposed lack of a right breast (Bk. 2, ch. 4). But Justin's translation was probably erroneous because the word is not thought to be of Greek origin. In a variety of tongues it can mean anything from breastless to breadless, eaters of strong foods, etc. Many late classical and medieval authors followed Justin's theory.

14. Bothmer notes that the attribution of the Theseion to Micon can only be conjectured, *Amazons in Greek Art,* p. 163.

15. John Maxwell Edmonds, ed. and trans., *The Fragments of Attic Comedy,* 3 vols. (Leiden: E. J. Brill, 1957–1961), I, 10008, II, 659.

16. These remarks appear in *Diodorus of Sicily,* trans. C. H. Oldfather, Loeb Classical Library (1967), VIII, pp. 340–41 n. 1.

17. Proclus's summary of the *Aethiopis* of Arctinus is in the Loeb Classical Library edition of *Hesiod and the Homerica* (1967), p. 507.

18. Thomas Day Seymour notes that some of the oldest manuscripts of the *Iliad* mentioned in various scholia were extended and included a last verse telling of Penthesilea's arrival at Troy. *Life in the Homeric Age* (New York: Macmillan, 1907), p. 628.

19. Bothmer, *Amazons in Greek Art,* p. 148.

20. See Margaret R. Scherer, *The Legends of Troy in Art and Literature* (New York: Phaidon, 1963), p. 221.

21. *The Aeneid of Virgil,* a verse translation by Allen Mandelbaum (New York: Bantam Books, 1971), p. 18. Copyright ©1971 by Allen Mandelbaum. All rights reserved. Used by permission of Bantam Books, Inc. All citations from Virgil are from this edition. (Throughout my text I have used the traditional spelling Vergil.)

22. See Xenophon *Mem.*; Plato *Resp.*, bk. 10.

23. See Harold Mattingly, *A Catalogue of Coins of the Roman Empire in the British Museum, IV, Antonius Pius to Commodus* (London: Trustees of the British Museum, 1968), p. 182.

24. See Jocelyn M. C. Toynbee, *Roman Medallions,* Numismatic Studies no. 5 (New York: American Numismatic Society, 1944), p. 135, n. 75.
25. Carl Robert, *Die Antiken Sarkophag-Reliefs,* vol. 2, *Mythologische-Cyclen* (Berlin: G. Grote, 1890), pp. 76–145, pls. 27–49.
26. Adolf Klügman, *Die Amazonen in der Attischen Literatur und Kunst* (Stuttgart: W. Spemann, 1875), p. 89.
27. Robert, *Mythologische-Cyclen,* 2: pl. 33.
28. An example of this bewilderment at Roman foibles is the unsigned article, "Amazon," in Pierre Devambez et al., eds., *The Praeger Encyclopedia of Ancient Greek Civilization* (New York: Praeger, 1967), pp. 32–33.
29. J. J. Bachofen, *Versuch Uber die Grabersymbolik des Alten* (Basel: von Helbing & Lichtenhahn, 1925), pp. 73–74.
30. For other theories on Amazons and death, see Klügman, *Die Amazonen,* p. 89; Annalina Levi, *Barbarians on Roman Imperial Coins and Sculpture,* Numismatic Notes and Monographs, no. 123 (New York: American Numismatic Society, 1952); J.M.C. Toynbee, *Death and Burial in the Roman World* (London: Camelot Press, 1971).

The Sword of Vengeance: Amazons in the Middle Ages

The Western medieval world was first and foremost Christian. Many historians argue that women found greater freedom and opportunity in the early and high Middle Ages than they had enjoyed in Roman times. For Amazons, however, conditions got considerably worse. Authors reinterpreted the classical ideal of excellence according to a Christian sensibility. Their heroes fought for God's glory as well as their own, and the goal of transcendence was reshaped into the hope of salvation. Amazons were no longer required to test the mettle of a hero. If these authors evoked the specter of the Amazon at all, their purpose was not to measure her prowess, but to vent their moral indignation. In a Christian world, the Amazon was almost irredeemably pagan, a violation of God's order who was destined to yield before the sword of vengeance and retribution.

Justin Martyr, a second-century Christian apologist, attacked the writings of the Greek poets as "permanent testimonials of madness and perversion." But Justin himself was versed enough in the very literature he defamed to join the dour Homeric boor Thersites in the vilification of the Greek hero Achilles. Justin contemptuously noted that this legendary figure who "conquered Troy and vanquished Hector . . . was overcome by a dead Amazon."[1]

Justin's younger contemporary, Clement of Alexandria, discussed Amazons as part of his survey of the different peoples of the world. The Amazons were singular in their ignorance of morality: "none of the Amazons have husbands, but, like animals, they go out from their own territories once

Martyrdom of Saint Agatha, eighteenth century, from *Book of Saints.*
(*Courtesy Print Collection, Art, Prints and Photographs Division, The New York Public Library, Astor, Lenox and Tilden Foundations*)

a year . . . and live with men of the neighboring nation; and if they bring forth a male child, they cast him away, and rear only females."[2]

Later church fathers like Bardesan and Paulus Orosius repeated Clement's theme of the "animal" nature of Amazon mating and practice of male infanticide. Paulus Orosius, a fourth-century author, found in Thalestris, whom legends credit as seeking the sexual favor of Alexander, an example of a "shameless Amazon."[3] For Orosius the Amazon nation was a sign of the error and disorder that characterized the world prior to the birth of Christ and the acceptance of Christian values. His only faint words of praise for an Amazon was to note that Sinope, the daughter of the Amazon queen Marpesia, "achieved a unique reputation for courage by reason of her permanent virginity."[4]

Despite the fact that at least one church father praised an Amazon who remained a virgin, the Amazon tended to resist Christian reinterpretation. Devout authors treated them as exemplars of lust and uncontrolled sexuality, rather than as models of virginity. It is true that the hapless third-century martyr Agatha suffered the removal of her breasts before she refused to renounce Christ, but the church hailed her as a saint, not as an Amazon. To be an Amazon, or to conquer an Amazon, is an act of great physical bravado: Christian heroism required a trial of both body and spirit. As the fourth-century apologist Lactantius explained, "to conquer the mind, and to restrain anger is the part of the bravest man. . . . For he is not to be thought braver who overcomes a lion, than he who overcomes the violent beast shut up within himself . . . or he who subdues a warlike Amazon, than he who conquers lust."[5]

In using the legends of the epic cycle to express ideas and values that conformed to their sensibility, Christian authors were simply following a tradition that had been established long before their day. It has already been noted how Dio Chrysostom sharpened his sophistic skills by asserting that Homer lied, and that Priam's city never fell to the Greeks. His *Trojan Discourses*, however, appear timid and restrained compared to the works of Dictys and Dares, two Greek authors who were roughly his contemporaries. Western authors knew Dictys and Dares through Latin translations of the fourth and sixth centuries. In this form these works became the chief sources for the Troy stories in the West throughout the medieval period. Dares and Dictys chose not to be known to their contemporaries; their claim to be of greater veracity than any previously known source on the Trojan War was based on their insistence that they actually fought in that war—Dictys, a Cretan in the camp of Idomenus; Dares, a Phrygian and follower of the Trojan Antenor. Dares could claim to have survived to write his memoirs, since Antenor in the end went over to the enemy, and was spared, along with his camp and following, from the vengeance and slaughter of the Greeks.

How could two accounts contemporary to the Trojan War suddenly appear on this earth more than a millennium after those critical events? How was that possible, when not one of Helen's jewels, not a shield or a sword, or ashes or bones, or treaties and vows kept or broken, had survived? Dares' and Dictys's stories were of the most urgent and vital fascination to the West. In the early Middle Ages there were several forces that served to bind the Western world together: the ever-widening arms of the Christian Church; the remembered unity of the Roman Empire; and among peoples who would later become known as the French, British, Germans, and Italians, and even Danes and Norwegians, the firm and unwavering conviction that their earliest ancestors could be traced back to refugees from war-torn Troy.[6] Thus it was widely believed that the Trojan War had shaped not only the events of the Bronze Age, but the very destiny of medieval Europe.

It is unlikely that either Dares or Dictys was a legend in his real or imagined time. No complete manuscript in Greek survives of either work. Their greatest influence was through Latin translations executed long after their time, in a medieval world that knew Homer only as a name.[7] The habit of accepting Dictys and Dares as authentic became firmly entrenched in the West, and the first systematic scholarly exposition of their fraud awaited the eighteenth-century Enlightenment.[8]

That Europeans preferred Dares to the Greek Dictys was understandable, since they saw themselves as having Trojan blood coursing through their veins. Dictys, however, was not without his admirers, and his supposedly pro-Greek account of the war does as much to diminish Homer's favorite Greek hero, Achilles, as that of the pro-Trojan Dares. On the other hand, neither Dictys nor Dares has anything very positive to say of Penthesilea and her Amazons.

Dictys's work is a relatively short prose narrative which, in many points, is at variance with Homer's *Iliad*. The medieval Latin manuscripts contain either an introductory letter or a preface explaining the sudden "discovery" of Dictys's *Journal of the Trojan War*. It was either an earthquake (according to the preface) or simply the overwhelming weight of time (according to the letter) that caused the collapse of a very old tomb and permitted shepherds to discover a tin box among the ancient remains. It contained the *Journal*, inscribed in the Greek language, but in ancient Phoenician characters. The shepherds took the tablets to scholars in Phaxis for transcription, and the rest of the story, we are asked to believe, is history. The result of these efforts was to make for the very first time an eyewitness account of the Trojan War available to all.

Some of Dictys's diversions from Homer and from the events of the epic cycle serve to deprecate the character of Achilles and to make his slaying of the Amazon queen Penthesilea an ordinary, indeed almost trivial, incident. By Book III of Dictys, it is already clear that Achilles really is not very different from the Trojan villain Paris, who dragged his entire nation into war because of his infatuation with Helen. In Dictys's account, Achilles would also sacrifice the good of his people to his personal amorous desires.

During a truce in the lengthy war, Achilles spied Queen Hecuba and her female entourage worshipping in the temple of Apollo, which was on neutral ground. Hecuba's party included her two unmarried daughters—the prophetess Cassandra, and Polyxena, who does not even figure in Homer's account. Achilles was immediately captivated by Polyxena's beauty and was determined to have her as his wife. Through a mediator he promised Hector he would end the war in exchange for the hand of his sister. Only his rage at Hector's insistence on a formal oath kept him from betraying the Greeks.

Achilles' love for Polyxena did not diminish, but he now understood that the only way to fulfill his desire was to win the war and gain her as part of his booty. Penthesilea's entry into Dictys's tale occurs when Achilles was suffering from a double burden weighing heavily on his spirit: his unrequited love and his unbearable grief at the death of his friend Patroclus at the hand of Hector. He was not in the least excited or disturbed over the arrival of the Amazons at the scene of the war. Penthesilea almost could have been expected, given the fact that "her race, being naturally warlike, was always conquering the neighboring peoples and carrying the Amazon standards far and wide." No passion. No terror. Just another gloomy fact of life. Even worse, Dictys presents no motives for Penthesilea's decision to oppose the Greeks: "Why she was coming to Priam's aid, whether for money or simply because of her love of war, was uncertain." Dictys also never explicitly states why Penthesilea wished to fight on the Trojan side, and portrays the Trojans themselves as puzzled on this point. There are, however, some hints that Penthesilea's support is somehow connected to her feelings for the person of Hector: when she learns of his death she wants to forget the whole project and go home. Hector did die in an attempt to greet her, leading a party of warriors that Achilles cut down in ambush as they tried to cross a river. The Amazon queen finally arrives in the besieged city to find the Trojans in utter despair: "Some of them believed that the army which Penthesilea had brought to aid Priam was now joined with Achilles; everything was adverse and hostile, all their power was broken and destroyed." But Penthesilea did not go home, nor did she join Achilles: "Alexander [Paris] gave her much gold and silver, and finally prevailed upon her to stay."

The reason the Trojans were willing to pay handsomely for Amazon aid is that, in Dictys's version of the story, Penthesilea brought with her considerable forces, including Amazons and "other neighboring peoples." She divided her army into archers, foot soldiers, and cavalry, to which she herself belonged. Her confidence in her army was so great that she led an attack on the Greeks entirely with her own forces, without any Trojan assistance. But she fared no better than the many hapless Trojans who had fought and died before her.

Dictys may have lessened Achilles' heroic stature by rendering an account of his supposed love for Polyxena, but he left the battle prowess of the hero of the classical Troy stories untouched. Achilles had only to locate Penthesilea among the cavalry of the enemy to hurl his spear and to wound her seriously. Conforming perfectly to the classical Greek artistic heritage, Dictys relates that Achilles "seized her by her hair and pulled her off her horse," no great feat now that she was incapacitated by her wound. Perhaps he kept her horse, but the Amazon herself he neither ravished nor cherished. He just left her in the field to die.

Dictys relates that when the Amazons saw their leader down, they panicked and lost all semblance of battle discipline. An entire army made a desperate dash for the gates of Troy with the Greeks close at their heels. The Greeks did not hesitate to cut down those who were unable to reach the safety of the city walls before the gates closed. But the Amazons were safe, because Dictys has the Greeks refrain "from touching the women because of their sex." The jeering Thersites of the epic cycle could not have put it better. How can we expect Amazons to evoke passion and terror when they are women, and this alone suffices to make them contemptible? Dictys depicts the Greeks deterred more by some undefined fear of pollution than by a reverence for the feminine.

After the dust of the battle died down, the Greeks roamed the field to survey the enemy dead and wounded, and of course, as victors, to claim their spoils. To Penthesilea's misfortune, they discover her, "still half-alive." As in the late classical accounts of the story, Dictys portrays the Greeks as pausing to marvel at her. But it is her "brazen boldness" that fills them with wonder. If she was beautiful, her beauty never moved Dictys, who would have us believe he stood near the dying Amazon queen. Nor did Dictys portray any of the Greeks as stirred to a semblance of compassion or pity, let alone admiration or love.

According to Quintus of Smyrna's later version, Penthesilea dies in the arms of a sorrowing and remorseful Achilles. In Dictys's story, Achilles is also the greatest defender of the Amazon. He is the only Greek who feels that the queen should be allowed to die where she fell. He did not even entertain the thought of giving her a funeral, or at least giving her a burial. He did not pursue his view that she should be left to die with any great strength or vehemence, for he failed to prevail over his companions, who hotly debated two ends even less kind: "It was decided to throw her, while still alive enough to have feeling, either into the river to drown, or out to the dogs to tear apart." Why did they single her out for death by drowning, or still worse, by mutilation? There must have been many on the field who lay dying, on whom the Greeks could have vented their rage, their scorn, their lust for vengeance. But who could be a better victim than an Amazon, who "transgressed the bounds of nature and her sex"? Diomedes supposedly made a decision for her drowning a point of personal honor. According to Dictys, Diomedes spoke to every Greek and pressed his view, finally gaining a unanimous vote in favor of drowning the Amazon queen. He did the job himself: "dragging her by the feet, he dumped her into the Scamander." Dictys interrupts his narrative to remark, "it goes without saying that this was a very cruel and barbarous act." But he has little trouble excusing the deed: "the queen of the Amazons . . . died in a way that befitted her foolhardy character."

Dares "the Phrygian" might well have agreed with him, although this imposter, supposedly describing the war from the point of view of one who fought on the Trojan side, does give Amazons somewhat more importance than they receive from Dictys. As a muse, however, Dares leaves much to be desired. The classicist Gilbert Highet described his Latin *Fall of Troy* (supposedly a word-for-word translation of a Greek original) as being of "extreme simplicity, verging on stupidity."[9] The Latin manuscripts of Dares are accompanied by a very brief letter penned by a Cornelius Nepos, who claims to have discovered the Dares text while studying in Athens. There is no further explanation of the circumstances of the "discovery."

Dares' account opens with the tale of Jason and the Argonauts. He then moves on to a first capture and destruction of Troy at the hands of Heracles under the reign of Lacomedon, Priam's father. This opening section, in particular, reinforces the judgment of Highet. To wit:

> Thus, reembarking, they departed from Phrygia.
> And set out for Colchis.
> And stole the fleece.
> And returned to their homeland.

Dares' account is so weighted on the Trojan side that his story has no Trojan villains. Alexander (Paris) never violated the hospitality of Menelaus of Sparta by running off with his wife. He did not steal Helen from Sparta. Helen went to the island of Cythera to worship at the temple of Venus. She wanted to see Alexander as much as he wanted to see her: "thus they met and spent some time just staring, struck by each others' beauty." As far as Helen's abduction is concerned, "she was not unwilling."

Dares interrupts his narrative to describe the major persons in his account. Unfortunately, though he would have seen her many times (if his claim to have participated in the Trojan War is to have any creditability), he tells us nothing of Penthesilea. But Helen is eulogized in his inimitable manner. After describing her twin brothers, Castor and Pollux, as "blond-haired, large eyed, fair complexioned, and well-built with trim bodies," he goes on to say that Helen resembled them: "She was beautiful, ingenuous, and charming. Her legs were the best: her mouth the cutest. There was a beauty-mark between her eyebrows." This is our only "eye-witness" account and description of the face that launched a thousand ships. Also, thanks to Dares, the peoples of Rome would always know that their "ancestor" Aeneas was "auburn-haired, stocky, eloquent, courteous, prudent, pious, and charming," and that "his eyes were black and twinkling."

In the classical epic cycle, both Memnon and Penthesilea arrive on the scene well into the conflict, after the death of Hector. In Dares' *Fall of Troy*, Memnon is in a sense promoted. He is present in Troy right at the outbreak of the war, and Priam makes him one of his commanders. Penthesilea has no such luck. It would, however, be incorrect to say that Dares diminishes her role in the war. As in Dictys, the love interest in Dares' account is between Achilles and Polyxena. But unlike Dictys, a love between Penthesilea and Achilles would have been impossible: in Dares' tale, Achilles is dead when Penthesilea arrives. Hecuba used her daughter Polyxena as bait to lure him to the temple of Apollo, where Alexander killed him. Dares notes that Hecuba devised, "like the woman she was, a treacherous vengeance." Dares forgot that he had earlier described Hecuba with the words "she thought like a man."

Though he was obviously no friend to women, Dares could not oppose the tradition of Penthesilea's martial skill. In his account the Greeks have tremendous difficulty resisting the onslaught of the Amazon queen and her army. Diomedes was only narrowly able to prevent her from setting the Greek ships on fire. Day after day she led a massive slaughter of the Greeks, while Agamemnon remained in his camp, determined not to fight until the arrival of Neoptolemus (Pyrrhus), the son of Achilles. Neither Penthesilea nor Neoptolemus found in each other an easy match: he "wreaked great slaughter," while she "proved her prowess again and again." They battle together for several days running: "Finally Penthesilea wounded Neoptolemus, and then fell at his hands: in spite of his wound, he cut her down."

Dares tells us not a word of how he killed her, or whether the Trojans or the Amazons were able to bury her. His omission of a death scenario for Penthesilea makes his otherwise tawdry and inept account a model of taste and discretion, when his *History* is compared to later medieval accounts in which Neoptolemus dismembers the Amazon queen on the battlefield.

A world in which heroes are cast not only as descendants of Peleus or Priam, but also as sons of Adam and Noah, had little respect or use for Amazons. In medieval times, Amazons no longer had the job of certifying heroes. The seventh-century work of Frédégaire, which names the Trojan prince Francus (originally Francion) as the founder of France, and the eighth-century account of Nennius, which names the Trojan prince Brutus as the founder of England, have not one word on the subject of Amazons. At least the Italian Trojan Aeneas has to contend, if only indirectly, with the Amazon figure Camilla. The later medieval elaborations on the stories of French and British Trojans posit combats with giants as the only larger-than-life trial of their manhood and bravery.[10] Neither Brutus nor Francus are persons of Homeric stature, and the entire medieval fascination with these homeless, defeated, and fleeing refugees from Troy has only the most remote relation to the classical ideal of heroism.

But if Amazons are missing from these early medieval accounts of European origins, they return to medieval literature by the eleventh century. The chronicler Ordericus Vitalis compared Isabel of Conches, a wealthy and powerful noblewoman, to "Camilla, the renowned virgin of Italy among the squadrons of Turnus," as Isabel rallied the ranks of her husband's forces. The author's knowledge of Amazons was not limited just to Vergil, for he added, "nor was she [Isabel] inferior to Lampedona and Marseppa, Hyppolyta, and Penthesilea, and other warrior-queens of the Amazons."[11] He named for the source of his information Trogus Pompeius, a historian of the first century B.C. whose work is lost to moderns, except for the third-century Latin summaries of them by Justin. Whatever the source or sources of his images, it seems clear that Amazons did not vanish entirely from European consciousness. William of Jumièges's eleventh-century *Histoire des Normandes* (History of the Normands), it is true, excludes Amazons from its account of the origin of the Goths. According to Jumièges, it was not a case of Amazons figuring in Gothic beginnings, but of Goths as the true ancestors of Amazons (not to mention Danes, Trojans, and just about everyone else).

In his *Histoire*, which he dedicated to William the Conqueror (d. 1087), Jumièges carefully remains within the constraints imposed by Christian belief. Given the fact that Christians must accept on faith the occurrence of a universal and catastrophic deluge at the time of Noah, Noah and his descendants must bear the burden of populating all the earth and constituting all nations. Medieval historians were secure in the belief that variations in the racial and linguistic characteristics of different peoples that might appear to be striking and irreconcilable to us, were at most superficial since all of living humanity descended from Noah.

Jumièges claims that Noah's youngest son Japhet had a son named Magog, who gave the last syllable of his name as the title of the Gothic race. He insisted that the Goths were a barbarian people with a difference, always more learned than the other nomadic tribes, "almost comparable to the Greeks."[12] He places the Goths originally as the inhabitants of the island of Scanza, in the middle of a sea. From Scanza, they branched out to form two peoples, one warring with the Egyptians and eventually settling in Scythia, and the other Gothic people laying the foundations of Denmark and becoming the Danish people.

Jumièges says that while the men of the "Scythian Goths" were off fighting the Egyptians on an unusually long campaign, their angry and neglected wives left their husbands' hearths. The women armed themselves, elected two queens to lead them, and formed the Amazon nation. He added the detail that these women burned off the right breast so they could hurl their darts, spears, and javelins with greater ease. In a period of less than one hundred years they conquered all of Asia, bringing it under the yoke of their very harsh domination. Without anywhere tying his account to exact dates, Jumièges tells his readers that he cannot linger over more details regarding the Amazons. But he advises the curious that "if you want to know more about them, read the history of the Goths."[13] Apparently after spawning Amazons, the Goths reabsorbed them. With Greeklike intellect and Amazonian courage, the Goths, Jumièges argues, were destined to have a most profound effect on history.

Although Jumièges was eager to underscore what he believed to be a close tie between Amazons and Goths, he was not the greatest champion of Amazons in the medieval period. A limited, yet somewhat fuller appreciation of the Amazon women appears in the work of Benoît de Sainte-More, a Norman author of two generations later.

Benoît was influenced by the medieval cult of romantic or courtly love that flourished in some of the French and Anglo-Norman courts of his day. His patron, Henry II of England, was (unhappily) married to Eleanor of Aquitaine, whose grandfather, William of Provence, had been one of the earliest troubadours. Eleanor may well have been the "riche dame de rich rei" (wealthy lady of the wealthy king) to whom Benoît dedicated his *Roman de Troie* (Story of Troy).[14]

Benoît's lengthy poem (more than thirty thousand lines) is a complete recasting of the Troy story into the idiom of the medieval world. Its heroes are great courtly knights, displaying prowess, generosity, and courtesy. The story is transformed into a series of tournaments, or extended battles, with Penthesilea dying at the conclusion of the twenty-third. To these contests, Benoît adds an epilogue detailing the treason of Aeneas and Antenor, the sack of Troy, and the homecoming of Pyrrhus and Ulysses.

Benoît treats two groups of women in his *Roman*—the women of the Trojan court and the Amazons who come to aid the Trojan cause. The Trojan women in the *Roman* behave like great medieval ladies who have the honor of watching their lovers perform in tournaments. They help their men arm, and during the third battle Benoît has them stand at their windows to observe the display of prowess.

Benoît's Amazons are more interesting, because Benoît sees them as a hybrid of both male and female virtues. They are great ladies and chivalrous knights at the same time, worthy of fighting for, and protecting, yet capable of doing the job of combat themselves. The fact that his Amazons do not resemble the women of his day creates no problem for Benoît. His Amazons have their own dimension in space. They come from a faraway nation belonging to the most oriental section of the world—the land of Feminie, or Amazoine.

The Feminie of Benoît's *Roman* is no ordinary place. The tradition of an exotic eastern nation inhabited only by women certainly preexisted Benoît's *Roman*, and most medieval geographies included a section on Feminie or Amazoine, a nation without men. For Benoît, who uses the names interchangeably, it is a land of rare and precious spices, full of extraordinary trees and herbs, and replete with rich and exquisite delicacies. Benoît's Amazons inhabit a veritable tropical paradise, sun-drenched and scented with spices and perfumes, exotic, mysterious, and luxurious. The Amazon women themselves are worthy of their setting, with their very clothing of silken and golden cloth.

Close to Benoît's Amazoine there lies an island on which only men live. During the months of April, May, and June, the women of Amazoine joyfully visit with males from surrounding nations. But it is only the brave and the valiant, the most beautiful and most highly esteemed of their members, whom the Amazons permit to mingle with the men and to conceive a child. Benoît's Amazons considered childbearing to be a privilege of those who had demonstrated their worth to their own Amazon society. Nowhere does Benoît suggest that the Amazons were man-hating. He depicts them as nurturing male infants for one year and then turning them over to their fathers. No man, young or old, is seen setting foot on their territory, which is completely cut off from the rest of the world. Benoît claimed that many of the women lived their entire lifetimes without ever laying eyes on a man.

He depicted his Amazons as making warfare their livelihood. Their renown as warriors was worldwide, and they were much sought after as fighting forces. Many women, Benoît claimed, left their nation to fight for pay. But it was not money that lured Penthesilea to Troy. To Benoît, the Amazon queen is "proz e hardie e bele e sage (line 23, 287)" (virtuous and strong, beautiful and wise), honored the world over for valour and her noble lineage (though Benoît excludes her genealogy). Benoît makes the Amazon queen the female equivalent of the ideal chivalrous knight. She came to Troy because she is a loyal vassal of Hector. She observes the code of chivalry and treats all knights with courtesy. Thus, in an incident that would have been out of character for the classical Penthesilea, she becomes a patron of the handsome young Greek "knight" Celidis, who dies early in the story. That she fought on the Trojan side, and he on the Greek, did not hamper their relationship. This sense of "noblesse" between gentlemen, even if they are fighting on opposing sides, was one of the virtues of the code of chivalry and of romantic love. Benoît depicts Penthesilea as the perfect gentleman.

One thousand warrior-women accompany Penthesilea to Troy, all combat trained and well equipped for battle, mounted on their richly ornamented Arabian horses. This colorful procession arrives in Troy to find that the gates of the city have been closed for two months in mourning: Hector is dead. Penthesilea is grief-stricken at the terrible news. Penthesilea's love for Hector is clearly adulterous, since in Benoît's, as well as all other versions of the story, Hector is a married man and the father of an infant son. But according to the rules of courtly love, marriage was no excuse for refusing to be a lover, and true love itself flourishes best outside of the bonds of matrimony.[15] Hence it was the death, not the marriage of the man whose love she sought, that ruined the happiness of the Amazon queen: in her great disappointment, she was, at least momentarily, ready to return to her country.

Unlike Dictys's version of the story (which Benoît acknowledges as one of his sources), Penthesilea does not have to be paid to stay at Troy; Benoît has Priam and the Trojan people joyously receive her. It is Penthesilea who vows to avenge Hector, and it is at her urging that Priam recovers the strength and will to reform his companies and prepare his warriors once more for battle. In promising Priam the combat services of her valiant young women, Penthesilea speaks as a courteous, generous, and loyal vassal.

Sitting astride a Spanish horse, her armor covering magnificent silk garments, Penthesilea led her splendidly attired companies, all noble and honored women (23, 481). Fighting along with them is Philemenis, who comes from a nation near that of the women, and is himself a powerful king and a fierce warrior. In addition to weaving Penthesilea's story with that of Philemenis, Benoît creates for the Amazon a whole series of exploits and achievements, filling in with elaborate detail deeds that Dares' account had presented only as sketches. Benoît's Penthesilea performs wonders in the field—she had only to thrust her sword and another Greek lay dead (23, 621–23). The beautiful Amazon queen struck Menelaus from his magnificent steed. She clashed with Diomedes and caused him to drop his sword. The Greeks fought fiercely against her, often forcing her to abandon a dropped sword or a wounded horse. But she was well assisted by her warriors, who always followed her instructions directly without fear or hesitation.

The Amazons were relentless, ceasing their battle only at nightfall. The Greeks suffered so many casualties and wounds they were forced to abandon their ground and retreat. The following day the Amazons nearly succeeded in setting the Greek ships on fire. Realizing that these warrior-maids could well turn the tide of the war, the Greek kings take counsel in their tents. They decide to send Menelaus, who had almost been killed by the Amazon queen, to fetch Pyrrhus (Pirrus), the son of the great and recently fallen Greek hero, Achilles. As in Dares' story, Benoît has the hapless Achilles, while lovesick for Polyxena, die in ambush in the temple of Apollo.

The Greek camp receives Pyrrhus joyfully, and they present the young "knight" with the armor of his father. He is their only hope against the Amazon queen. Benoît's Penthesilea proves to be no easy match, even for the son of an Achilles. However, right from the start of the struggle, he makes a noticeable dent in Amazon strength and morale. They and the Trojans quickly see that Pyrrhus is no longer a child, but a strong and mature knight, who fought and bore his father's armor well. Yet the twenty-second battle was still a victory of Trojans and Amazons over the Greeks. It is in this round of the struggle that Benoît depicts Penthesilea as winning her most stunning triumphs.

In preparation for battle the Amazons sing a hymn, and Benoît tells us that the beauty of their voices was such that they hardly sounded like mortal women. Then these angels mount their horses and ready their weapons for contest. Penthesilea struggles with Ajax-Telemon with so much force that both warriors are thrown from their horses and have to continue their combat on foot. Victory is hers as she fells him with a mighty blow of her lance. Her maidens quickly help her remount. At the moment of her victory, some bleeding and badly wounded Paflogonians rush up to the Amazon queen and seek her help in freeing their king, Philemenis, who is her neighbor and good friend. Loyal companion that she is, she promptly devises a plan for his rescue. Pyrrhus observes the preparation for the venture, and in anger and with a great deal of sarcasm, he approaches Penthesilea and remarks:

> Turn around, my noble knight—
> You allow yourselves to be treated too roughly . . .
> Bearing arms is tedious and disagreeable
> When women take the field against us.
> (24, 079–88)

Her response to Pyrrhus is bold, but it ducks the question of whether women belong in warfare. Penthesilea does not speak in the defense of the female sex, but only of her own Amazon community:

> You believe that we are
> Like ordinary women
> With bodies weak and feeble:
> That is certainly not our situation.
> We are young maidens
> Cleansed of evil conduct and of luxury . . . !
> (24, 091–97)

She adds that Amazons not only had the military skill to defend their own lands, but also fought well enough to make the bearing of arms their profession. She warns Pyrrhus that since he is the son of the man who killed Hector, she bears a special enmity toward him. Hector was the greatest knight the world had ever known, and Pyrrhus cannot escape her wrath or the sting of her lance.

Their exchange of threats and menaces ends as they are separated by a large crowd of Greeks and Amazons, fighting a fierce and bloody battle. During the course of the melee, she is able to free Philemenis, whose gratitude is boundless. Benoît portrays him as returning the favor only after Penthesilea's death. He depicts a sense of camaraderie and loyalty among Priam's allies, but no romance. The love interest in the *Roman de Troie* is reserved for the tale of Achilles and Polyxena, and for Benoît's original story of Troilus and Briseida—later elaborated by Chaucer, Boccaccio, and Shakespeare (as *Troilus and Cressida*). Benoît's Amazons speak like great and courteous ladies, sing like angels, fight like the bravest of knights, and die like butchered animals.

But before death claims Penthesilea, she again and again triumphs in battle. As the action of the fight whirls by her, she finds herself with Pyrrhus in view. They engage in a furious battle, in which she wounds him critically in the chest, head, and face. She had grabbed him by the faceplate of his helmet, and might have inflicted a mortal wound had Polydamas not separated them, coming to the assistance of his half brother. It was a difficult day for all the warriors. The Amazons and Trojans could almost taste the victory they came close to possessing, and for the Greeks there was bitterness and humiliation, but not defeat. And on both sides the losses were appalling. Benoît claims that ten thousand lay dead, and that the need by both sides to bury the bodies led to talk of a truce.

In the series of encounters that Benoît groups together under the heading of the twenty-third battle, luck is initially on the Amazon side. Penthesilea and Pyrrhus had become special hated enemies. They make a point of seeking each other out in battle, making a special effort to exchange blows, both mounted and on foot. Such was their rage and fury that reconciliation was unthinkable. On the fateful last day of their struggle, it was Penthesilea who drew the first blood, with her lance actually breaking off within Pyrrhus's chest, so she could not draw out the tip to strike again. Still unsatisfied, she prepared herself to continue the struggle. She had not completed the lacing of her armor, or placed her helmet on her bare head, when suddenly, all at once and without warning, she spied Pyrrhus charging toward her. Though badly wounded himself, he made one superhuman effort and struck a mighty blow on her shoulder. Her arm fell to the ground, severed from her torso. Unhorsed, she lay on the ground half dead. In spite of the strength of her army and of the Trojans fighting with it, the Greeks were able to take an unusually cruel vengeance against her. The ringing sound of the clash of steel could be heard all about her. When the dust settled and all was silent, her brains lay sprawled on the new fresh green grass, and all her limbs lay in pieces.

Meanwhile, Pyrrhus, badly wounded, had lost so much blood that he cried out in fear and trembling. In panic he thought he saw his soul departing from his body. But this did not come to pass: the Greeks carried him back to his tent where, in time, he healed.

Benoît gives the Amazons two responses to Penthesilea's death. At first, they hunger for blood and vengeance. With renewed ferocity, they attack the Miridonians (Pyrrhus's people), while the Trojans fight the remaining Greeks for half the day, until, Benoît writes, their grief outweighed their will to fight. At this point, Benoît conforms to Dictys's story, and depicts the Amazons as totally demoralized and disheartened by the death of their queen. Like Dictys, he has them make a dash for the gates of Troy, adding the misogynistic detail that many thousands of them died in the crush and pressure of the panic-stricken crowd.

Benoît depicts Penthesilea as mourned by both sides, which suggests that he had sources of the Troy legends available to him in addition to Dares' and Dictys's. He even has the Greeks pause to admire her beauty "like nothing born of living" (24, 435)—an incident that appears completely absurd given Benoît's description of Penthesilea's bloody and dismembered corpse. It was hardly the material for romance. Pyrrhus, her killer, is driven not to love, but to a sense of knightly honor. It is his belief that the Amazon queen deserves a proper burial and tomb. In conformity with Dictys, Benoît presents Diomedes as the champion of those who would seek vengeance and retribution from the Amazon's corpse. Pointing out that she alone was responsible for the death of at least ten thousand Greeks (this seems to be Benoît's favorite number), he adds, "it would be a sad tale to tell/if there were no condemnation" (24, 449–50).

But even Diomedes rejected anything as cruel and violent as throwing her to the dogs. After obtaining the consent of his companions, he dragged her remains to the River Es-

chandre whose waters were so deep "only the gods could
fathom them" (24, 460), and over Pyrrhus's objection, hurled
her to the deep.

This disposal of the queen's remains would appear to be
without a doubt final, yet Benoît depicts her women as re-
trieving her body (and presumably all the pieces thereof)
from the river at the time of the peace negotiations between
the Greeks and the Trojans. They took the body within the
walls of Troy, and there set about the task of embalming it.
King Philemenis, undoubtedly mindful of the fact that Penthesilea had helped to free him when he was captured, stated
his intention to carry the Amazon's remains back to her realm,
adjacent to his nation. He manages to leave Troy before the
Greeks vent their wrath, carrying the body on a magnificent
imperial chariot, followed by the four hundred thirty Amazons who survived the war. Benoît does not give his readers
the exact location of Penthesilea's tomb and monument, but
he does make the claim that these are described by Pliny (25,
795).

Benoît's work displays the faintly positive image of women
that was so much a product of the doctrine of courtly love.
No other medieval Troy tale echoes even his limited appreciation of Amazon beauty, and of the strength and prowess
of these heroic women. Nor do succeeding works reflect the
chivalry that Benoît attributes to Pyrrhus in his dealings with
Penthesilea. Benoît's Pyrrhus defeats the Amazon queen fairly
in a one-to-one combat, like a true knight and gentleman. If
his soldiers so take advantage of the fallen queen, it is only
after Pyrrhus already has dealt her a mortal blow. Yet she
was unquestionably killed and mutilated at the pen of this
"friend" of women.

It follows that Amazons were to fare immeasurably worse
in the hands of later authors who were unmoved by, or even
opposed to the ideas of romantic love. Joseph of Exeter, like
Benoît, wrote in the court of Henry II, but his Latin *Bellum
Troianum* is quite different in spirit from Benoît's *Roman de
Troie*. Scholars like M. A. Joly see Exeter's work as an attempt
to discredit and counteract the "scandalous" amorous creations and details in Benoît.[16]

In Exeter's poem the entire role of women is diminished. No longer do ladies assist Hector in putting on and removing his armor. No longer do the women watch the battles from the windows of Troy. His Penthesilea is a fierce and formidable warrior, not a courtly lady. She is neither a patron of young knights nor a true and loyal friend of neighboring kings. And there is absolutely nothing womanly about her; she wears none of Benoît's silks: "her appearance was rugged, her garments were faded."[17] Although her battle gear matched that of the richest knight, "she detested the gold with which her arms had been decorated. If you listened to her laughter, or her speech, if you looked closely at her eyes, you would observe nothing frivolous or weak: in all things she did the woman lay hidden."

Exeter has the Greeks observe the Amazon in utter amazement, "for in the Peloponnesus women are timid creatures and never bear arms." Menethus the Mycenaean has nothing but scorn for the Trojans for allowing "girls lobbing their distaffs" to join their cause. But ignoring his own scruples, Menethus resolves that though "it is a base thing for men to pound timid girls to the ground, I nevertheless will go to give battle." It would have been better for him had he never ventured to fight the Amazons, for he dies a horrible death, torn to pieces by Penthesilea's spear and the bolting of his own horse.

Pyrrhus, wearing the armor of his dead father, which is a bit too big for the yet boyish span of his shoulders, spies Penthesilea and decides to challenge her. Joseph of Exeter appears to be unfamiliar with the epic tradition that made the Amazons daughters of Mars, and represented Mars as flying into a violent rage, a tantrum of divine dimensions, upon the slaying of Penthesilea. Instead, Exeter naively follows the misogynist tradition of his own day and depicts Mars as aiding Pyrrhus. Male gods aid male protagonists, and the goddesses Minerva and Juno assist Penthesilea, who "was a woman like them." He represents Penthesilea as striking the first blow, with the tip of her lance becoming irretrievably buried in his shield. With the Amazon thus disarmed, Pyrrhus is able to inflict a fatal wound in her left breast. As she fell dead to the ground, her group of maids fell apart, "as fear, the weakness of their sex, returned easily to them." The author makes no mention of the disposal of Penthesilea's remains.

Joseph of Exeter's bare and unadorned Latin prose work was not the most popular in the medieval world. That distinction went to Guido de Colonna's (late thirteenth-century) *Destruction of Troy*. Because Guido wrote in Latin, his work found a wider audience and served as the basis for more translations than Benoît's French *Roman de Troie*. Guido de Colonna's work is closely modeled on Benoît's poem, but in relating the fate of Penthesilea and her confrontation with Pyrrhus, he makes a critical change in the succession of events. As in Benoît, Penthesilea is the first to draw blood, and she gives Pyrrhus a serious injury. The tip of her lance remains embedded in his body. The Greeks notice his dangerous wound, and it is at this point that several of them surround the Amazon, break and remove her helmet, and wound her all about her head. She is already badly injured when Pyrrhus, bleeding profusely from his own injury, comes along and more from rage than necessity uses what appears to be his last strength to lop off her arm. Pyrrhus, to be sure, is still a great and chivalrous knight, but Penthesilea is no longer regarded as a proper object of his courtesy. Chivalry was a code of behavior practiced between social equals. The fact that fair play was no longer a necessary consideration in the battling of the Amazon queen shows that she is outside the rules. War is a man's game that women, even Amazons, are not permitted to play, and any female who stumbles into this masculine sphere may be exterminated without the slightest regard to justice and fairness.

Similarly, John Lydgate's *Troy Book* (early fifteenth century) keeps Guido's order of events: Penthesilea wounds Pyrrhus, the Greeks surround her destroying her helmet and armor, and Pyrrhus then attacks and cuts off her arm. Lydgate adds the detail that Pyrrhus himself hacks her body to pieces, as does the *Laud Troy Book* (circa 1500). In both versions the Greeks throw her body into a deep lake, and it is miraculously fished out to be given to the Trojans for burial during the peace negotiations.

This genre of literature, with its bold and brazen Amazons who are dismembered by furious and avenging knights, begins to fade in popularity with the late medieval authors. Authors like Joseph of Exeter, Guido de Colonna, John Lydgate, and others had already eliminated Amazon sexuality. Their cruel and bloodthirsty warrior-women were utterly unlovable, and indeed were hideously dismembered. They are never even given a chance to inspire anything resembling amorous devotion—how can you love a woman who is chopped up like a jigsaw puzzle? But in the hands of Chaucer and Boccaccio, Amazons were to suffer still another blow, and their image was even further weakened: they were shorn of their warrior determination and prowess.

The Hippolyta of Chaucer's "Knights Tale" is only incidentally an Amazon. It is her sister Emily who is a beauty, and neither woman has formidable strength. Hippolyta is just the woman whom Theseus happened to marry, and she is hardly noticeable. Her Amazon past is far behind her, and she is a dutiful and obedient helpmeet.

Boccaccio's Amazons are equally devoid of passion and prowess. Of the one hundred and four lives of women Boccaccio presents in his *De Claris Mulieribus* (Concerning Famous Women), one deals with Penthesilea, and two others discuss pairs of Amazon queens (Orithya and Antiope, Martesia and Lampedo). Boccaccio's purpose in relating these lives is as much to draw moral lessons as it is to tell interesting and entertaining stories. But he has no consistent moral principle to draw from his discussion of the warrior-women. His Penthesilea is a virgin, and he presents Orithya as "marvelous and very praiseworthy for her perpetual virginity"[18]—an epitaph he could just as easily hang on a nun as an Amazon. In a like manner he uses the lives of Martesia and Lampedo to comment on the necessity for careful education of girls. His discussion of the first Amazon queens begins with a rather confused retelling of Justin's story of two outcast Scythian princes who migrate to Cappodocia near the shores of the Thermodon with their wives and families. In Boccaccio's version, the widowed women of Cappodocia, not the abandoned Scythian wives, resolve to have no further discourse with men, form a female community, and become Amazons. Re-

gardless of their origin, it is clear that Boccaccio judges them
to be very bad women, murderers not only of the remaining
males in their group, but also of any infant sons fortune
brought to them as the result of random mating with their
neighbors. As he saw it, their malevolent behavior could be
explained by the fact that "they did not have the same concern
in raising girls as we have with ours. For, having discarded
the distaff, the wool basket, and other womanly tasks, they
practiced hunting, running, continual war-like exercises,
archery and similar skills, and they hardened the grown girls
in the aptitudes and strength of a man." He raises the same
point, that female behavior must be learned, in his discussion
of Penthesilea. Through their rigorous training, she and her
women had become more manly in arms "than those who
were made men by nature but were then changed into women
or helmeted hares by idleness and love of pleasure."

To the traditional medieval tale of Penthesilea, Boccaccio
adds a detail of his own invention: Hector was still alive when
she came to Troy (in the hope of having a child by him), and
he had ample opportunity to observe her in battle and to
note both her beauty and her bravery. But their love was
never consummated, for Boccaccio depicts her as falling dead
among the Greeks she had just recently hurled to the ground.
At any rate, the entire episode is just a minor but entertaining
detail. Boccaccio's main goal in writing about Penthesilea is
to exhort men to manliness, not to praise and honor brave
women.

By the time we reach one of the last of the medieval Troy
stories, Raoul Lefèvre's *Le Recueil des hystoires troyennes* (1464)
and William Caxton's *The Ancient History of the Destruction of
Troy*—a late-fifteenth-century English translation of the same—
the Amazons have become almost unrecognizable. Lefèvre
has a chapter entitled "How Hercules and Theseus fought
together against the Damosels of Scythie, & c." If one knew
nothing of the supposed Scythian origin of Amazons, one
could skim this chapter without ever realizing that it deals
with them. The "Damosels of Scythie" are of an extremely
hybrid stock: they are a rebirth of Benoît's courtly Amazons
without sexuality or danger. Lefèvre's Amazons are more

concerned with social propriety than with military success. His versions of the old Amazon stories are almost irredeemably silly. A "damosel strangely arrayed" approaches Hercules on behalf of the "Queen of Scythie, Ladies of Egypt and of Cappodocia." She has come with the message that the women she represents are enemies of Egypt, and since Hercules is of "Egyptian lineage," he and Theseus must either "submit to the ladies or give battle." They agree to a battle in which "two knights will fight two ladies." Thus Hercules and Theseus came to fight two sisters of Queen Synope, Ypolite (Hippolyta) and Menalipe.

When the four first meet, they are on horseback. But their first encounter places all four "combatants" on the ground. Finding themselves "lying on the erthe . . . shame and abashment smote them onto their hearts."[19] After much blushing, they rise to draw their swords and "fight" on foot. Hercules overcomes Menalipe, but Theseus needed Hercules's encouragement before he could best Ypolite. The quarrel ends without any drawing of blood or violation of the rules of courtesy. Queen Synope sends her arms to Hercules as a token of his victory, and Theseus, who fell in love with his opponent, carries her back to Athens as his bride.

Lefèvre's attempt to cloak the story of Penthesilea in the same desexed courtly idiom works less successfully. The quarrel between Penthesilea and Pirrus (Pyrrhus) had too long a tradition for Lefèvre to change its ending. Penthesilea is a "Lady and Queene, a very noble virgine and a strong fighter," who brings "a thousand virgins" to Troy for the love of Hector.[20] After having been "knighted" by "Thelamon" and presented with the arms of his father, Achilles, Pirrus proceeds to perform his bloody deed: after being badly wounded by the Amazon, "he gave her so great a stroke with his sword, that hee cutte her arm off the body, where of the saide Penthesilea fell downe deade, to the earth, and Pirrus was not yet content, smote the body and cut it into two pieces."[21] At this point the author appears to lose interest in his "noble virgin."

Oddly enough, Lefèvre created his pure, courtly, and spineless Amazons around the same time that another author was creating works that restored these women to beauty, prowess, and sexuality. But the second author was a woman, and the difference in gender was crucial to the authors' depictions of Amazons. Christine de Pisan (1363–1431) was probably the first woman ever to write about Amazons, and almost certainly the first person ever to understand Amazons as a symbol not just of transcendence, but transcendence for women. Pisan clearly understood *Amazon* as a superlative, and used the term to signify women as superb, wonderful, and glorious. How else could she have called her mother "strong and free, and more worthy than Penthesilée"? (*Mutacion de Fortune*, i. v). This extraordinary expression of a daughter's love and admiration for her mother identifies a voice sounding on behalf of women in the midst of centuries of silence.

Later in the same work, in a section where she weaves autobiography with allegory, Pisan insists that at the moment of her widowhood fortune changed her into a man, and that she has remained male for thirteen years since that event. These "facts" do roughly accord with actual occurrences in the life of Christine de Pisan. She wrote the *Le Livre de la Mutacion de Fortune* (The Book of the Changing Fortune) in 1403, thirteen years after the death of her husband. As a widow with three small children, she did not, as in her allegory, actually change sex, but she did function as a male. Continually staving off lawsuits against her husband's small estate, she supported her family by seeking noble patrons for her poetry of love and morality. She had the advantage, through her birth and marriage (her husband had been a secretary; her father, a physician and astrologer), of knowing people in court circles who could help her gain the support of kings and princes, counts and dukes.

Her claim to have changed sex is every bit as remarkable as her tribute to her "amazonian" mother. But Christine de Pisan did not originate the theme of gender change. The whole plot of the *Mutacion de Fortune* is based on the Ovidian idea of metamorphosis.

Christine de Pisan did not create original materials. Her major works are all reworkings, usually poetical renditions, of the various texts that were available to the authors of her day. Again and again her works reverberate with stories encountered elsewhere, and historians and literary critics have made elaborate and detailed studies that trace and identify the various sources she employed in sections of her works. Christine de Pisan moralizes, borrows, imitates, and even copies freely according to the custom of her day, as did Chaucer, Boccaccio, and later Shakespeare. What makes this author's work fresh is not her material, but her attitude toward it. Her feminism permeates her work, and the basic tales and themes that served as a foundation for all late medieval and early Renaissance literature in the West spring from her pen transformed. A new sensibility emerges. Everywhere the actions are the same, and yet they are different. Christine de Pisan cannot write about Amazons without boasting. She had a strong sense of sisterhood with these women who lived without men, and in all the difficulties she encountered in her own life the model of these Amazon women must have been a source of comfort and meaning.

The story she loved best is the one she tells three times: in *Othéa*, in *The Cité des dames*, and in the *Mutacion*.[22] It is a story of male pride and vanity crushed beneath female strength and competence. It deals with Cyrus, the founder of the Persian Empire. Since antiquity, the figure of Cyrus had been used by authors to illustrate the ephemeral and fragile character of all human endeavor. Plutarch represents Alexander, during his triumphant and stunning conquest of Persia, coming upon the tomb of Cyrus and being moved by the inscription,

> O man, whosoever thou art and whensoever thou
>   comest,
> for I know that thou wilt come,
> I am Cyrus, and I won for the Persians their empire,
> Do not, therefore, begrudge me this little earth
> which covers my body.
>
> (Alex. 69. 2)

The tradition that Cyrus met his death at the hands of a warrior-queen goes back at least as far as Herodotus. A description of the exact nature of his demise is also in Hero-

dotus, although it is unlikely that Pisan had direct access to
this source. The story relates that Cyrus had killed the son
of Queen Tomyris, and her punishment of the great king,
after she captured him in a long and furious battle, was to
oversatisfy his thirst for blood. First, his warriors (his "bar-
ons" in Pisan's version) were slain before his eyes, and their
blood was drained into a huge vessel. Then Queen Tomyris
ordered the decapitation of Cyrus, and tossed his head into
the fresh blood. The moral that even the mighty fall, in
Pisan's rendering, takes on the additional message: one must
never underestimate the power of a woman, nor the fury or
intensity of the rage of a woman wronged. Next to the triumph
of Tomyris, the fate of Cyrus shrinks to an insignificant detail.

According to Pisan's rendering of the story, Heracles and
Theseus did not repeat Cyrus's fatal error. When they launched
their attack on Amazoine, knowing well the formidable strength
and prowess of the women they planned to attack, they avoided
the light of day and waited for the cover of darkness. Even
then the contest became deadlocked in a fierce struggle between Heracles and Menalipe, Theseus and Hippolyta—both
women being sisters of the Amazon queen Sinope. Pisan
changes the emphasis of the traditional tale by insisting that
the battle was a close shave for the two heroes. She dwells
upon the theme that the scales could have easily tipped the
other way, with the Greek warriors losing. Theseus and Heracles are overwhelmed with respect for their opponents—
now their captives—and in the case of Theseus, his awe and
admiration turn to love of the beautiful Hippolyta (*Mutacion*,
Bk. 6, lines 13840–55). To the great rejoicing of the Greeks,
he brings her back to Athens as his bride.

Pisan tells the same event in *Cité* (Bk. 1 ch. 18), where she
places even greater emphasis on the sexual attraction between
the Greek heroes and their captive Amazon princesses. It is
only after the men have carried the women aboard their ships
and there stripped them of their armor, that they discover
the extraordinary beauty of the women. Thus, what began
as a routine task in the work of warriors—the detention of
prisoners—unexpectedly becomes a pleasure. Pisan notes the
"extreme joy" the men experienced in the company of their

captives—how out of chivalry they demanded no ransom for the women, how Theseus married Hippolyta because he could not bear the idea of being parted from her, and how she bore him a son, Hippolytus, who was a very great "knight."

Finally, even the tale of Pyrrhus's defeat of Penthesilea takes on an entirely new meaning in Pisan's rendering. This is another of her most cherished stories, and she appears to have found as much inspiration in Penthesilea as she did in her "Thamaris." In her moralizing *Othéa*, the queen of "Damazoine" represents to Pisan the virtue of charity more clearly than anyone else in "knyghthoode." She exemplifies this through her willingness to use her own strength and that of her great army to avenge Hector, even though his death at the hand of Achilles has thwarted her desire to express her love for him.

In Pisan's *Mutacion*, it is the still living Hector who loves Penthesilea, and small wonder, "For in all the world no one knew/Of a man who had as much prowess" (6.17, 568–9). Hector dies, and Penthesilea vows revenge. The arrival of Pyrrhus at the scene of the battle does not disturb the Amazon, and although they fight together with great vigor, he is unable to defeat her. It is Penthesilea who wounds Pyrrhus and so severely that the Greeks carry him off the field as they would a dead man. But Pyrrhus miraculously survives, filled with hatred for the Amazon but also very aware that he cannot best her in a fair and honorable fight. Thus, according to Pisan, he deliberately schemed to have his men encircle the queen and separate her from her warriors. When this was done, he and "Thalamon Ajax" together close in for the kill: "C'estoit dure chose a veoir!/.II. chevaliers contre une dame" (6. 17, 874–5) (It was a terrible thing to behold/ Two knights against one woman!). In *Cité* (1.19) Pisan repeats essentially the same version of the story, adding a few details that further tarnish the character of Pyrrhus. The wound Penthesilea inflicted on this hero caused him great agony. His pain was exacerbated by his humiliation. Pyrrhus was ashamed at having been beaten so badly by a woman. In order to ensure that his fellow warriors would cooperate with his plan to isolate and encircle the Amazon, he promised them great gifts and riches for carrying out the deed. Perhaps he feared that some inner sense of chivalry might otherwise deter them. At any rate, he set no bounds on the injury they might render Penthesilea, only reserving for himself the final death blow.

So Pyrrhus waits and watches. When he sees bright and lovely yellow hair, he knows the Amazon's head has been bared and that his men have begun their ghastly deed. Pyrrhus moves in and dashes out the brains of the queen whom Pisan called the chief, the most splendid of all women on earth.

In *Cité*, Pisan emphasizes that the death of Penthesilea at Troy was not the end of the Amazon state. In the universal history she presents in *Mutacion,* she includes an account of Alexander meeting with an Amazon queen, which she accepts as proof positive of the exceptionally long and continuous duration of the Amazon state (7. 48). This was another of Pisan's favorite themes: in the course of human history, in which nations continually rise and fall, the land of Amazoine had one of the longest durations in time—more than eight hundred years (Cité 1. 19).

Christine de Pisan was very much of her time and her works are based on the very same texts that scores of late medieval and early Renaissance authors used to express misogynist ideas. Either Amazons were seen as so hateful and unnatural that they were butchered on the field, or they were made into perfect "ladies of Scythia"—palatable to woman-haters because they were made utterly devoid of any sexuality and womanliness.

It is against the background of these works that the unique quality of Christine de Pisan's works truly becomes apparent. While male authors waved the swords of vengeance and retribution and used the Amazon image to glorify themselves, Christine de Pisan created Amazons of strength, sensuality, prowess, and competence and made them speak for women. While men continued to dream, at least for the next few centuries, of conquering Amazons, even of carving up Amazons, Christine de Pisan demonstrated that women could use the Amazon to stake a claim to a share in the art and work of civilization.

Notes

1. *The Writings of Saint Justin Martyr*, trans. Thomas B. Falls, in Ludwig Schopp, ed., *The Fathers of the Church* (New York: Christian Heritage, 1949), p. 431.
2. *The Recognitions of Clement*, IX, 24, in *The Ante-Nicene Fathers*, ed. A. Cleveland Coxe (New York: Scribners, 1925), VIII, 188.
3. Paulus Orosius, *The Seven Books Against the Pagans*, trans. Roy J. Deferrari, in *The Fathers of the Church*, Vol. L, ed. Roy Joseph Deferrari et al. (Washington, D.C.: Catholic University Press, 1964), p. 36.
4. Ibid., p. 104.
5. *The Works of Lactantius*, trans. William Fletcher, vol. I, *Institutes*, in *Anti-Nicene Christian Library*, ed. Alexander Roberts and James Donaldson, vol. XXI (Edinburgh: T. & T. Clark, 1871), Book I, Chapter 9, p. 22.
6. The best scholarly discussion and list of sources for all these European "Trojans" are in M. A. Joly, "Benoît de Sainte-More et le *Romain de Troie*," *Mémoires de la Société des Antiquaires de Normandie*, ser. 3, 7 (1869): 599–635.
7. Gilbert Highet asserts that Homer was lost and available only in incomplete fragments to Benoît. The first known Latin translation in the West after classical times was the copy of the *Iliad* and *The Odyssey* presented by Boccaccio to Petrarch in the mid-fourteenth century. See *The Classical Tradition*, rev. ed. (New York: Oxford University Press, 1967), pp. 53, 84.
8. Their fraud was exposed in the early eighteenth century by Jacob Perizonius. See. R. M. Frazer, Jr., ed. and trans., *The Trojan War, The Chronicles of Dictys of Crete and Dares the Phrygian* (Bloomington: Indiana University Press, 1966). All citations are from pp. 79–80, 87–88, 135, 141–143, 160, 162–63 of this edition. Used by permission of Indiana University Press.
9. As cited by Frazer, ibid., p. 15.
10. For Brutus, see *Historia Britonum of Nennius*, ed. and trans. James Henthorn Todd (Dublin: Irish Archeological Society, 1848); Geoffrey of Monmouth, *The Chronicles of the Kings of Britain*, trans. Peter Roberts (London: E. Williams, 1811); and George Gordon, "The Trojans in Britain," in *Essays and Studies by Members of the English Association*, vol. IX (Oxford: Clarendon Press, 1924). For Francus, see "Comment s'est formée la légende de l'origine Troyenne des Francs," in Edmont Faral, *La Légende Arthurienne* (Paris: Librarie Ancienne Honoré Champion, 1929), I, 263–93.

11. *The Ecclesiastical History of England and Normandy*, trans. Thomas Forester (London: Henry Bohn, 1854), II, 494.

12. Guillaume de Jumièges, *Histoire des Normands*, in M. Guizot, ed. and trans., *Collection des mémoires relatifs à l'Histoire de France*, Vol. XIX (Paris: Brière, 1826), p. 10.

13. Ibid., p. 9.

14. Benoît de Sainte-More, *Roman de Troie*, from Leopold Constans, ed., *Société des Anciens Textes Francais*, 6 vols. (Paris: Firmin Didot, 1904–09; reprinted by Johnson Reprint Corp., New York, 1968), 13. 468. All citations are from this edition. I am following the usage of the United States Library of Congress National Union Catalogue of pre-1956 imprints, and spelling Benoît's name as de Sainte-More rather than Benoît de Sainte-Maure.

15. For the rules of courtly love, see the classic statement by Andreas Capellanus, who was the confessor of Marie de France, in *The Art of Courtly Love*, trans. John J. Parry (New York: Columbia University Press, 1941).

16. "Benoît de Sainte-More," p. 859.

17. Joseph of Exeter, *The Iliad of Dares Phrygius*, trans. Gildas Roberts (Capetown: Balkema, 1970), p. 78. All citations from Joseph of Exeter are from pp. 78–79 of this edition.

18. Giovanni Boccaccio, *De Claris Mulieribus*, trans. Guido A. Guarion (New Brunswick, New Jersey: Rutgers University Press, 1963), p. 4. All citations in text are from chs. 11, 18, and 30, pp. 23–66.

19. Raoul Lefèvre, *The Ancient History of the Destruction of Troy*, trans. William Caxton (London: Thomas Creede, 1596), p. 306.

20. Ibid., p. 359.

21. Ibid., pp. 360–61.

22. Christine de Pisan, *The Epistle of Othea*, trans. Stephen Scrope, Early English Text Society, no. 264 (Oxford: Oxford University Press, 1970); ch. 57, *Cyte of Laydes* (London: Henry Pepwell, 1521), bk. 1, ch. 17; and *Le Livre de la Mutacion de Fortune*, ed. Susan Solente (Paris: Picard, 1959), bk. II, lines 9535–9802. All citations are from these editions.

↰ The Net of Fantasy

Before Europeans had a precise knowledge of the face of the earth, they did not feel compelled to sort their dreams into bins labeled true or false, probable or impossible. Their hazy and inexact geographical knowledge conspired with the accounts of the earliest voyages of discovery to produce a genre of romance literature that was an expression of their visions and their fantasies, of the world Renaissance Europeans hoped to encounter.[1] They had always been certain that somewhere, as yet unknown or perhaps forgotten, or lost through carelessness or want of daring, there existed a place where all their desires for wealth, fame, sex, and glory could be fulfilled. The faraway lands in the writings of Boiardo, Ariosto, Montalvo, Sidney, Spenser, and Shakespeare were places of this world. They were paradises occupied not by angels, but by Amazons, along with fantastic beasts and unlimited wealth. In a world where all things seemed possible, the imagination of European men was kindled and fired by Amazon dreams.

It was not that medieval authors like Benoît had neglected to describe the land of Amazoine, or Feminie; Benoît and others did so in great detail. But somehow, with the first voyages of discovery, the enchanted places and their inhabitants became at once more fantastic and more accessible. Medieval adventurers like Marco Polo and Sir John Mandeville had ventured east and managed not to fall off the edge of the world. By the fifteenth century their relations found an ever-widening audience with the invention of the printing press and the proliferation of vernacular translations. Their accounts, and the first reports of Columbus's voyages, lined the shelves of every literate man, right next to the purely fictitious "lying histories." And in a world where Amazon dreams were daily blossoming, and even coming true, who could tell the lie?

Marco Polo indisputably traveled to the east in the thirteenth century, and, in the area of the Arabian Sea, he described women whom he did not call Amazons, although they observed some customs identified with them. According to Marco Polo, the women lived on one island, and their men on another thirty miles away. These people, both male and female, were baptized Christians but observed the customs of the Old Testament, with the men abstaining from sex with their wives when the women were pregnant. The men cohabited with their wives only three months a year (March, April, and May)—not unlike the Amazon societies described by Benoît and Pisan. The men claimed "they could not live" if they remained with their wives for longer than was customary.[2]

According to this account, the women raised their male children until the boys were fourteen, when they were sent off to live with their fathers. But Marco Polo does not refer to the inhabitants of Female Island as Amazons, and his account consigns them to traditional women's work: weeding, tending, and feeding. They had nothing to do, he claimed, except care for their children, and till and reap the crops that their husbands sowed during their last visit.

Sir John Mandeville, a traveler of the fourteenth century, did not hesitate to affirm the existence somewhere in the east of an island called Amazonia, or Feminye. "It is inhabited only by women, because they will suffer no men amongst them to be their sovereign."[3] When these women desire male company, they march to the lands of men, for "they have loves that use them." The women remain no longer than eight or ten days, and then go home. If they bear any "knave child," they either keep him until he can go about and feed himself, or they kill him. The females all have one breast seared—noblewomen, the left, so they can better carry a shield, and the daughters of footsoldiers the right, to shoot better with bows.

In spite of the caste system that Mandeville ascribed to them, he wrote that they elected their queens, and that the Amazons always selected the woman most worthy in arms and outstanding in valor. So excellent was their prowess that "they go oftentimes in solde to help other kings in their wars, for gold and silver as other soldiers do."

Mandeville gave a whole new twist to the Amazon story when he claimed that the ten lost tribes of Israel lay trapped in a valley between two enormous mountains, far to the east, beyond the land of Cathay, and that they yield tribute for the land "to the Queen of Amazonia, the which that maketh them to be kept in close full diligently." The mountains are much too high to permit escape, and the single straight passage from that country is a desert where men cannot survive, because "it is full of dragons, of serpents, and of other venomous beasts." But in spite of the diligence with which the Amazon queen guarded the Jews, "nonetheless men say that they shall go out in the time of anti-Christ, and that they shall make great slaughter of Christian men."

Whatever the danger of these lost Jews may have been, Europeans were as anxious to find them as they were the Amazons. They were also looking for a powerful Christian ruler, who, like the Jews, had somehow been "lost." Both Marco Polo and John Mandeville mentioned coming upon the realm of the fabulously wealthy brother-in-Christ, Prester John, somewhere in the east. In the late fifteenth century, the opening of Spanish and Portuguese trade with India, the appearance of popular vernacular translations of Polo and Mandeville, and Nicolas Conti's report from India that he docked at an island that was only one mile away from the country of Prester John,[4] all converged to arouse a strong interest in this missing king. The first French printed edition of the letter of Prester John appeared in 1500, soon to be followed by at least twenty others, and English translations also appeared in the early sixteenth century.[5]

Dating from the middle of the twelfth century, the original Latin letter is one of those spectacular hoaxes in which Western medieval culture abounds. Claiming to be the king of India, "Prester John" addressed his letter to the emperor of Rome and the king of France. He proposed that the three of them join together to liberate the holy sepulcher from the infidels, and, in fact, he invited all the rulers of the West to enter into his service, for he already had forty-two monarchs serving under him. He promised wealthy estates and high administrative offices to those who answered his call and accepted his offer. He claimed to be as old as Methuselah (give or take a hundred years) and to rule a vast and wealthy realm inhabited by all kinds of exotic beasts. These included dromedaries, wild horses, one phoenix, griffons, and also "wild bulls of seven horns, white bears, and the strangest lions of red, green, black, and blue color." Prester John also boasted of three different kinds of unicorns, with horns colored either green or black or white, and of lions clever enough to kill them by causing the unicorns to impale their horns in the stock of a tree.

Prester John's subjects were hardly less exotic than the beasts of his kingdom. He had some with the heads of men and the bodies of horses below the waist. These loved to eat raw flesh, and they were often captured, chained, and kept as curiosities. There were also some with human bodies and dogs' heads. In his realm, he reported, were cannibals so ferocious that they ate the flesh of their own parents. He boasted of "horned men who have but one eye in front and there are four on back." Not surprisingly, Prester John said that among the horned men there were women who fit the same physical description (who else would marry a horned man?).

Forty-two days' journey from the land of the horned men lay the land of Great Feminie, also under John's dominion. He seemed anxious to stress that the women of Feminie were his subjects, for he wrote, "Do not think it [Feminie] is in the land of the Saracens, for the one we are talking about is in our country." John's Feminie had three queens "and many other ladies who hold their lands from them." Each queen had under her immediate command "one hundred thousand armed women, not counting those who drive the carts, horses, and elephants, with the supplies and food."

He assured his readers that these women fought as bravely as men. Nevertheless, these warrior-women lost none of their sexual appeal, and fortunate men could stay with them up to nine days time, "during which he can arouse himself and make them conceive." Those who stayed longer died, either because sex is dangerous, or the women murderous, or both.

John's Feminie must have been very close to the place for which we all yearn, for he described Feminie as encircled by a river wide and deep named Cyson (Gehon or Gihan in the Latin editions), "that flows from the terrestrial paradise." Also from paradise, John claimed, came the River Ydonis, which separated his realm from that of the Saracens. Beneath its gently flowing waters lay precious stones of every description, numerous as pebbles in a creek. Very near to this river lay a wonderful fountain, and all who bathed therein emerged not one day older than thirty-two, even if they entered into its miraculous waters twice or three times that age.

It mattered little to European readers of the fifteenth and early sixteenth centuries that the "original" letter of Prester John dated from hundreds of years before their time: had not travelers like Mandeville verified his account? And the earliest reports of Columbus's voyages seemed to bring these fantastic places and experiences even closer within reach: had not Columbus sailed very near to the terrestrial paradise, and wasn't it only the adversity of the winds which prevented him from reaching the rich and luxurious island of Martinio, inhabited by women alone?[6] True accounts were fantastic, reality without adornment was splendid—the world had more riches than any person could carry and magic waters which could bring eternal youth.

For two hundred years European literature, first Spanish and Portuguese, then Italian, French, German, and English, was laced with Amazon dreams. In the quest for the good, the true, and the beautiful, knights who lived forever struggled against the most impossible odds, fighting monsters and giants, battling with the aid of Christian Amazons, or against infidel Amazons, whom they conquered and converted, loved, married, and tamed, in a land of fantastic beasts, ever-lurking perils, and ever-unfolding delights. They were victims of illusion and enchantment. They fell in and out of love. Unknowingly, they drank the waters of disdain, only to have

their magic spell broken by the waters of love. They fought
for hours on end only to discover beneath the armor of a
formidable enemy, a long-lost sibling, or ever faithful lover,
long ago snatched away by a raging tempest or bloodthirsty
pirates. The rewards for their endeavors were beyond any
dreaming—unspeakable wealth and everlasting glory. They
emerged from all adventures vindicated and victorious,
crowned kings and emperors, with hardly a pause to savor
delight before riding off to the next adventure.

What was the motive behind this prolific outpour of creative imagination? Amazons had always inhabited the realm
of fiction, but the women of the Renaissance "lying histories"
were not just make-believe: they were fantastic. They rode
to battle on the backs of wondrous beasts, they fought with
the help of trained griffons, and dressed themselves in golden
cloth embroidered with jewels of every description. They
ruled vast nations, and men all over the world hailed their
beauty, their wealth, and their power. Many literary critics
have struggled to comprehend this surfeit of fantasy.[7] Was
the Renaissance reading public credulous and naive? Did
men doggedly retain the belief that the world is incompre-
hensible and unpredictable? Or was it, as Irving Leonard
argued, the counterpart of modern movies and melodramas,
"a pleasant escape from the harsh monotony of an essentially
primitive existence"? But Leonard himself argues that the
lying histories were more than hypnotic daydreams, more
than escapism, that their readers found in them "authentic
portrayals of life" from which they derived behavior patterns
and manners, as well as "ideas of larger reality and excitement
to greater endeavors."[8] Perhaps John O'Connor, in his study
Amadis de Gaule, expresses the point most aptly when he states
that the admirers of that romance "found in it a mirror of
the world as it ought to be."[9] If the events described therein
were not exactly true, they should be. The lying histories met
a yearning that had lain dormant for centuries, since men
had dreamed of Penthesilea dying in the arms of Achilles.
They were at once the expression of a certain recovery of
nerve, and the desire to be excellent, to be superlative, to
transcend the limitations of one ordinary lifetime. One has

only to note the incredible energy and optimism of those Amazon dreams to recognize unmistakable signs of confidence, of willingness to rise to an occasion, regardless of its danger, its novelty, or its challenge.

In a time when the face of the earth daily was changing its aspect, the Amazon provided authors with an image that was both exotic and reassuring. The Western world had under its belt one thousand years of a literary tradition which told that men of true grit could win a contest with an Amazon. If these women were fantastic, the new generation of heroes spawned by the romances was even more so. In his Amazon dreams, every would-be hero could cast his net—to capture, to kill, or to love his Amazon.

Was this the proper business of Christian men? Some moralists responded with a resounding negative. The Spanish humanist Vives said it would be better to be illiterate, or even to be blind, than to succumb to the poison of the romances. He declared that they were written "by idle and irresponsible individuals devoid of culture and full of vices and filth." Vives had utterly no patience for the works that he considered irredeemably silly: "One hero kills twenty men, another thirty, and another riddled with six hundred wounds and left for dead, promptly recovers, God willing, and returns to the fray against two giants and kills them, thereupon sallying forth weighted down with so much gold, silver, precious stones, silks, and other things that a Genoese carrack could hardly carry them away. What idiocy it is to take pleasure in such stupidities."[10] This same worried moralist believed that the romances had already ruined the young men of Spain, that their only thought now was "to dishonor young women and to shame matrons."[11] He could scarcely number the souls lost through the power of the pen.

The work moralists abhorred the most was *Amadis de Gaule*, a sixteenth-century collection of romances, loosely held together by a more or less continuous story line, and running twenty-one volumes by the end of that century. Its seemingly endless episodes borrowed their elaborate stories from a great variety of sources—pagan, Christian, classical, and medieval. The cycle traced the fortunes of Amadis down to the adventures of his great, great, great, great grandson. It is utterly ahistorical. Amadis's son Esplandian, and his issue, devote themselves to the most Christian mission of helping the Emperor of Constantinople save his city and its holy relics from the hands of the "Turks." The fact that the city had been already lost in 1453 is cheerfully ignored. It is never too late for brave and true knights to stem the tide and spin the globe in their direction. *Amadis* had five different authors, who accordingly produced their volumes in their own Spanish or German or Italian. It was translated into a spectacular variety of languages, including Hebrew. All over Europe readers clamored for more and more, and if the mark of genius escaped it, its authors could at least console themselves with popularity.

In 1605 Miguel de Cervantes paid tribute to *Amadis* in his brilliant spoof of the romances, *Don Quixote de la Mancha*. The lying histories are the obvious cause of the madness of Don Quixote. Cervantes was able to use an inquisition and inspection of Don Quixote's library by a cast of ridiculous and self-righteous characters, a curate and a barber, as a vehicle for commenting on the literature of his day, as well as some of the more boorish reactions to the same.

Cervantes's curate looks at the four books of *Amadis de Gaule* and announces that this was "the first romance of chivalry to be printed in Spain, and the beginning and origin of all the others." But he did not speak these words to save the book: "for that very reason I think that we should condemn it to the flames without any mercy whatsoever."[12]

It is the barber who wins a reprieve for *Amadis*: "I have heard that it is better than the other books of this sort that have been composed, and in as much as it is unique of its kind, it ought to be pardoned." The curate agrees to spare *Amadis* "for the moment," but the next book the barber hands him is the *Exploits of Esplandian*, "the legitimate son of Amadis de Gaule." The curate had no problem rendering an immediate sentence for Esplandian—the Old Testament prophets may have spared the sons from the iniquities of the fathers, but Cervantes's curate would spare them from the fathers' grace as well: "the father's merits are not to be set down to the credit of his offspring. Take it, Mistress Housekeeper, open that window and throw it out in the stable yard; it will make a beginning for that bonfire of ours."

Cervantes's curate may have consigned Esplandian to the flames, but the reading public of Europe, and even of the Spanish outposts in America, did not concur. Between 1570 and 1588, in Spain alone, Esplandian, or Book V of *Amadis de Gaule* went through ten editions and was as popular, or even more so, than the first four books, which dealt with Amadis alone.[13] Book V may have been of poor aesthetic value, but it nevertheless burned in men's minds, kindling and rekindling the fires of imagination and desire. Today the English edition is not found in most libraries, so we must bear the happy burden of relating Montalvo's wonderful, if improbable story. He began with words that he knew would captivate his readers: "Now you are to hear the most extraordinary thing that ever was heard of in any chronicles, or in the memory of man. . . . Know then, that on the right hand of the Indies, there is an island called California, very close to the side of Terrestrial Paradise, and it is peopled by black women, without any men among them, for they live in the fashion of Amazons."[14] Not only were these women beautiful, they also were "of strong and hardy bodies, or ardent courage, and of great force."

California was no ordinary place, but as an island it was "the strongest in all the world, with its steep cliffs and rocky shores." The women lived "in caves wrought out of the rock with much labor." They shared their homes with griffons, which they trapped and raised. Although the griffons were enormous beasts, the women had no trouble in maintaining them, for "they fed them with the men they took prisoners, and with the boys to whom they gave birth." Of course Montalvo assured his readers that California had an abundant variety of wild animals in addition to the griffons, but it was very poor in mineral resources. The women were forced to fashion their arms and the harnesses of the wild beasts they rode in one metal alone, "for in the whole island, there was no metal but gold."

Now it came to pass that one day a representative of the
pagan sultan Armato sailed to California to seek the aid of
Queen Califia and her Amazons at the siege of Constantinople. Of all the Amazons, the queen was "the most beautiful . . . of blooming years, and in her thoughts desirous of
achieving great things, strong of limb, and of great courage."
She knew that peoples from all over the world were fighting
Christians, but "she did not know what Christians were." Not
that Armato need worry. Califia and her Amazons had so
much hope of "plunder and glory and getting to see the
various peoples of the world" that they readily agreed to join
the alliance against the Christians, whatever they were. It
took a veritable fleet to carry all the women, their food, and
their golden armor, the wild beasts which they rode to battle,
etcetera. One entire boat was loaded with five hundred griffons, who "from the time they were born . . . were trained to
feed on men." Califia's strategy, which she carefully explained
to her pagan allies, was to hold back from battle until her
griffons cleared the Christians from the walls of Constantinople. The next morning, the pagans waited behind while
Califia and her women rode to the front in their armor of
gold, "all adorned with the most precious stones, which are
to be found in the island of California like the stones of the
field for their abundance." The women mounted on their
assorted fierce beasts, and then released the now starving
griffons from their cages.

In vain the desperate Christians struck at the griffons with
arrows, swords, and lances: "their feathers were so tight joined
and so stout, that no one could strike through to their flesh."
Thinking the city taken, the sultans ordered their troops to
climb ladders over the walls. If Califia herself hardly knew
what a Christian was, her griffons could scarcely be expected
to distinguish between male friends and male foes. They had
been trained to attack all men. They were no longer hungry,
having dined on a hearty diet of Christian warriors. So the
griffons contented themselves with swooping up the Turks
in their enormous claws and carrying the terrified pagans to
great heights before releasing them to plunge to their deaths.
Her easy victory denied her, Califia had to order the griffons

recaged, and she and her women mounted the ladders up the walls of Constantinople to join the furious battle that was raging within. Both she and her Amazons placed "before their breasts such breastplates as no weapon could pierce," but the rest of their armor was "all of gold, which covered their legs and their arms." From the streets and alleys of Constantinople archers fired at them "with arrows and darts which pierced them through the sides, so that they received many wounds, because their golden armor was so weak." Yet, the Amazons did well in conventional combat (that is, without griffons). The author did not cease to marvel at "the things the Queen did in arms, like slaying knights or throwing them wounded from their horses." She lost two hundred of her women in the attempt to take the city.

Nightfall brought battle to a close with heavy casualties on all sides. In the meantime, the Christian ranks had been swollen by defending knights arriving from all over the West to help save the besieged city: among their ranks were Amadis of Gaul and his son Esplandian. They are greeted by a challenge brought by a richly attired "black and beautiful" damsel. The note read:

> Radiaro, Sultan of Liquia, shield and rampart of Pagan Laws, destroyer of Christians, cruel enemy of the enemies of the Gods, and the very Mighty Queen Califia, Lady of the great island of California, famous for its great abundance of gold and precious stones: we have to announce to you, Amadis of Gaul, King of Great Britain, and you, his son, Knight of the Great Serpent, that we are come into these parts with the intention of destroying the city of Constantinople, on account of the injury and loss which the most honored King Armato of Persia, our cousin and friend, has received from this bad emperor.

The note closed with a personal challenge, which Amadis and Esplandian accepted. But in the meantime Califia was utterly captivated by her messenger's description of Esplandian's beauty, and she asked the sultans to arrange a safe conduct for her so that she might view her famous enemies. The Christian princes were at first reluctant to grant her visit, but Lisuart, king of Great Britain and liege lord of Amadis of Gaul, could not see any harm in the request: "it is a good thing to see the most distinguished woman in the world."

So, with permission for the visit in hand, Califia retired to her shipboard quarters to prepare for the events of the next morning. Here Montalvo depicts her as writhing in conflict, torn between the woman and the Amazon. She lay awake all night, unable to decide whether to appear before Amadis and Esplandian in her armor, or in womanly dress (which, fortunately, she had packed and taken with her, knowing that nothing is more fickle than fortune and the weather). Luckily, her sleeplessness took no toll on her beauty, and with daybreak, having resolved that "it would be more dignified to go in the dress of a woman," she put on her dress "all of gold, with many precious stones" and a wonderful turban, also of gold and gems. But her primping was really in vain, for she was outshone by her mount, the most extraordinary beast ever to be observed by human eyes: "It had ears as large as two shields, a broad forehead which had but one eye, like a mirror; the openings of its nostrils were very large, but its nose was short and blunt. From its mouth turned up two tusks, each of them two palms long." Lest we should form a mental picture of a one-eyed elephant (which would have been erroneous), Montalvo supplied more detail: "its color was yellow, and it had many violet spots upon its skin. . . . It was larger than a dromedary, had its feet cleft like those of an ox, and ran as swiftly as the wind, and skipped over the rocks as lightly . . . as do mountain goats." Montalvo gives no impression of the total beast, but he does note that "its flank and haunches and breast were very beautiful."

Califia rode on this beast, and two thousand women, also very richly attired, led by twenty damsels whose long trains "falling from each beast dragged four fathoms on the ground," followed her. In a rather signal display of bad faith, the Christian princes carried their arms, because "they had not much confidence in the promise of the pagans."

Califia and Esplandian spotted each other immediately. He hardly noticed her, but Califia felt herself stricken by the "resplendent beauty" of his eyes: "she was softened and broken by that sight and by her amorous passion, as if she had

been pressed between mallets of iron." Before Esplandian
her Amazon prowess threatened to vanish. "She saw that by
any delay she should expose herself to the risk of dishonor,
by being turned to that native softness which women of nature consider to be an ornament. . . ." Califia decided to let
the sultan take on Esplandian, while she herself would fight
Amadis. She bid the Christian kings farewell, promising to
return "in 'a different dress.' Then, taking the two older kings
by the hand, she permitted them to help her mount up on
her strange steed." Esplandian, the quintessential hero, says
nothing at all to her. Indeed, what code of gentlemanly behavior can prepare a knight for addressing an Amazon? She
might as well have been naked, or bearded, or both. For
although he thought her very beautiful, "he considered it as
very dishonorable that she should attempt anything too different from what the word of God commanded her, that the
women should be in subjection to the man, but rather should
prefer to be ruler of all men, not by her courtesy, but by
force of arms, and above all, he hated to place himself in
relations with her, because she was one of the infidels whom
he mortally despised and had taken a vow to destroy."

But Amadis was prepared for the situation. He did battle
with the Amazon without sacrificing any of his gentlemanly
courtesy. He never drew his sword against her, but instead,
after they unhorsed each other, he chose to fight with a
fragment of her own lance that had become embedded in
his shield. She perceived the insult. When she asked why he
had not drawn his sword, he replied: " 'I have always been
in the habit of serving women and aiding them; and, as you
are a woman, if I should use any weapon against you, I should
deserve to lose all the honors I have gained.' " Furious that
Amadis ranked her a woman, Califia fought even more vig-
orously, until Amadis pointed out to her that Esplandian had
bested the sultan. But she will not surrender—Califia wanted
to fight another round. She struck him on his head as hard
as she could, and thinking that she had surely split his skull,
she was unprepared for his blow. It was so hard, it broke the
lance fragment with which he had been fighting, and caused
her to drop her sword. At last, Califia surrendered. The

Infanta (who was Esplandian's fiancée) received the prisoners most graciously, even bringing Califia "a rich robe and head-dress" so the queen could shed her armor.

As soon as Califia saw the great beauty and the noble lineage of the Infanta, she knew that she must yield to her. Here was the woman worthy of Esplandian. It was not just the strength of her enemy which had captured her, but also his faith. Sounding like a dutiful Christian daughter, she asked Esplandian, " 'seek, if it please you, to take for my husband some other man, who may be the son of a king, or be of such power as a good knight ought to have, and I will become a Christian. For, as I have seen the ordered order of your religion and the great disorder of all the others, I have seen that it is clear that the law which you follow must be the truth while that which we follow is lying and falsehood.' "

Happy to comply with her request, Esplandian, who was now emperor of Constantinople (with the gracious retirement of his father-in-law), presented her to Talanque, his cousin and her future husband. From the very outset she was the model of wifely obedience and submission: " 'Thou shall be my lord,' " she told Talanque, " 'and the lord of my land which is a very great kingdom.' " But she surrendered more than the freedom of one former Amazon: " 'For thy sake, this island shall change the custom which for a very long time it has preserved, so that the natural generations of men and women shall succeed henceforth, in place of the order in which the men have been separated so long.' " This was quite a change for a nation of women who, according to Montalvo's story, were wont to carry the heads of their defeated male enemies at the ends of their spears. Califia proceeded to marry her sister Liota to Talanque's brother-in-law, and she solemnly observed the conversion and baptism of all her women. The conversion of the rank and file brought the possibility that they, too, might someday become dutiful Christian wives. Montalvo's hero, Esplandian, son of Amadis of Gaul, conquers an entire population of Amazons.

Under several authors, the romance was extended another seventeen books, with various Amazons appearing in many of the episodes. In spite of the fact that Montalvo had described the Christianization of the Amazon army, as well as their vow to stay in the proper womanly sphere, Califia reappears in Book VII, back to her old fighting ways. This time, however, she is fighting on the Christian side.

In Book VIII, there is Zahara, an Amazon queen, who Amadis's grandson Lisuart fights in much the same manner as Amadis had fought Califia, that is, without drawing his own sword. In that same book, Lisuart's son, Amadis of Greece, assumes the costume of Néréide to see his beloved lady Niquée. Neither Caesar nor the emperor Commodus would have found this behavior reprehensible. If a man would be a woman, then let him be an Amazon. But his Néréide was a very fetching Amazon, and Niquée's father Brazilique falls for him at first sight, which greatly complicates the affairs of the lovers. Similarly, in the disguise of the Amazon Daraïde, Agesilan, a great-grandson of Lisuart but a chip off the old block, is able to gain the proximity of his beloved Diane. His rival for her love, Arlanges, uses the same trick.

Amazons abound in this world of all things possible, which includes any number of varieties of arrangements between the sexes. In Book XII a mighty storm brings the heroes ashore on the Isle of Canabee, an Amazonian community ruled by Queen Florelle. But it has lost its pure Amazonian character. Zahara, the queen of the Caucasus, drafted fifty thousand trained female archers to help Abra, the queen of Babylon, fight Lisuart of Greece. While the women of Canabee were fighting, the men took the opportunity to rebel. The peace settlement was something of a compromise—men could not carry arms or govern; male children could not inherit, since inheritance was restricted to the female line; if women chose to marry, they were to be the heads of the household; and any man having sex with a woman not his wife was to be burned alive.[15]

Book XIII introduces another Amazon princess. She is Penthasilée, the daughter of Queen Calpendre, obviously named for her famous foremother. She fights with twenty thousand warrior-maids each mounted on a unicorn with their bridles, their clothing, and their arms all trimmed in

gold. Behind them followed a triumphal carriage pulled by
four Ethiopian "rhinocerons." In front of them marched their
daughters, who, like their mothers, had their right breast
seared in infancy so they could better handle the bow. Pages
in golden cloth walked at their side, followed by seven beautiful queens, their vassals, and their unicorns, etcetera. The
dress of the princess Penthasilée was so sumptuous "she seemed
more like a fairy than a human."[16] But alas, she cannot carry
a sword or wear full armor, because the princess has not yet
taken the vows of knighthood. So chivalrous is the now quite
elderly Amadis, that he cannot refuse the request to knight
the princess, although she is fighting on the side of the enemy.
After she solemnly promises to obey the rules of chivalry
without ever intentionally doing wrong or causing injury,
Amadis receives Penthasilée into knighthood. She and her
mother then fight his great, great, great-grandson Agesilan
(who is helped by his mother). The quarrel ends with mutual
respect, with Christians and Amazons forming an alliance,
which served to anger greatly all the pagans.

There are so many Amazons in the cosmos of *Amadis* that
the brave Christian knights cannot hope to pacify all of them.
Amazons reemerge in Book XXI with the realm of the Amazon Castora. Any man who happens by must take a woman
for two years on pain of death, and all children from their
union become the property of the state.[17] It is in this same
book that Amadis finally dies, after more than one hundred
years of the most faithful service to Christianity, exhibiting
to the last prowess in love and war, his heroism so many times
verified by his killing and his loving of Amazons. And those
who read of his adventures dreamed that they, too, could
conquer death and dying, and be famous all across the earth.

In 1533 a worried Spanish diplomatic official hastened to
report to his superior, who was secretary to the emperor
Charles V, news of a rumor circulating in the region of the
capital of Spain: " 'I can hardly exaggerate how much cre-
dence has been given to the report that seventy large ships
had come into the harbors of Santander and Laredo, bringing ten thousand Amazon women who had come to mate
with Spaniards.' " They came for the very same reasons that

Thalestris supposedly had sought out Alexander, in days of old, "because of the reputation for valor and virility of our men." This report was difficult to refute, given the primitive communications system, as well as the shared beliefs of large segments of the population of sixteenth-century Spain. Amazons in great numbers inhabited the world everywhere, and once again, as in antiquity, they were within range of the experience of the brave. Spanish men were so superlative that "any Amazon who became pregnant would give fifty ducats to the man concerned for his work." This offer had quite an effect on customary transactions between the sexes in the capital district of Valladolid: it caused "the rates of the local 'ladies of pleasure' to drop because of such a large and wealthy competition, and because their men customers were so well remunerated for their trouble. And rest assured that this has been considered so well founded here that nothing else has been talked about."[18]

Sixteenth-century Spaniards were not the only men who had Amazon dreams, who saw themselves as heroes in a life every bit as exciting as a novel, and who found in the lying histories the true story of life as it ought to be. Readers throughout Europe read *Amadis*, and this romance was a major influence on the literature of Italy and England, as well as France and Germany.

It is impossible to sort out the precise origin of the stories in the most popular of the sixteenth-century romances. One of the earliest works was Matteo Boiardo's *Orlando Innamorato*, dating from 1484. It was a sparse work, which Ludovico Ariosto completed and continued with his *Orlando Furioso* in 1516. But during the intervening years Boiardo's work served, in prose translation, as the first three books of a popular Spanish romance called the *Mirror of Knighthood*.[19] The Italians returned the compliment by devouring the work of Montalvo which was published in Rome in 1519, but almost certainly known (in the Spanish original) before that date.[20]

Boiardo's *Orlando Innamorato* dealt with Hector, as well as with Penthesilea (who saved Hector's sword to pass it on to the hero, Roland), and introduced a virago, or Amazon, named Marfisa, a "young Indian queen"[21] who vowed to capture three Christian kings—Charlemagne, Gradasso, and Agrican. She was a great warrior, and her opponents included the Christian Amazon Bradament. The story line was a complicated tangle with a markedly Oriental quality. It had fairies, giants, monsters, and all kinds of enchantments and spells. It was a mixture of reverie and nightmare.

Ariosto's work managed to be a dazzling tale of adventure and at the same time mock the genre. To this day its ironic wit makes it a joy to read. His fighting heroine Marfisa and her companions survive a storm at sea only to land near "Lymisso, Tropoly, or Satila" on a coast ruled by Amazon women. The sea pilot explained to Astolfo, the English duke, that according to the traditional rule of the women, all newcomers to this nation were put to a special test:

> The sole shall escape, that runs at tilt so well,
> As first to make ten men of theirs fall,
> And next in venery and flesh delight
> And satisfie ten women in one night.[22]

All men who failed the test, or any part of it, the Amazon women killed or enslaved. The motley group of ill-fated traveling knights drew lots to see which of them would venture his luck at the challenge posed by the Amazon women: which of them would dare to kill ten knights and still survive to give sexual pleasure to ten damsels. It was their assumption that Marfisa would be excluded from the lottery, for although she was a warrior of the greatest skill, "for the second daunce she was not fit" (19. 49). But she insisted on being included in the drawing of lots, and of course Ariosto had her win. Marfisa then announced her intention not only to gain the freedom of herself and her fellow travelers, but to make that hostile shore safe for all travelers forever—to end that malevolent Amazonian state.

Naturally, her performance in the first part of the test was astounding. Marfisa wrote the book on being a superheroine. Like her twentieth-century daughters, Wonder Woman and the Bionic Woman, the results of her contests were never in doubt. Ordinary blows of ordinary men had neither the power nor even the possibility of harming her. It is doubtful that all the technology and wealth of the modern world could conspire to produce one such as Marfisa. Witness the fate of her first nine opponents:

> She bath'd her blade in blood up to the hilt,
> And with the same their bodies all she mangled,
> All that abode her blowes, their bloud was spilt,
> They scaped best that here and thither ranged,
> Or those whose horses overthrown at tilt,
> Lay with their masters on the earth intangled.
> Thus of nine enemies remained none,
> For all were kil'd, or maim'd, or overthrown.
>
> (19. 56)

At last, there remained only one knight for her to conquer, the Black Knight. She had saved the best for the last. They both grabbed sturdy lances and awaited the signal for the start of the combat. Their battle was furious:

> The speares in spels and sundry pieces flew,
> As if they had been sticks or cane,
> Yet of the blowes to both did hurt ensew,
> Their steeds were welnigh brought into their bane,
> Quite overthrown in all the peoples view.
> As though their legs had quite from them been tane,
> So both horses tumbled on the ground.
> Yet both themselves from hurt were safe and sound.
>
> (19. 61)

They fought for hours on end without any conclusion. When darkness fell the knight invited Marfisa and her companions to spend the night at his castle so they could complete their combat in the morning. It was also important to spare Marfisa from the rage of the ninety widows she had created, for each hero who passed the Amazons' dual trial of defeating ten men and then deflowering ten women, became the husband of those ten women. All of the nine knights whom Marfisa killed that day had passed the test.

As Marfisa removed her helmet, the Black Knight was astonished to learn that his opponent had been a woman, and Marfisa was amazed to find "That the knight did by his face appeare/ To be a boy, of age but eighteen yeare" (19. 70).

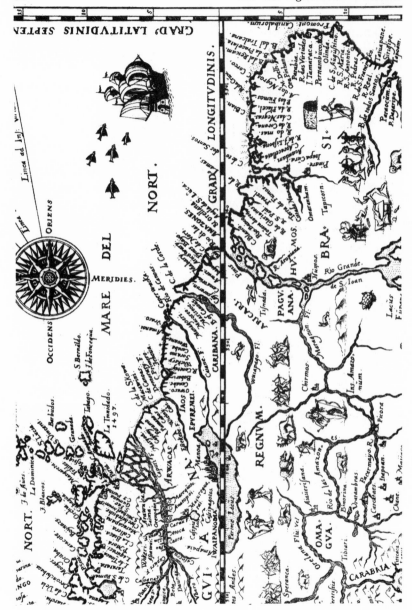

Amazons, headless men, and cannibals in South America, from
Levinus Hulsius, *Voyages*, Part IV, 2d ed. (Nuremberg, 1618). (*Courtesy
Rare Books and Manuscripts Division, The New York Public Library,
Astor, Lenox and Tilden Foundations*)

All she said to him was, I am Marfisa: "And she need to say no more,/For all the world had heard the rest before" (20. 4). Her opponent, a knight named Guidon, turned out to be a long-lost cousin of the English duke in her own party, and with their combined cunning and daring, and with the help of the duke's magic trumpet which caused all who heard it to freeze in terror, the group escaped from the Amazonian shore. And splendid Marfisa never did have to deflower the ten maidens.

In his very apt description of the geographical confusion Europeans experienced in the early sixteenth century, Sanders suggested that this was but a brief moment in time; that Europeans had only to await the results of a few more Portuguese voyages to know the world as it actually is.[23] But as in so many instances in the history of ideas, what could happen does not. Just because men had some more information does not mean they possessed the power or the desire to break the spell, and like a lingering melody, the enchantment of Amazon dreams went on and on.

Even Tasso's *Jerusalem Delivered*, which he wrote in the most Catholic climate of Counter-Reformation Italy two generations after Ariosto, did not elude the spell. First published in 1580, the work dealt with actual historical events—the Christian conquest of Jerusalem in 1099. But it had its Amazon, Clorinda, nursed by a lioness in her infancy. Tancred, the great Christian hero, wounded her mortally in battle. In a scene reminiscent of Penthesilea's death, Clorinda falls by the hero's sword, and like Achilles, Tancred lived to regret his act:

> But when he saw her gentle soul was went,
> His manly courage to relent began:
> Grief, sorrow, anguish, sadness, discontent,
> Free empire got and lordship on the man,
> His life within his heart they close up pent,
> Death through his senses and his visage ran;
> Like his dead lady dead seem'd Tancred good,
> In paleness, stillness, wounds, and streams of
>   blood . . . [24]

Even the thought that he had been able to fulfill her dying wish for baptism, that she died Christ's "child and handmaid dear," did little to cheer him for the loss of the beautiful Amazon.

Clorinda's death destroyed neither the Amazons nor the fantasies Europeans fashioned to ensnare them. The vogue for these warrior-women and for the romances about the realms in which they and the great heroes who conquered them held sway was only beginning to boom in England, where the influence of *Amadis* and the many generations after him was strongest in the 1570s. In his *Defense of Poetry*, Sir Philip Sidney argued that he "had known men, that even with reading *Amadis de Gaule* (which God knoweth wanteth much of a perfect poesy) have found their hearts moved to the exercise of courtesy, liberality, and especially courage."[25]

Whether or not his own behavior resulted from reading *Amadis*, Sidney himself was something of a model of courtly perfection: he excelled in courtesy, arms, and chivalry. He was cupbearer to Queen Elizabeth, and he frequently donned body armor and participated in tournaments and other knightly festivities held at Elizabeth's court. In his *Countess of Pembroke's Acadia*, he used a theme that had appeared in *Amadis of Greece*—that of a knight disguising himself as an Amazon in order to gain the proximity of his lady. Though Sidney knew *Amadis*, there are also precedents for knights in Amazon attire in classical history and in mythology. The great hero Heracles was forced to spin by the wicked Queen Omphale. Sidney may have had this legend in mind. His hero, Pyrocles, for the sake of love, disguised himself as the Amazon Zelmane. His cousin Musidorus warned him, "this effeminate love of a woman doth so womanize a man that, if he yield to it, will not only make him an Amazon, but a launder, a distaff spinner, or whatsoever other vile occupation their idle heads can imagine and their weak hands perform."[26] Pyrocles responded that he was unable "to think light of the sex of whom I have my life. . . . I was to come to it, born of a woman, and nursed of a woman. . . . And truly we men, and praisers of men, should remember that, if we have excellencies, it is reason to think them excellent creatures of whom we are—since a kite never brought forth a good flying hawk."[27]

Sidney was the patron of Edmund Spenser, who no doubt shared Sidney's admiration for *Amadis* and love for the heroic. Why else would Spenser have set his great work in Faery Land? In the Proem of Book II of his *Faerie Queene*, Spenser somewhat playfully identifies its setting as the New World:

> Right well I wote most mighty soveraine . . .
> Sith none, that breatheth aire, does know,
> Where is that happy land of Faery. . . .

> But let that man with better sence advize
> That of the world least part to us is red:
> And daily how through hardy enterprize
> How many regions are discovered,
> Which to late age were never mantioned.
> Who ever heard of th'Indian Peru?
> Or who in venturous vessell measured
> The Amazons huge river, now found trew?[28]

In the same manner, Spenser suggests, might we not find "Faeryland"?

Spenser's poem, however, is far more about a dimension of human experience than it is about an existent or imaginary portion of space. In a letter of 1589, he explained, "In that Faery Queene, I meane glory in my generall intention, but in particular I conceive the most excellent and glorious person of our soveraine Queene, and her kingdom in Faery Land."[29] To praise Elizabeth, Spenser created Gloriana, queen of Faery Land, and Britomart, a beautiful, virtuous, reformed, and rather boring Amazon—though she is easily a match for Ariosto's Marfisa as well as Tasso's Clorinda. But Spenser's idea of fame and heroism was closely tied to his notion of defending right order in the world. And essentially that meant that his Faeryland was a place where man stepped into a magical and heroic dimension, but women, even those of superlative skill in battle, were to remain subordinate to

men. As in classical times, Spenser's Amazons exist only as
vehicles for male transcendence.

Spenser spoke most directly on the topic of right order in
his treatment of Radigund, an evil Amazon. He explained
that she fell upon her malevolent ways when she was cruelly
disappointed in love. Spurned by the knight she loved,

> She turn'd her love to hatred manifold,
> And for his sake vow'd to doe all the ill
> Which she could doe to knights: which now she doth
>   fulfill.

> For all those knights, the which by force of guile
> She doth subdue, she fowly doth entreate.
> First she doth them of warlike armes despoile,
> And cloth in womens weedes: and then with threat
> Doth them compell to worke, to earnee their meat,
> To spin, to card, to wash, to wring:
> Ne doth she give them other thing to eat,
> But bread and water, or like feeble thing,
> Them to disable from revenge adventuring.

Spenser very astutely saw that the most degrading, the very
worst thing that can ever befall a man is to be treated like a
woman. Sir Turpine, his narrator, stated, "I rather choose
to die in lives despight,/Then lead that shameful life, unworthy of a knight." But Artegall, the "Elfin knight" (and
Spenser's hero), was not at all frightened away. He immediately determined to put an end to Radigund's cruelty and
to the unnatural order of her state. After a full day of bloody
and indecisive combat, Radigund sent her maid Clarin, or
Clarinda, to propose a private contest between herself and
Artegall. Clarinda quoted her queen as saying,

> . . . if I vanquishe him he shall obay
> My law, and ever to my lore be bound;
> And so will I, if me he vanquish may,
> What ever he shall like to doe or say.

He accepted, and at the appointed time Radigund rode to
the battle in an outrageous costume—silver strands, milk
white satin, and "ribbands diversely distraught" flowed over
her armor. Her skirt was "short tucked for light motion/up

to her ham," and her legs were covered with "mailes" that showed above "painted buskins . . . basted with bands of gold on every side." She is both woman and warrior. As a warrior, however, she proved no match for the "Elfin knight." But as Artegall ripped off her helmet, at a point when he would have cheerfully removed her head, too (for such was his rage), the woman accomplished what the Amazon could not:

> He saw, his senses straunge astonishment,
> A miracle of natures goodly grace
> In her fair visage voide of ornament,
> But bath'd in bloud and sweat together ment. . . .
>
> At sight thereof his cruel minded hart
> Empierced was with pittiful regard,
> That his sharpe sword he threw from him apart,
> Cursing his hand that had that visage mard.

Now, "damned by the doome of his owne mouth," he was forced to serve Radigund:

> Then tooke the Amazon this noble knight,
> Left to her will by his owne wilfull blame,
> And caused him to be disarmed quight
> Of all the ornaments of knightly name. . . .
> In stead whereof she made him to be dight
> In womans weedes, that is to manhood shame
> And put before his lap a napron white . . .

After she clothed him properly for his new station in life, Radigund led him to the dungeon where she kept most of her captives:

> There entered in, he round about him saw
> Many brave knights, whose names right well he knew,
> There bound t'obay that Amazons proud law,
> Spinning and carding all in comely rew,
> That his bigge hart loth'd so uncomely so uncomely
>   vew. . . .
>
> Amongst them all she placed him most low,
> And in his hand a distaffe to him gave,
> That he thereon should spin both flax and tow:
> A sordid office for a mind so brave:
> So hard it is to be a woman's slave.

Spenser compared his hero with Hercules, "who for Iolas
sake . . . did apply/his mightie hands the distaff vile to hold."
This inversion of right order was a natural effect of Radigund's defiance of nature:

> Such is the crueltie of women kynd,
> When they have shaken off the shamefast hand,
> With which wise Nature did them strongly bynd,
> T'obay the heasts of mans well ruling hand . . .

But it was Spenser's intent to flatter his queen, not to offend
her. It was probably for Elizabeth's sake that he added,

> But vertuous women wisely understand,
> That they were borne to base humilitie,
> Unlesse the heavens them lift to lawfull soveraintie.

It is understood that Elizabeth is one of those few who the
heavens allowed to rule.

Spenser did allow his evil Radigund one all too human
emotion: she could not help falling in love with her newly
captive "Elfin knight." She sent Clarinda, her most trusted
servant, to propose to Artegall the exchange of his bands of
iron for bonds of love. But Clarinda herself conceived a passion for Artegall and betrayed her queen by bringing false
reports to the knight, of Radigund's ever increasing disdain.
Clarinda proved false to Radigund because in this unnatural
state there could be neither faithfulness nor loyalty. It was a
wrong order, and those who served it were necessarily wrong-
hearted. For Radigund, Spenser could permit no redemp-
tion. Her violations against nature were so great there was
nowhere in heaven or earth, even in Faery Land, where she
could find forgiveness. When Britomart, the Amazon of right
order, came to free her knight and the other captives, Radigund met her match. Though they fought like "a tigre and
a lioness," in the end Radigund fell beneath the avenging
sword.

While Artegall and the other former prisoners were re-
covering from the degradation and deprivation of their imprisonment, Britomart reigned as princess. She saw her first
task as returning to "normal" relations between the sexes:

> And changing all that forme of common weale
> The liberty of women did repeale,
> Which they had long ursurpt; amd them restoring
> To man's subjection, did true justice deale.

Britomart risked her own life to serve Artegall, and spent her toil on returning him back to health, only to stand "full sad and sorrowful" as he rode off to his next adventure. She wisely understood that, as with any fine knight, Artegall's honor depended upon his constant experience of trials and adventures, and this idea comforted her, while "womanish complaints she did represse."

Spenser's Britomart, as well as Shakespeare's Hippolyta (in *A Midsummer Night's Dream*), were tamed subordinate wives. So too was Anthony Gibson's Hippolyta who defeated Theseus in battle but married him anyway "on mere grace." She became such a "serviceable" wife, that when Theseus received a wound from a bull's horn on one of his heroic ventures, Hippolyta licked his wound and restored him to health.[30]

Mark Rose, in his *Heroic Love*, suggested that the correct ordering of the domestic sphere was a major motif in Elizabethan drama;[31] Jean Gagen in *The New Woman* argues that would-be Amazons trading their autonomy for the love of a man is the theme of a series of seventeenth-century English plays.[32] But the Elizabethan authors who killed off hopelessly evil Amazons, and fashioned from the rest perfect wives, were not speaking primarily about married love: they were reasserting and bolstering the primacy of male dominion. For Elizabethan men the popularity of the age-old theme of conquering and overpowering Amazons had a special significance. Even if their ruler was a queen, and even if experience should continue to unfold more and more strange and new peoples, they could comfort themselves with the belief that the basic relations between the sexes were fixed throughout space. These relations were eternal verities of nature and everywhere unchanging.

In her essay "Woman on Top,"[33] Natalie Davis argued that the image of women pursuing traditional male activities is often, but not always, invoked to reinforce traditional values. Sometimes role reversals function to challenge or weaken the

old and established ideas and values. Yet it is difficult to find
any message in favor of female emancipation in the frequent
references to Amazons in Elizabethan literature. Perhaps the
proof of the pudding lies in the fact that only a single minor
poet is known to have directly addressed Elizabeth as an
Amazon.[34] Similarly, a cartoon showing the queen as a one-
breasted, bow-wielding virago, whose Amazonian body is also
a map of Europe, was of foreign (Dutch) origin. Had the
image of Amazons been clearly positive, Elizabeth would have
been deluged with tributes to Antiopa, Orinthia, Hippolyta,
and Penthesilea. But this genre of Elizabethan literature does
not exist, because the Amazon image was ambivalent. To call
Elizabeth an Amazon would have been to praise her and
insult her at the same time. It would have been calling her
extraordinary, superlative, and also an aberration of nature.
For every heroic Britomart is a close relation to an evil Radigund, and a jeering Thersites lies in the lurk to mock and
ridicule every adoring Achilles.

And, too, the occasional appearance of Amazons in Renaissance masks and pageants should not be understood as a
celebration of women. In the French courts of Henry II and
Henry III the male courtiers who dressed as Amazons at
particular functions were undoubtedly testifying to the enormous vogue of *Amadis of Greece*, and possibly of certain aspects
of classical history and mythology. When Shakespeare included a mask in which Amazons sing and dance in *Timon
of Athens*, when Amazons appeared at the 1594 ceremonies
for the christening of Prince Henry (heir to James I), and
figured in Ben Jonson's 1609 *Masque of Queens*, Amazons were
once again serving as ladders to transcendence and glory.
Just as Amazons had certified the heroes of old, they were
now invoked to certify royal stature and authority.

In early modern times Amazon dreams played a particularly important function. Amazon women represented the
transcendent, almost supernatural character of the many trials
and challenges that lay ahead in regions awaiting discovery
and exploration. Since the very, very brave and the very, very
great could trap them and tame them, Amazons represented
most of all an affirmation of the strength and the ability of
Western man to conquer and master these newfound worlds.

Notes

1. For an excellent comment on the state of European geographical confusion see Ronald Sanders, *Lost Tribes and Promised Lands* (Boston: Little, Brown, 1978), p. 110.
2. *The Travels of Marco Polo*, trans. Ronald Latham (London: Penguin Books, 1958), p. 269.
3. *The Travels of Sir John Mandeville*, ed. A. W. Pollard (New York: Dover Publications, 1964), pp. 103–4. All citations from Mandeville are from this edition, pp. 103, 105–6.
4. See the "Journey of Hieronimo di Santo Stefano," in R. H. Major, ed., *India in the Fifteenth Century* (London: Hakluyt Society, 1857), 1st ser., no. 22, p. 4.
5. For a discussion of the popularity of the work, see Vsevolod Slessarev, *Prester John, The Letter and the Legend* (Minneapolis: University of Minnesota Press, 1959). All citations from Prester John are from this edition, pp. 67–79.
6. Cecil Jane, ed. and trans., *The Voyages of Christopher Columbus* (London: Argonaut Press, 1930; reprinted by DaCapo Press, New York, 1970), p. 264.
7. See, for example, A. Bartlett Giamatti, *The Earthly Paradise and the Renaissance Epic* (Princeton, New Jersey: Princeton University Press, 1966); Thomas M. Greene, *The Descent from Heaven* (New Haven: Yale University Press, 1963); Robert M. Durling, *The Figure of the Poet in Renaissance Epic* (Cambridge, Massachusetts: Harvard University Press, 1965).
8. Irving A. Leonard, *Books of the Brave* (New York: Gordian Press, 1964), p. 14.
9. John J. O'Connor, *Amadis de Gaule and Its Influence on Elizabethan Literature* (New Brunswick, New Jersey: Rutgers University Press, 1970), p. 18.
10. Cited in Leonard, *Books of the Brave*, p. 68.
11. Ibid., p. 69.
12. Miguel de Cervantes Saavedra, *The Ingenious Gentleman Don Quixote de la Mancha*, trans. Samuel Putnam (New York: Viking Press, 1967), p. 52. All citations are from this edition, pp. 52–3.
13. See Henry Thomas, *Spanish and Portuguese Romances of Chivalry* (Cambridge, Massachusetts: Harvard University Press, 1920), p. 67.
14. Sir Edward Everett Hale, *The Queen of California . . . with a Translation of the Sergas of Esplandian* (San Francisco: Colt Press, 1945). All citations from *Esplandian* are from pp. 15–44 of this translation.

15. *Le Douzieme livre d'Amadis de Gaule*, traduit nouvellement d'espagnol en français (Anvers, France: Guillaume Silvius, 1573), p. 318.

16. *Le Trezieme livre d'Amadis de Gaule*, traduit nouvellement d'espagnol par I. G. P. (Lyons, France: Francois Didier, 1577), p. 281.

17. O'Connor, *Amadis de Gaule*, p. 95.

18. Cited in Leonard, *Books of the Brave*, p. 56.

19. Ibid., p. 110.

20. See Thomas, *Spanish and Portuguese Romances*, p. 183.

21. [Matteo Maria Boiardo], *The Orlando Innamorato*, trans. from the Italian of Francesco Berni, by William Stewart Rose (Edinburgh, Scotland: W. Blackwood, 1823), p. 101.

22. Lodovico Ariosto, *Orlando Furioso, Sir John Harrington's Translation*, ed. Graham Hough (London: Centaur Press, 1962). All citations are from Cantos 19 and 20 of this translation.

23. Sanders, *Lost Tribes*, p. 110.

24. Tasso, *Jerusalem Delivered*, trans. Edward Fairfax, ed. Henry Morley (London: George Routledge, 1890), p. 265 (bk. 12, v. 70).

25. Sir Philip Sidney, *Defense of Poetry*, in *Selected Prose and Poetry*, ed. Robert Kimbrough (New York: Holt, Rinehart and Winston, 1969), p. 124.

26. Ibid., p. 327.

27. Ibid., p. 328.

28. Edmund Spenser, *The Faerie Queene*, from *The Complete Poetical Works*, ed. Neil Dodge (Boston: Houghton Mifflin, 1908). All citations are from Book V, cantos 4–8 of this edition.

29. Letter to Sir Walter Raleigh, 23 January 1589, ibid., pp. 136–7.

30. Anthony Gibson, *A Woman's Worthe* (London: John Wade, 1599), pp. 5,37.

31. Mark Rose, *Heroic Love* (Cambridge, Massachusetts: Harvard University Press, 1968), p. 140.

32. Jean Gagen, *The New Woman* (New York: Twayne Publishers, 1954), see especially "The Amazons," pp. 163–77.

33. Natalie Davis, "Woman on Top," in *Society and Culture in Early Modern France* (Stanford, California: Stanford University Press, 1975).

34. See Winifried Schleiner, "Divina virago: Queen Elizabeth as an Amazon," in *Studies in Philology*, vol. 75, 2 (1978): 163–80.

The Confrontation

When he set sail to the west across the Atlantic, Columbus was no more looking for Amazoine than he was searching for America. His letters and diaries disclose all the dreams he crumpled in his pockets and the visions he stuffed into his chests when he dared to be first to venture across the Ocean Sea. He sought golden temples and pagodas; powerful mandarins clothed in heavy silks adorned with gold and jewels; tiny, delicate, elaborately clothed ladies; pepper, cloves, and cinnamon; luxury and mystery; unspeakable wealth, fame, and glory. It was the East that beckoned him, and his Most Catholic Kings (as Ferdinand and Isabella were called in their day) penned a letter of introduction for Columbus to present to the Grand Khan, as if the descendants of Kubla Khan still reigned, the China Marco Polo described was unchanged, and their messenger was to sail across space and time. They wisely threw in two additional and identical letters with the names and titles of the recipients left blank, so Columbus could fill them in correctly as the occasion demanded. For he was bound for the East, and he was the official representative of the power and authority of the Spanish throne in the Orient. The letter was sufficiently vague to meet all eventualities and arrogant enough to demonstrate its majestic origin:

> From the statements of certain of our subjects and of others who come to Us from Your Kingdoms and Domains, we have learned with joy of Your esteem and high regard for Us and Our nation and of Your great eagerness to be informed about things with Us. Wherefore, we have resolved to send You Our Noble Captain, Christopherus Colon, from whom You may

learn of Our good health and Our prosperity and other matters
which We have ordered him to tell You on Our part. We
therefore pray You to give good faith to his reports as You
would to Ourselves. Ready and eager to Please You. From Our
City of Grenada, 30 April, 1492.[1]

The naiveté of Ferdinand and Isabella's letter to the Grand
Khan illustrates the extremely rough and semimythical state
of European knowledge of the East—a field of learning where
"Prester John," Marco Polo, and Sir John Mandeville wrote
the textbooks. The beliefs in exotic peoples and animals,
magical fountains of youth, the earthly Paradise, and Amazons were not inventions of the moment, but deeply ingrained convictions of the centuries, boasting classical,
medieval, as well as Renaissance sources.

Thoroughly steeped in the misinformation of his day, Columbus was simply a man in search of fortune and fame who
had somehow managed to reconcile his goals with a deeply
ingrained and devout Christianity. He hoped to do what few
believed possible and none had dared: to reach the East by
sailing west.

Little did he guess, his detractors and the naysayers were
absolutely right. His mission was impossible—not because the
Ocean Sea was unnavigable, but because it was larger than
Columbus in his wildest dreams ever imagined. According
to Samuel Eliot Morison, Columbus underestimated the size
of the world by at least 25 percent.[2] But even with his incorrect estimate of the girth of the globe, his daring and
courage to venture such distances would seem extraordinary
had he not been beckoned and heartened by another siren
spawned by medieval geography—the false but seductive belief that Asia stretched far into the western realms of the
globe. Columbus treasured and heavily annotated his personal copy of Pierre d'Ailly's *Imago Mundi*. This work, penned
before the introduction of Ptolemy in the West, assured him
that the distance between Morocco and the eastern coast of
Asia was not very great, and that it could be navigated in a
few days with favorable wind. He was also wooed by the
apocryphal Book of Esdras (VI, 42), whose statement "six
parts hast thou dried up" was interpreted by many to mean

that the ocean is only one-seventh of the globe. And finally, the medieval cosmology that Columbus used as a foundation for his plans and dreams also included the sweet but spurious promise that he was not sailing into a void, that he would never be very far from the sight of land. For surely there would be many islands at which he could stop for rest and refreshment on his way to the "Indies." The sixth-century Irish monk Saint Brendan discovered many lovely islands on his (legendary) voyages, including one that bore his name. The Florentine scientist and humanist Toscanelli himself suggested to Columbus the mythical Antilia as a convenient resting point en route to Asia. Part of Columbus's reward from Ferdinand and Isabella, in addition to a tax-free 10 percent share in all booty he might gain, and the title "Admiral of the Ocean Sea," was the promise that he would be viceroy and governor of any mainlands or islands he discovered.

Armed with enough misinformation to believe that he could almost walk west to China, Columbus also possessed as a back-up system a navigational skill that many a modern sailor contemplates with awe and envy. And though the hopes founded upon myths one by one proved false, his gifted ability to ride the waves never failed him.

After more than a month at sea, Columbus and his crew sighted land. By Columbus's own reckoning they had sailed through day and night halfway around the world. Surely the island they had in sight was Japan. In fact, it was Hispaniola (modern-day Haiti and Dominican Republic), and Columbus was only one-quarter around the globe. He never wavered in his conviction that he had reached the Orient. No matter that he found not one pagoda or temple, or that the natives (even assuming that they owned gorgeous silk robes) pre-ferred to wear nothing at all. This was the East, and in an attempt to prove to the world that he had reached his des-tination, Columbus fastened his hopes on locating the Island of Martinio, which, according to what may have been a native tradition, was inhabited by women who lived without men. (The question of how much the natives, Columbus, and his Arabic interpreters understood each other is very much open

to debate and speculation.) Martinio sounded like the Island
of Female, which Marco Polo had located in the China Sea.
If only Columbus could capture a few of these women, no
one could dispute his claim of reaching the East. In Columbus's letter to his sovereigns dated February 15, 1493, he
reported finding gold, rhubarb, cannibals, and women who
lived without men. Whether the women of Martinio were
truly the descendants of the Amazons of old mattered little
to Columbus: his main motive was not, as had been in the
case of the classical heroes, to associate himself in some way
with Amazons, but to associate himself with Marco Polo and
stand on the ground on which he had stood. He added one
detail that was not in Marco Polo's *Travels*: the women of
Martinio had as their lovers ferocious cannibals who eagerly
devoured any human flesh they could get. He never explained why the men chose to father the women's offspring
rather than eat the women. He only noted that the women
"use no feminine exercises, but bows and arrows of cane . . . and
they arm and cover themselves with plates of copper, of which
they have plenty." He added that nearby on an island "there
is countless gold."[3] At least one scholar has seen Columbus's
description of Carib women and their wealth as the inspiration for Montalvo's Book V of *Amadis de Gaule*, with Queen
Califia and her Amazons clad in golden armor.[4]

The Italian humanist Peter Martyr d'Anghiera, who in-
terviewed Columbus when he returned to Spain in 1493,
greatly elaborated on Columbus's account in his *Decades of
the New Worlde*. Richard Eden translated the 1503 Latin original into English in 1555, when it became one of the first
English books on America. Eden's translation included Peter
Martyr's commentaries, which made Columbus's reports about
Martinio and its inhabitants sound exotic, forbidden, and
enticing:

> it is inhabited only with women: To whom the Cannibals have
> accesse at certain tymes of the yeare, as in owlde tyme the
> *Thracians* had to the *Amazones* in the Island of *Lesbos*. The men
> children, they sende to theyr fathers. But the women theye
> keepe with themselves. They have great and strong caves or
> dennes in the ground, for which they fly for safeguarde if any

American Amazons in their April mating season, from Levinus
Hulsius, *Voyages*, 1st ed. (Nuremberg, 1598). (*Courtesy Rare Books
and Manuscripts Division, The New York Public Library, Astor, Lenox
and Tilden Foundations*)

man resorte unto them at any other time then is appoynted. And there defend themselves with bowes and arrowes, agenst the violence of suche as attempte to invade them.

Though Columbus tried, "he could not at this tyme approache to this Ilande, by reason of the Northenortheast wynde which blew so vehemently from the same; wheras they nowe followed by Eastsoutheaste."[5]

Like Columbus, Americus Vespucci also encountered warrior-women in what eventually became America, and also like Columbus, the public regarded these women as proof that he had reached the East. Vespucci's "Amazons" were even sexier than those of Columbus: they were not the mistresses of cannibals, they were cannibals themselves. The supposed events of Vespucci's voyage of 1502 were reported by Sebastian Münster in his *Universal Cosmology* (which was translated into English in 1553). Münster wrote that Vespucci and his crew dropped anchor off the shore of an island in the "West Indies." They found the natives unwilling to communicate with them: the two men they sent ashore to examine the island for spices and potential riches of all kinds vanished. When a group of women appeared at the shore, the explorers decided that the best means of establishing communication would be to send a young man "beyng very strong and quicke" ashore, thinking naively that the attractiveness of the young sailor would surely move the women to communicate and to disclose all the secrets of their island. But unfortunately, Münster states, it was not their sexual appetite that this hapless sailor aroused. After looking him over carefully, and feeling the textures of his clothing, the crowd of women increased by one: "there came suddenly a woman down from a mountayne, bringing with her secretly a great stake, with which she gave him such a stroke behynde, that he fell dead on the earth." The men of the island shot arrows at the men on the ships, who responded with volleys of gunfire. Meanwhile, before the eyes of the horrified sailors, "the women also which had slayne the yong man, cut him in pieces even in the sight of the Spaniardes . . . shewing them the pieces, and rosting them at a great fyre."[6]

The sailors got the message and left in search of friendlier

American Amazon-Cannibals, from Hulsius, *Voyages*, 1st ed. (*Courtesy Rare Books and Manuscripts Division, The New York Public Library, Astor, Lenox and Tilden Foundations*)

natives. The image of Amazon cannibals made a powerful impression on the European mind, and an engraving of one-breasted women simultaneously cooking and stabbing a couple of men strung by their feet from a limb appeared as late as 1603 in an edition of Hulsius's *Voyages*.

After his second voyage, Columbus was certain that he was in the East. He and his crew had been attacked by female archers on the island of Guadeloupe, where he also found extensive evidence of cannibalism. Surely this was the island Marco Polo had described.

It was on his third voyage that Columbus discovered the presence of a huge freshwater bay, indicating the presence of a great river (the Orinoco) which, he reasoned, must necessarily belong to a substantial land mass. He had in fact sailed along the continent of South America, and he wrote to his sovereigns, "Your highnesses have won these vast lands which are an Other World. . . ."[7] The historian Samuel Eliot Morison cautioned,

> By *Otro Mundo* it must not be inferred that Columbus grasped the correct relation of his discoveries to the Old World; he merely meant (as Vespucci did, when, later, he called the same regions *Mundus Novus*) that it was a world unknown to the ancients or to Ptolemy. Columbus never abandoned his theory that Cuba was a cape of southeast China, or that west and south of it lay the "Golden Chersonese," the Malay Peninsula. South and Central America, from Paria to Honduras, he believed to be a newly discovered continent tailing off from the Malay Peninsula such as Indonesia actually does; and the main object of his next voyage was to find a strait between them.[8]

Edmundo O'Gorman, in *The Invention of America*, presents a map that is a composite of several sketch maps made by Christopher Columbus's son, Ferdinand Columbus, from 1503 to 1505.[9] Its most outstanding feature is South America hanging from the mainland of China. It is an extraordinary testimony to a unique point in time, to a radical transformation of the globe which was itself to yield, indeed vanish, before a greater knowledge. The map kept alive, for the moment, Columbus's belief that sailing west was a reasonably efficient route for reaching the East. So great were the expectations of the explorer and his sovereigns that he would reach India, that Columbus carried on his fourth voyage a letter of introduction from Ferdinand and Isabella for him to present to the Portuguese explorer Vasco da Gama. Da Gama had set out in 1502 to repeat his feat of reaching India by sailing around Africa, and with the existence of the Pacific Ocean still unknown, it did not seem unlikely that Columbus and Da Gama might, in fact, meet somewhere in the Indian Ocean. The letter urged the two great explorers to treat each other with kindness and courtesy. But a continent and an ocean several thousand miles wide decreed that such a meeting would never occur.

Columbus himself came close to discovering the futility of that letter of introduction. As Morison notes, he spent New Year's Day of 1503 at what is the present-day harbor of Cristobal, in the Panama Canal Zone.[10] Had he used a small craft to sail up the Chagres River, and then hiked over only twelve miles of land, he would have discovered the great unknown sea. Confronted by the fact that he had not reached the East, would this great man have parted with the "Indians" and man-hating warrior-women of his dreams? Would he have seen his "Other World" with fresh eyes? If so, he would have greatly transcended the imaginative and conceptual bounds not only of his contemporaries, but also of many subsequent generations. No matter that America was not part of China—native Americans were fixed forever as Indians,[11] and the belief that the New World abounds in Amazons has proven almost as long lived.

By the early decades of the sixteenth century, the earth was yielding its mysteries. In 1522 Magellan circled the globe. Cortés had already conquered Mexico and received from Emperor Charles V the title "Discoverer of the South Sea," for such was the first name for the Pacific Ocean. America was not part of Asia after all, but some place about which the old authorities, Christian and otherwise, had been so strangely silent. If they knew about America, then why had they failed to speak plainly on that matter? Was America Paradise, as Columbus once thought,[12] or was it the Apocalypse, a gateway to evil, sin, and destruction? And who were all these people? What god had created them and put them in this strange wilderness? Were they also sons and daughters of the children of Adam and Eve? Were they our sisters and brothers? All these questions were of grave importance, and they threatened to undermine the foundation of the European perception of the cosmos. For if they were answered in the affirmative, if God created Indians, if Indians were children of Adam, if these naked and strange people were our brothers and our sisters, then some fundamental alterations in what had been commonly accepted as boundaries of experience and of human nature had to be made. There was indeed much more to heaven and earth than had been grasped in our philosophy. On the other hand, a negative answer to these questions was unthinkable. For to say "Indians" were not the work of our God was tantamount to denying God and all the omnipotence revealed by Faith. Few early modern Europeans were prepared to accept a godless world and to confess that they were so utterly alone in a universe they could not comprehend. Most Europeans agreed with the sixteenth-century Spanish historian, Antonio de Herrera, and his wonderfully ambiguous statement, "since all the race of man descends from *Adam* and *Eve*, it is plain that [native Americans] must come from us; but we are so little acquainted with the extremities of the earth, that nothing can be positively asserted."[13] Europeans could assure themselves that even if the Bible did not speak of America, the Indians were *probably* their brothers. It was Herrera's conviction that claiming to know anything more on this question was tantamount to asserting the ways of God in America, surely a mark of hubris, folly, and presumption.

There were thinkers who tried to comprehend the culture of the Indian as a sort of regression, or a degenerative state of human culture. More interesting were the first attempts to formulate a rudimentary theory of human cultural evolution, to suggest that at an early stage of their development, Europeans were once very much like the Indians. Among the earliest engravings on America, which were rendered by Théodore de Bry from sketches made by John White, were amusing and imaginative representations of early Picts and Britons, "to show that the Inhabitants of great Bretannie haue bin in times past as sauuage as those of Virginia."[14]

Most Europeans probably chose not to see America at all, viewing it as unworthy of their intellectual curiosity. There was a definite time lag in European interest in the newfound world: between 1480 and 1609, for example, twice as many French books appeared on Turkey than on North and South America combined.[15] Books on the East Indies and Asia also exceeded the number of those on America. Not until the Spanish conquests of Mexico and Peru, and the spectacular wealth they yielded, did some at least begin to comprehend the enormous import of including America in the cosmos. By the mid-sixteenth century, the historian Francisco López de Gómora characterized the discovery of America as the greatest event in human history since the creation of the world and the coming of Christ.[16]

For many dreamers, explorers, or both, America was the site of all things strange and wonderful. As late as the end of the sixteenth century there was a report of a sighting of a unicorn in Florida, and earlier accounts included a feathered monkey that sang like a nightingale, blue men with square heads, cannibals who lived to be one hundred and fifty, monsters, ferocious sea animals, and bones of giants.[17] Some of these adventurers were determined to follow the rainbow and make their dreams come true: Antonio de Herrera reports that Spaniards and Indians, searching for the magical fountain of youth with its reputed ability to wash away the ravages of time, were so thorough that "there was not a River, or Brook, nor scarce a Lake, or Puddle in all Florida, but what they bathed themselves in."[18]

Some thinkers, once having decided to contend with America, chose to deny its novelty. They strained their eyes to find familiar scenes, and their ears to hear their favorite melodies. "Indian" tongues sounded as strange as Hebrew (whatever that sounds like); could these naked red-skinned peoples be the Ten Lost Tribes of Israel? Bartolomé de Las Casas, the first bishop and one of the earliest chroniclers of the West Indies, theorized that the Indians of America were the de-

scendants of the Hebrew tribes that Alexander the Great
enclosed behind the gate that separates the Western world
from Gog and Magog, and the further parts of Asia.

Mid-seventeenth-century Antonio de Montezinos, a Mar-
rano who had visited South America, arrived in Amsterdam
to raise money for his cause. While in America, he had met
some Indians who claimed they deserved every bit of the
harsh treatment the Spanish dealt them, because they had
badly treated the holy people. When Montezinos returned
to Quito and demanded to meet these "Holy People," he was
led to three men who greeted him with, "Shema, Yisroel,
Adonai Elohenu Adonai Ehod." (Hear, O, Israel, the Lord
our God, the Lord is One.)[19] Montezinos seems to have vanished along with the monies he raised from wealthy Dutch
Jews to bring these mysterious people the "twelve bearded
teachers" and other aids they supposedly requested. The theory that native Americans are remnants of the "lost" Hebrew
tribes persists to this day in some quarters (most notably, as
part of the Mormon creed), and it is of note that one of the
earliest Hebrew congregations in America, established in New
York in 1730, called itself "Shearith Israel" (the remnant of
Israel).

The other favorite theme of those who insisted on seeing
America as the realm of the familiar, was the finding of
Amazons in America. Like the ten Hebrew tribes, they too
had roots in the very beginning of time. They too were known
to the ancients, and due to a reprehensible failure in the
memory bank of mankind, they too had somehow been "lost."
Granted that Penthesilea died at Troy, what happened to the
tens or hundreds of thousands of women who fought val-
iantly beside her? Achilles, or Pyrrhus, could not have destroyed them all. The theory that the surviving Amazons
migrated to America appeared more than plausible in some
quarters. Andrewe Thévet, who penned his *New Founde Worlde*
in 1568, offered two theories for the arrival of the Amazons:
"some think that after the warre of *Troy*, for thither they
went . . . they scattered abrode, and wandered heere and there.
Others think that they are come from certain places of *Grecia*
in *Affrica*, from whence a cruell king chased them. We have

many histories of their acts and feats of warre . . . "[20] Whatever the occasion of their migration to America, Thévet accepted their presence there as factual, and he even cited cases
in which Spaniards actually battled with the women.

The assumption that Amazons were in the New World was
a very convenient one precisely because so many of the explorers, starting with Columbus and his experiences on Mar-
tinique, did in fact encounter fighting women, sometimes
fighting alone, sometimes in the company of men, and sometimes leading the men. Not only did the women of America
make war, but they also were involved in the political and
economic leadership of some cultures. As Lewis Hanke writes,
"The Spaniards . . . made in America their first acquaintance
with a matrilineal society. The queens and princesses they
met both titillated them and scandalized their sense of propriety. The mores of a society in which males did not make
the rules were different from their own, and as 'civilized'
persons have done around the world, they unhesitatingly
condemned the unfamiliar culture pattern and proceeded to
break it down."[21]

In giving native Americans an Amazonian origin, the
Spaniards were following the example of the Greeks. Two
thousand years earlier, Herodotus had attempted to understand the Sauromatians by postulating that they were a cross
between Scythians and Amazons.

The assumption that Amazons were present in America
did more than merely help male Europeans to comprehend
the customs and practices of native American cultures. It
immensely magnified the lure of the New World by extend-
ing a challenge of sexual conquest which hitherto existed only
in fantasy. For Amazons are in the superlative voice, rep-
resenting heroic valour and heroic sex. Didn't Theseus, king
of Athens, who surely could have chosen any maiden, marry
the Amazon Hippolyta? Wasn't Achilles smitten even with
the bloodstained corpse of Penthesilea? Remember how the
Amazon Thalestris burned for Alexander? She lingered thirteen nights in his tents before she could quench her desire.
The ancients understood that no hero could really try his
mettle in love or in war without an Amazonian encounter.

Most delicious of all the dreams was the version where the
hero wins his battle only with the most extraordinary display
of skill and daring, thereby conquering not only the sword,
but also the heart of his Amazonian opponent. His reward
is a love affair which brings him to a whole new dimension
of erotic experience, a passion before which all former diversions paled. Even if the details of names and encounters
had been forgotten, or never perfectly learned, there was
something erotic in the mere mention of Amazons.

Although most medieval authors stripped Amazons of their
physical desirability, the sexual element is clearly present,
with redoubled force, in Renaissance and Elizabethan literature. Even more, the notion that Amazons are sex-starved
women who diligently seek out valorous men for their own
pleasure as well as for the propagation of their race was so
well nurtured by the romance literature that it became the
common possession of the populace, which tied Amazons to
fantasies of sex as well as wealth.

According to the stories that were current in the Spanish
harbors of Laredo and Santander in 1533, the Amazons who
were about to descend upon Spain because of the great virility
of Spanish men were willing to reward the men richly "for
their trouble." For the popular literature of early modern
Europe also placed great emphasis on the vast riches of the
Amazons. The notion that these women had abundant resources actually had its origin in medieval, rather than classical sources. Wealth and generosity were two of the virtues
of the chivalric ideal, and in the hands of authors following
the tradition of Benoît de Sainte-More and his *Roman de Troie*,
the Amazon was the perfect female counterpart of the proper
knight. Renaissance romances gave Amazons sexual as well
as financial appeal, and Califia and her golden armor, her
extraordinary beauty and wealth, were to play a part of great
importance in the New World.

To European men America seemed like a dream fulfilled,
and its chroniclers fanned the flames of lust, desire, and
greed. In 1526, Gonzalo Fernández Oviedo, in his *Natural
History of the West Indies*, gave the following information about
the females of that part of the world: "The principall woman

Bo Svenson and Anita Ekberg in the twentieth-century version of the Amazon dream, *Gold of the Amazon Women.* (*Courtesy The National Broadcasting Company, Inc.*)

when theyr teates faule or be come loose, beare them up with
barres of golde of the length of a spanne and a halfe, wel
wrought, and of such byggenesse that sume of them way
more then two hundreth Castilians or ducades of golde. These
barres haue holes at both th[e] endes, wherat they tye two
smaul cordes made of cotton at euery ende of the barres.
One of these cordes go[e]th ouer the shulder, and the other
vnder the arme where they tye togyther, so that by this meanes
the barre beareth vp theyr teates." Oviedo emphasized that
the activities of these women were not like those of European
wives and mothers: "Sum of these chiefe women go to the
battayle with theyr husbandes, or when they them selues are
regentes in any prouinces, in the which they haue all thynges
at commaundement and execute th[e] office of generall cap-
itaynes. . . ." As further evidence of their impudence, these
women "cause them selues to bee caryed on mens backes."[22]

Of course, those operating at a distance, like the private
entrepreneurs who financed many of the expeditions of exploration and conquest, had to accept the gold without the
sex and the danger. But many of them drew up contracts
with their paid adventurers which required them to search
for Amazons.[23] These capitalists mandated the Amazon search
not because of any interest in anthropology, but rather because of a firmly held conviction widely shared in early modern times: the gold is where the Amazons are. And if this be
not the fabric of reality, it is still very much the stuff of which
dreams are made, serving as inspiration for sci-fi and adventure stories even of today, as witnessed by a prime-time airing
in March 1979 of a made-for-television film called *Gold of the
Amazon Women.*

But the conquistador, that almost larger than life hero,
had no need for modern reveries. His ambition was more
than adequately fired by the tales of his own age. Reminiscing
about his participation in the conquest of Mexico in the 1520s
Bernal Díaz del Castillo wrote, "we saw so many cities and
villages built in the water and other great towns on dry land
and that straight and level causeway going towards Mexico,
we were amazed and said that it was like the enchantments

they tell of in the legend of *Amadis*. . . . . some of our soldiers even asked whether the things that we saw were not a dream?"[24]

All the dreams that men had dared to dream were coming true, and the world was more wonderful than men had hoped. Even the most tantalizing and titillating inhabitants of the regions of early modern fiction slipped without any difficulty from the realm of fantasy to reality. Montalvo published Book V of his *Amadis* in 1510, and throughout the 1520s, as Mexico and more and more of South and Central America fell under Spanish rule, the story of Queen Califia and her realm of California went through edition after edition. European men believed that Amazons almost certainly existed in America, and no explorer could hope to earn his pay without diligently searching for them, or better still, finding them.

In 1518 the clergyman Juan Díaz, a member of an expedition exploring along the west coast near the island of Yucatan, reported sighting a beautiful tower at a place the natives said Amazons inhabited. He also saw many similar towers "seemingly in towns," all along the shore.[25]

The fact that Antonio Pigafetta, an Italian seaman who accompanied Magellan and chronicled the great voyage around the world, reported Amazons in the East, near Java Major, changed nothing. The major thrust of the search for Amazons was in the New World, and as the exploration of the new lands progressed, Amazon sightings increased.

In 1524, Hernando Cortés, the conqueror of Mexico, expressed to his emperor Charles V his plans to seek out even more wealth: a captain who he had sent out to explore to the south brought him

> an account of the chiefs of the province of Ceguatan, who affirm that there is an island inhabited only by women without any men, and that, at given times, men from the mainland visit them: if they conceive, they keep the female children to which they give birth, but the male, they throw away. This island is ten days journey from the province, and many of them went thither and saw it, and told me also that it is very rich in pearls and gold. I shall strive to ascertain the truth, and, when I am able to do so, I will make a full account to Your Majesty.[26]

The expedition Hernando Cortés sent to seek out the Amazons was commanded by his kinsman, Francisco Cortés. A member of this party was Nuño de Guzmán, a man determined to find Amazons and gold on his own. Guzmán wrote Charles V in 1530, referring to his plans for further exploration in the Pacific Ocean, "I shall goe to find the Amazons, which some say dwell in the Sea, some in an arme of the Sea, and that they are rich, and accounted of the people for Goddesses, and whiter than other women. They use Bowes, Arrows, and Targets; have many great Townes; at a certain time admit men to accompanie them, which bring up the males as these the females issue, & c."[27]

Meanwhile, in the late 1530s, Juan de San Martín y Alonso de Lebrija reported that he and his party, while exploring modern-day Colombia, had come within three days' march of some fabulously wealthy Amazon women. The latter became pregnant by some male slaves whom the women summoned and dismissed according to their desire and whim. Only his inability to move "some mountain ranges in the way"[28] kept the determined conquistador from his goal—for the moment.

Fifteen forty-two was the Year of the Amazon in America—the year in which the search reached its most fevered pitch, and left an indelible impression on the Americas. For in 1542 the mighty South American River received the name "Amazon," almost at the same moment that the rocky coast of the southwest of North America became for all time known as the home of Califia and other Amazon dreams—"California."

The clearest account is of the naming of the river. Not content with the incalculable treasure his conquest of Peru yielded for himself, the marquis Don Francisco Pizarro sent his brother, Gonzalo Pizarro, in search of the fabled city of El Dorado and the Land of Cinnamon. The party set out in 1539 from Quito and headed south, finding a broad river with dense forests on either shore. Pizarro and his men built a boat so they could sail from one side of the river to the other, exploring and procuring food. When they found nothing to eat, but heard reports of victuals just ahead, Pizarro sent one of his captains, Francisco de Orellana, with a party of men to sail ahead, obtain provisions, and then turn back to rescue the now starving adventurers. He seems to have expected to fulfill his mission, but after three days the current of the river carried Orellana so far from Pizarro's camp that either through treachery (for his party had all the gold the expedition had uncovered thus far) or through a practical assessment of his situation (for it was now virtually impossible to turn back), he took command in his own name. It was thus under Orellana's leadership that the group of Spaniards had a number of rather dangerous and extraordinary adventures that led to the naming of the Amazon River. There is a first-hand account of these events penned by Gaspar de Carvajal, a Dominican friar who went with Orellana and received a wound in his side and lost an eye for all his troubles.

Carvajal describes the privation of the group that cast their lot with following the mighty river as "so great that we were eating nothing but leather, belts and soles of shoes, cooked with certain herbs, with the result that so great was our weakness that we could not remain standing, for some on all fours and others with staffs went into the woods to search for a few roots to eat."[29]

Finally, on New Year's Day of 1542, Orellana and his men met with some friendly Indians who fed them. Orellana was a remarkably gifted linguist, and Carvajal notes that his captain was able to communicate with these Indians in their own language, "for to a certain extent he could understand them." All the while the Spaniards feigned indifference to gold, and the Indians decked themselves in more and more precious ornaments. For once, the Spaniards concentrated only on their survival, and paused at this friendly village just long enough to build a larger ship in the hope that the river would lead them out to the sea. As they worked, an old native named Aparia "informed us of the existence of Amazons and of the wealth further down the river."

Orellana continued to converse with Indians they encountered further down the river, and friendly natives kept the Spaniards supplied with turtles and parrots. Carvajal claimed that Orellana's understanding of native tongues was "next to

God, the deciding factor by virtue of which we did not perish [somewhere] along the river, for, had he not understood it, neither would the Indians have come forward with peaceful intentions, nor should we have met with success in these settlements. . . ."

But further down the river their good fortune ran out. The Indians were less friendly, the Spaniards frequently had to fight to procure their food. One day they happened upon a sizable village, which contained a large public square. In its midst they found a remarkable structure:

> there was a hewn tree trunk ten feet in girth, there being represented and carved in relief [thereon] a walled city with its enclosure and a gate. At this gate were two towers, very tall and having windows, and each tower had a door, the two facing each other, and at each door were two columns, and this entire structure that I am telling about rested upon two very fierce lions, which turned their glances backwards as though suspicious of each other, holding between their forepaws and claws the entire structure. . . .

Even more extraordinary than the structure was the response the Spaniards received when they questioned the natives about the monument and its purpose:

> the Indian answered that they were subjects and tributaries of the Amazons and that the only service which they rendered them consisted in supplying them with plumes of parrots and macaws for the linings of the rooves of the buildings which constitute their places of worship, and that [all] the villages which they had were of that kind, and that they had that thing there as a reminder, and that they worshipped it as a thing which was the emblem of their mistress, who is the one who rules over all the land of the aforesaid women.

The Spaniards left this village, and discovered another one downstream, with a similarly carved tree trunk in its square. Here the Indians put up a fierce resistance. The explorers met more and more hostility, for, Carvajal writes, "we came suddenly upon the excellent land and dominion of the Amazons." Here, hordes of Indians fought on and on against the Spanish crossbows and arquebuses. Though the invaders' weapons were vastly superior to their own, and there seemed to be no rational hope for resistance, the Indians fought in such great numbers, "it seemed as if it rained arrows." It proved impossible for all the Spanish to escape injury, and one Indian arrow pierced right through Carvajal's rib cage. He wrote that if it had not been for the thickness of his clothing, "that would have been the end of me."

The Spaniards were amazed to see the extent to which the Indians suffered losses and seemed ever-willing to resume a hopeless fight. Carvajal's explanation is, "I want it to be known what the reason was why these Indians defended themselves in this manner. It must be explained that they are subjects of, and tributaries to, the Amazons." Carvajal explains that when these women learned of the invasion, they themselves came to monitor and participate in the battle: "there came as many as twelve of them, for we ourselves saw these women, who were fighting in front of all the Indian men as women captains." The women fought courageously and enforced the most rigorous military discipline upon the men: "the Indian men did not dare to turn their backs, and anyone who did turn his back [the women] killed with clubs right before us."

Carvajal's description of the women suggested they were of a different racial stock from the ranks of their male warriors. He thereby added fuel to the notion that they were in fact descendants of the Amazons of old, though he never explicitly states this: "These women are very white and tall, and have hair very long and braided and wound about the head, and they are very robust and go naked, [but] with their privy parts covered, with bows and arrows in their hands, doing as much fighting as ten Indian men."

These remarks end Carvajal's eyewitness account of the Amazon women. Before Orellana's party left what they believed to be territory ruled by Amazon women, they captured a young Indian man whom Orellana took on board their ship in the hope of learning his language and gaining more information about his nation and its female rulers. In the meantime, they continued their journey down the river, ever hopeful of reaching the waters of the Atlantic, their passport to the safe Old World.

They had many encounters with natives whose response to them was clearly hostile. In one such battle, the unlucky Carvajal writes, "they hit no one but me, for they planted an arrow right in one of my eyes, in such a way that the arrow went through to the other side, from which wound I have lost the eye and [even now] I am not without suffering and free from pain." Better to be hungry and steer a safe course through the middle of the river than again to risk such wrath and misfortune. As they made their way downstream Orellana began to question their captive, "because he now understood him by means of a list of words that he had made." The Spaniards learned that the women they encountered earlier lived in the interior of the country, at least seven days' journey from the shore. Fortunately, this Indian, being a servant of one of the vassals to the Amazons, had often traveled to the nation of the women to transport tribute from his overlord. The interrogation indicated a great multitude of women: "The Captain asked if these women were numerous: the Indian said they were, and that he knew by name seventy villages, and named them before those of us who were present." They learned that the women lived in stone houses with regular doors and windows, and that their villages were connected by a network of roads, well-maintained and guarded.

The women were unmarried, but when they desired the company of men they obtained males by capture. This was a debilitating form of imprisonment, the Indian reported (in perfect conformity to that male fantasy which knows neither the bounds of time nor space). In the same manner, "an Indian farther up had told us that anyone who should take it into his head to go down to the country of these women was destined to go a boy and come back an old man." And, if no men happened their way, "They assembled a great horde of warriors and went off to make war on a very great overlord whose residence is not far from that of these women, and by force brought them to their own country for the time that suited their caprice, and after they found themselves

pregnant they sent them back to their country . . . and af-
terwards, when the time came for them to have children, if
they gave birth to male children they killed them [or] sent
them to their fathers, and if female children, they raised them
with great solemnity and instructed them in the arts of war."

The women the Indian described were not without a government. Perhaps the Spaniards were thinking of Montalvo's
Queen Califia when they learned that "among all these women
there was one ruling mistress who subjected and held under
her hand and jurisdiction all the rest, which mistress went
by the name Coñori. He said that there was [in their posses-
sion] a very great wealth of gold and silver . . . [in the case
of] all the mistresses of rank and distinction their eating utensils were nothing but gold and silver." These women, the
Indian related, observed a religion of their own. They worshipped in elaborate temples "lined with heavy wooden ceil-
ings covered with paint of various colors." These were no
humble churches: "they had many gold and silver idols in
the form of women, and many vessels of gold and silver for
the service of the Sun."

These women dressed in fine woolen garments and placed
upon their heads "crowns of gold, as wide as two fingers."
The Indian tried to describe the various exotic animals upon
which the women traveled about their land, which, Carvajal
admits, "we did not succeed in understanding about."

The Indian captive who supplied all this information died
on the island of Cubagua, the first Spanish port Orellana's
group reached after their arduous journey down the river.
From there they embarked to Spain, to report to the king
what Carvajal called "this new and great discovery . . . of this
river, which we hold to be the Marañón." But the river was
never again to have that name. López de Gómora complained, in what was to be a futile protest, that since Orellana
and his companions arrived in Spain and told of their adventures, "many write and say 'River of the Amazons' and
there have gathered together so many parties to go there."
Gómora believed that native American women were inca-
pable of sacrificing their sexuality for loyalty to, and main-
tenance of, an Amazonian community, "being as they are very

voluptuous."[30] Later, Antonio de Herrera concurred with
him: "in regard to the Amazons, many have expressed the
opinion that Captain Orellana ought not to have given this
name to those women nor ought he have affirmed on such
a slim foundation that they were Amazons, because in the
Indies it was not a new thing that the women should fight
and draw their bows, as has been seen in some of the Wind-
ward Islands in Cartangena and its neighborhood, where
they showed themselves to be as valorous as the men."[31] But
the deciding factor was that few European men of this time
were able, or willing, to distinguish between women who
fought with great success and ferocity, and Amazons. As
opponents of women, they risked looking ridiculous; as enemies of Amazons, their struggle was heroic.

The naming of California also had its origins in the fondest
fantasies of male European invaders of America—their hopes
for fame and glory, material wealth, and sexual fulfillment.
If Don Francisco Pizarro had looked beyond his fabulously
lucrative conquest of Peru and sent his kinsmen further to
the south and east, Hernando Cortés was not content with
Mexico and sent his kin scurrying to the west and north. For
Cortés and Pizarro were like the heroes of popular fiction,
and theirs was an unending quest and series of adventures.
They were not ordinary men, and every conquest, no matter
how great, was only a temporary ending—and the signal for
a new beginning. Like Amadis of the romances, they seemed
to expect to live forever, to be hale and always conquering
even at the age of one hundred. In the search for gold and
for Amazons, there is no growing old, and no wound that
will not heal. Poor old half-blind Carvajal could express his
pain, but never regret. And that common-man-turned-con-
quistador, Díaz de Castillo, at the age of something past eighty,
totally blind and deaf as well, felt compelled to record his
experiences in Mexico, for they were no ordinary human
endeavor: "there is so much to think over that I do not know
how to describe it, seeing things as we did that had never
been heard of or seen before, not even dreamed about. . . . I
stood looking at it and thought that never in the world would

there be discovered lands such as these, for at that time there was no Peru, nor any thought of it."[32] Castillo wrote that Mexico City evoked for him the wondrous cities Montalvo had described in *Amadis*. There is little reason to doubt that Book V of *Amadis* was the inspiration for putting California on the map. The romance literature of fifteenth- and six-teenth-century Europe enormously influenced the conquistadors and their perceptions of themselves and their experiences.[33]

Montalvo had placed Queen Califia's California on an island "on the right hand of the Indies" and within reach of Constantinople by sea. The long peninsula off the west coast of Mexico was long mistaken by explorers for an island, and Montalvo's romantic and vague geographical description could well be construed to signify the west coast of Mexico and North America: it was precisely in these areas that knights brave and true branched out to find the Amazons and the gold. And here, goaded by native Americans who feared them and tended to respond to all questions with a positive nod, they believed they were within reach of their heart's desire.

Hernando Cortés sent a detailed list of instructions to his kin Francisco Cortés, to go and seek the Amazon realm in the area of Colima (on the west coast of Mexico). He described these women as following the practices, in the matter of re-production, which are detailed in the *"istorias antiguas."* Irving Leonard argues that by "ancient histories," Cortés was in fact referring to the romances or novels of chivalry, those "lying histories" which so many a common man could not distinguish from reality, or actual historical accounts of the same.[34] From their descriptions of their "finds" in North and South America, the Spaniards in general seem to be more familiar with the Amazons of the romances than with the warrior-women of the classics. Details like the searing or removal of one breast do not appear in the Spanish reports.

Cortés and his kin seem to have reserved the name "California" for the Gulf of California, and referred to the peninsula projecting from the coast of Mexico as "Santa Cruz."

Yet it was California and the gold of Queen Califia that they sought, and by 1542 Jan Rodríquez Cabrillo sailed along that western coast, recording in his journals that he traveled along the shore of California. Santa Cruz thereby went the way of the Marañón River and America in the end had to yield to the Amazonian heritage her conquerors insisted on bestowing upon her. The Amazon River and California remain as testimony to the power of Amazon dreams.

One did not have to be Spanish to search for Amazons and gold. A desire for wealth, fame, and adventure was sufficient. Of course, the wealth of the sixteenth-century Spanish throne, much of which had come from American ventures, permitted extensive expeditions. Even before Carvajal's account, Juan de San Martín y Alonso de Lebrija reported learning from natives of what is now Colombia, during his 1536–39 exploration, of a community of Amazons who used slaves to assure their procreation. Although the Spaniards kept "getting more and more news that they existed and that they were very rich in gold," impassible terrain kept them from reaching the Amazons.[35]

Similarly, Augustín Zárate, a secretary of the Royal Council in Spain, reported in 1543 a province inhabited exclusively by women, located in the south of Chile. According to Zárate, these women had a queen named Gaboimilla, which in the local native tongue meant "heaven of gold." She and her women, however, sent most of their riches to Leuchengorma, a powerful chief to whom they were subject. Zárate did not manage to meet either the exotic chief or his alluring vassals.

In the same year as the report of the Chilean Amazons, Hernando de Ribera and a party of fifty-two men set out from Asunción (the capital of modern Paraguay) on a series of adventures, the account of which, Leonard remarks, "seems a vague paraphrase of Montalvo."[36] Natives told the group that they were within ten days' journey of some very large settlements of women who lived under a queen. They owned "white" and "yellow" metal in great quantities, and all their household utensils were of these metals. They mated with men of a neighboring tribe during a prearranged season of the year, with the women raising the resulting female off-spring and training them for war, sending the males to the men, etcetera.

If Ribera did indeed take his inspiration from Montalvo, a German in his company named Ulrich Schmidt (Ulrich Schmidel in the Spanish, or Hulderich Schmidel in the English translations) seemed more schooled in the writings of the ancients Strabo and Pliny. He wrote an account of his travels on the River Plate in 1567, some twenty-five years after the deeds. Most prominent in his memory after all those years gone by were the reports of Amazons he received from natives. The women lived on an island that could be reached only during certain times of the year, and then only by small boat or canoe. Otherwise, the extreme flooding of the surrounding area made the women inaccessible. Schmidt's Amazons, like Strabo's, have only one breast, the other having been seared off in childhood "that they may be more fit to handle their weapons and bowes. For they are warlike women, making continual war with their enemies."[37] Schmidt got his information from an Indian chief who spoke with the group and presented them with some silver and a plate made of solid gold. These, the Indian claimed, he received as spoils of war when his people fought with the Amazons some time ago. It was to Schmidt's ever-lingering remorse that he had arrived during the wrong season, and floods, or more likely swamps, kept him from the prize that was just outside his reach.

The close association of Amazons and gold received further reinforcement at the end of the sixteenth century from the pen of Sir Walter Raleigh. He spoke of Amazons in his *History of the World*, and in even greater detail in his *Voyages of Discovery to Guiana*, which he published in 1596. He assures his readers that his information on Amazons was correct, since it came from the lips of a native cacique, or chieftain, who had observed the Amazons with his own eyes. By carefully questioning this chief Raleigh learned that the Amazons "do accompany with men but once in a year, and for the time of one month, which I gather to be in April. At that time all the kings of the borders assemble, and the queens of the Amazons; and after the queens have chosen, the rest cast lots for their Valentines. This one month they feast, dance, and drink their wines in abundance."[38] This image of Amazons in wild abandon captured the imagination of others, and the April orgy Raleigh described became one of the (rather explicit) illustrations of Volume I of Hulsius' *Voyages*. From this month of pleasure came pregnancy, which was a duty to their community. If they "be delivered of a son, they return him to the father, if a daughter, they nourish it and retain it; and so many as have daughters send unto the begetters a present, all being desirous to increase their own sex and kind; but that they cut off the right dug of the breast I did not find to be true."

Perhaps the Amazons of Guiana dispensed with the mutilation described by authors of late antiquity: they were not for that reason any less formidable. Raleigh claims that he learned that "if they took any prisoners . . . they used to accompany with those at what time soever, but in the end, for certain, they put them to death; for they are said to be very cruel and bloodthirsty, especially to such as offer to invade their territories." The motives for invading the Amazons were mainly pecuniary, for "these Amazons have likewise great store of these plates of gold, which they recover for exchange, chiefly for a kind of green stones. . . . Of these I saw divers in Guiana; and commonly every king, or cacique, hath one, which their wives for the most part wear, and they esteem them as great jewels." For the next two centuries scholars and adventurers spoke of the virtue of these green Amazon stones.[39]

In general, Raleigh found Guiana to be a land of marvels, containing, in addition to Amazons, many of the wonders Sir John Mandeville had described seeing on his "journey" centuries earlier. Raleigh claimed there existed in Guiana a tribe called the Ewaiponoma, whose people were entirely without heads: "they are reported to have eyes in their shoulders and their mouths in the middle of their breasts, and their long train of hair groweth backward between their shoulders." Raleigh knew this to be true "because every child in the provinces of Aeromaia and Canui affirm the same."

Hence, in the eyes of Raleigh, Mandeville was vindicated.
Although Mandeville's reports were taken for fables for many
years, "since the East Indies were discovered, we find his
relations true of such things as heretofore were held incredible."

In his book on Guiana, Raleigh also published what he
claimed were Spanish letters he intercepted at sea in 1494,
in which the Spanish tag Guiana "Nuevo Dorado" because
the wealth of gold they found there reminded them of the
fabled city of El Dorado. In the hope of extricating himself
from royal disfavor, Raleigh made an unsuccessful appeal to
royal greed. He proposed that Queen Elizabeth should give
him more men, money, and ships to capture more of Guiana.
He suggests, at the conclusion of his *Voyages*, that Elizabeth
could easily win the respect of the Guianian Amazons, indeed, even serve as a model and example for them to em-
ulate: "these women shall hereby hear the name of a virgin
who is not only able to defend her own territories and her
neighbors, but also to invade and conquer so great empires,
and so far removed." But Elizabeth failed to accept the challenge he offered her, and Raleigh ended up in prison rather
than on a ship headed for the Amazons and the gold of
Guiana.

Raleigh recorded in his *History of the World* that many of
his readers took his accounts of Amazons in Guiana "for a
vain and unprofitable report." Hence he included a survey
of the Amazons of antiquity in his *History*, citing all the classical sources including those authors who questioned the very
existence of Amazons. He himself takes a moderate stand:
Amazons have existed in the past and do exist now, but not
all the stories authors have related about them are true. The
tale of the Amazon queen Thalestris and Alexander may not
be factual, "yet, as we believe and know that there are elephants, though it were false that Alexander fought with one;
so we may give credit unto writers making mention of such
Amazons, whether it were true or false that they met with
Alexander."

A generation later, the Jesuit father, Acuña, who served

as rector of the Portuguese college at Cuença, concurred with
Raleigh. Acuña traveled with Pedro de Texeria on a voyage
down the Napo and Amazon rivers in Paria, and he published
a journal of his adventures in 1641. He spoke of the Amazon
as if it were a person:

> it would be very strange, that, without good grounds, it should
> have usurped the name of the river of the Amazons, and that
> it should desire to become famous, with no other title than a
> usurped one: nor is it credible that this great river, possessing
> so much glory at hand should desire to glorify itself by a name
> to which it has no title. . . . But the proofs of the existence of
> the province of Amazons on this river are so numerous, and
> so strong, that it would be a want of common faith not to give
> them credit.[40]

To prove his point, Acuña cites no thirdhand sources. He
claims he deliberately ignores what others learned from the
natives: "I will only dwell upon that which I heard with my
own ears, and carefully investigated, from the time that we
entered this river. There is no saying more common than
that these women inhabit a province on the river, and it is
not credible that a lie could have spread throughout so many
languages, and so many nations, without such an appearance
of truth." Most of what Acuña reports on the women is information that he himself gained from a "careful" questioning of the natives, particularly of the Tupinambas tribe. He
learned, of course, just about everything that he already knew:

> The Amazons are women of great valour, and they have always
> preserved themselves without the ordinary intercourse with
> men; and even when these, by agreement, come every year to
> their land, they receive them with arms in their hands, such
> as bows and arrows, which they brandish about for some time,
> until they are satisfied that the Indians come with peaceful
> intentions. They then drop their arms and go down to the
> canoes of their guests, where each one chooses the hammock
> that is nearest at hand (these being the beds in which they
> sleep); they then take them to their houses, and, hanging them
> in a place where their owners will know them, they receive the
> Indians as guests for a few days.

Then, after some time, Acuña states, the men peacefully returned to their own country. Of the children who were the end result of this mating, Acuña was certain that the women raised the girls to be warriors like themselves. Acuña had less certain information regarding the male infants: "an Indian, who had gone with his father to this country when very young, stated that the boys were given to their fathers, when they returned in the following year. But others, and this account appears to be most probable, as it is most general, say that when the Amazons find that a baby is a male, they kill it." Acuña concluded: "time will discover the truth, and if these are the Amazons made famous by historians, there are treasures shut up in their territory, which would enrich the whole world." This was the good father's vision of the future. There is nothing un-Christian about dreams of unspeakable wealth, as long as these are visions of wealth shared. The Amazons must be found, and forced to disgorge their wealth for the good of all humankind.

But while Acuña fixed his vision on South America, the dreams of others involved other locations. Shall America alone yield Amazons, when the men who explored Africa were just as worthy and just as brave as those who went to the "Indies"? Of course not. Amazons and gold seemed, by the end of the sixteenth century, to be turning up all over the world.

Earlier in that century, the Portuguese passed along the east coast of Africa on their way to India. It was Vasco da Gama who first established this sea route to the East with his voyage of 1502. A Portuguese official named Duarte Barbosa published his notes and memoirs of some of these voyages when he retired in Venice in 1563.[41] He described a powerful central and south African state that was extremely rich in gold, which he called "Benamatapa." Its king "always takes with him into the field . . . a great band of warriors, and five or six thousand women, who also bear arms and fight." Further north toward India, Barbosa notes that the island of "Caotara" (Socotra) was, "as the Moors will have it," in the past an island of Amazons. He seems not to discredit the Moorish tradition, because he believed "some trace of this appears even yet, for the women manage and rule their estates, and their husbands take no part therein."

About five years after the publication of Duarte Barbosa's work, a Portuguese merchant named Duarte Lopez visited east Africa. When in Rome he held a series of interviews with an Italian scholar named Filippo Pigafetta, and the result was their *Report of the Kindgom of Congo*, which they published in 1591. By the time of the appearance of this work, the name Benamatapa was replaced by Monomotapa, and its location. moved further to the south, to the site of modern-day Rhodesia. It was thus with a grain of truth that Lopez wrote that the kingdom of Monomotapa "abounds in gold mines," and with some speculation that he added, "It is said that from these regions the gold was brought by sea which served for Solomon's Temple of Jerusalem."[42]

The emperor of Monomotapa ruled over a huge territory, and like the Romans of old, his massive armies were divided into legions. Among these, "those most renowned for bravery, are the female legions, greatly valued by the Emperor, being the sinews of his military strength. These female warriors, whose weapons are bows and arrows, burn the left breast with fire, in order to prevent it being a hindrance in shooting, as was the custom of those Amazons of olden time, so greatly lauded by the writers of early profane history." In fighting, too, these women followed tactics that resembled those of the ancient Amazons: "in battle they resort to very warlike manoeuvres, retiring at times as if put to rout, and taking flight, yet turning around to assail their adversaries with arrows; and, on seeing the enemy elated with victory, already beginning to disperse, they suddenly turn and repulse them with great slaughter. So that on account of their wiles and cunning, as well as rapidity of action in battle, they are held in great dread in those regions." In their manner of living, too, the women are more like the ancient Amazon communities than they are the ordinary subjects of Monomotapa: "the king grants them certain lands, where they live alone, but at various periods they mix with men chosen by themselves; and any male children born amongst them are sent to these men's houses, but the females are kept apart by themselves, and brought up in the arts of war."

Even more compelling than the Lopez-Pigafetta description of these women, was their account of the Amazons' most hated enemies. These were fierce and voracious cannibals called the Jagas who fought for the Monemugi. Any contest between the emperor of Monomotapa and his dreaded Monemugi enemies always boiled down to a heated and bloody battle between the Amazons, fighting as the elite troops, and final hope of the emperor, against the Jagas.

Lopez argued that in spite of the great skill of the Amazons, battles between them and the Jagas were so intense one could hardly tell the victor till the dust of the battle cleared. The Jagas were so frightening they hardly resembled men: "they are black and of formidable appearance, and mark the upper part of the lip and cheeks with lines burnt with hot iron. They also have a custom of turning their eyelids inside out, the skin of which, being black, the whites of the eyes give a terrifying and diabolical expression to the countenance. They are large in stature, but ill-proportioned, and live like wild beasts, and feed on human flesh." Their military strategy, Lopez wrote, involved carrying full-size leather shields, which allowed them to duck their enemies' arrows, while they hurled their darts, using noises to terrify their enemies: "thus by warlike stratagems they torment the enemy, inducing him to bring out his arrows to no purpose against their targets, and when they see them all spent, the Agagi [Jagas] renew the fight with redoubled vigour, putting to flight and killing their adversaries." But the Amazons always fought their finest battles against the Jagas, "being well assured if taken by their foes, they would be devoured. Therefore they fight with redoubled vigour so as to conquer, and by all means escape from such a savage and cruel multitude; nevertheless, the warfare causes great slaughter on both sides."

The Lopez-Pigafetta account of the Congo also speaks of a recent Jaga invasion on Monomotapa, during which the king and his court took refuge on an island on the River Zaire, while the Jaga enemy created havoc and set fire to the kingdom. The terror of this invasion was such that "forced by necessity, the father sold his son, and the brother his brother, everyone resorting to the most horrible crimes in

order to obtain food." In the end, the emperor of Monomotapa understood the invasion to be the scourge of the heavens, and he surrendered himself and his soul to the Christian
god, and his state and its gold mines to the king of Portugal.

A modern scholar, Joseph C. Miller, wrote "A Requiem
for the 'Jaga,' "[43] laying to rest a convenient myth that masked
a Portuguese intervention in the Congo on behalf of a native
king confronted with an uprising not of "Jagas," but of his
own people. Miller points out that these Jagas were also convenient to "private merchants and public officials" who used
them "to defend the morality of the slave trade by pointing
to the bellies of the 'Jagas' as the only alternative fate awaiting
the oppressed Mbundu and Kongo villages." Also, slaves captured in the interior of the country, upon whom no export
duty was ever paid, were said by their captors to have served
as victuals for the Jagas: "A slave allegedly consumed on the
battle field conveniently left no more traces than one shipped
surreptitiously to Brazil." And, perhaps the clinching argument is that there is no native Congo tradition telling of these
cannibals, and their story lives only in the white man's journals. Neither the Jagas, nor the Amazons who fought so
ferociously against them, have left behind any testimony to
an actual historical existence.

The sixteenth century represented a new stage in the war
against the Amazons. European men found the land of Amazoine in several locations in Africa and America, and they
did not shy away from the warrior-women. Boldly they ventured forward in a test of their courage and determination,
and warred against the Amazons. In the end, Amazoine had
to yield to its European masters, and the Amazon queens
disappeared into obscurity. Whether they saw themselves
as Heracles and Theseus attacking Themiscyra, or, more
likely, as Amadis and Esplandian defending the Christian
faith at the gates of Constantinople, the men who fought
the Amazons were beckoned on to adventure by the promise of wealth, fame, and sex, and just a bit of everlasting
glory.

Notes

1. Samuel Eliot Morison, ed. and trans., *Journals and Other Documents on the Life and Voyages of Christopher Columbus* (New York: Limited Editions Club, 1963), pp. 30–31.
2. Samuel Eliot Morison, *Christopher Columbus, Mariner* (Boston: Little, Brown, 1942), p. 17.
3. Ibid., Appendix containing some letters of Columbus, p. 211.
4. Ruth Putnam, "California: The Name," *University of California Publications in History*, vol. IV (Berkeley: University of California Press, 1916), pp. 294–346.
5. Pietro Martire d'Anghiera, *Decades of the New Worlde*, in Richard Eden, trans., *The First Three English Books on America*, ed. Edward Arber (New York: Kraus Reprint Co., 1971), Book II, p. 69.
6. Sebastian Münster, *Universal Cosmology*, in ibid., p. 39.
7. S. E. Morison and Maurice Obregón, *The Caribbean as Columbus Saw It* (Boston: Little, Brown, 1964), p. 167.
8. Ibid., pp., 167–68.
9. Edmundo O'Gorman, *The Invention of America* (Bloomington: Indiana University Press, 1961), pl. iv.
10. Morison, *Christopher Columbus*, p. 177.
11. See Robert Berkhofer, *The White Man's Indian* (New York: Alfred A. Knopf, 1978); Francis Jennings, *The Invasion of America* (Chapel Hill: University of North Carolina Press, 1975).
12. Morison, *Christopher Columbus*, p. 151.
13. Antonio de Herrera, *History of the West Indies*, in *A Collection of Voyages and Travels in VI Volumes*, vol. V, 3rd ed. (London: Messrs. Churchill for Henry Lintot & John Osborn, 1746), p. 596.
14. See Paul Hulton and David Beers Quinn, *The American Drawings of John White* (Chapel Hill: University of North Carolina Press, 1964), vol. II, pls. 64–67.
15. See Lewis Hanke, *Aristotle and the American Indian* (Bloomington: Indiana University Press, 1959), p. 2.
16. Ibid., pp. 4–6.
17. Ibid.
18. Antonio de Hererra, *The General History of the Vast Continent and Islands of America*, 6 vols. trans. John Stevens (London: Jer. Batley, 1725), II: 3.
19. Ronald Sanders, *Lost Tribes and Promised Lands* (Boston: Little, Brown, 1978), p. 264.

20. Andrewe Thévet, *New Founde Worlde* (London: Henrie Bynne-
    man for Thomas Hacket, 1568), page misnumbered 74 (be-
    tween 103a and 103b).
21. Hanke, *Aristotle*, p. 51.
22. In Eden, *First Three English Books*, p. 238.
23. Irving A. Leonard, *Books of the Brave* (New York: Gordian Press,
    1964), p. 36.
24. Bernal Díaz del Castillo, *The True History of New Spain*, ed.
    Genero Garcia, trans. Alfred Maudslay, vol. II (London: Hak-
    luyt Society, 1910), p. 37.
25. Cited by Leonard, *Books of the Brave*, p. 46.
26. Hernando Cortés, *The Five Letters*, trans. F. A. MacNutt, vol.
    III (New York: 1908), p. 177.
27. In Putnam, "California," p. 325.
28. In Leonard, *Books of the Brave*, p. 57.
29. *The Discovery of the Amazon*, according to the Account of Friar
    Gaspar de Carvajal and other documents, trans. Bertram T.
    Lee, ed. H. C. Heaton (New York: American Geographical
    Society, 1934). All citations from Carvajal are from pp. 172–
    234 of this edition. Used by permission of American Geo-
    graphical Society.
30. In ibid., p. 26.
31. Ibid., pp. 26–27.
32. Díaz del Castillo, *The True History*, pp. 37–38.
33. On the question of the origin of the name of the state of
    California, see Leonard, *Books of the Brave*, p. 351; Edward
    Everet Hale, *The Queen of California* (San Francisco: Colt Press,
    1945); and Putnam, "California," pp. 294–346.
34. Leonard, *Books of the Brave*, p. 49.
35. Ibid., p. 57.
36. Ibid., p. 61.
37. In Samuel Purchas, *Purchas, His Pilgrimes*, 5 vols. (London:
    William Stansby for Henrie Fetherstone, 1625), IV: 1358.
38. Sir Walter Raleigh, *The History of the World, in Five Books*, to
    which is added Sir W. Raleigh's *Voyages of Discovery to Guiana*,
    6 vols. (Edinburgh: Constable, 1820). All citations from Raleigh
    are from vol. VI, pp. 36–37, 76, 101 and vol. IV, p. 312 of
    this edition.
39. See especially M. de La Condamine, *Relation abrégé d'un voyage
    fait dans l'interieur l'Amérique Méridionale . . .* (Paris: Chez la Veuve
    Pissot, 1745), pp. 140–2.
40. In *Expeditions into the Valley of the Amazons, 1539, 1540, 1639,*

ed. and trans. Clements R. Markham (London: Hakluyt Society, 1859, reprinted by Burt Franklin, New York, n.d.). All citations from Acuña are from pp. 41–134 of this edition.

41. *The Book of Duarte Barbosa*, trans. Mansel Longworth Dames, vol. I (London: Hakluyt Society, 1918), 2d ser., no. 44 (1918): 12–60.

42. *A Report of the Kingdom of Congo and of the Surrounding Countries*; drawn out of the Writings and Discourses of the Portuguese, Duarte Lopez, by Filippo Pigafetta (Rome: 1591), ed. and trans. Margarite Hutchinson (London: John Murray, 1881). All citations are from pp. 97–125 of this edition.

43. Joseph C. Miller, "A Requiem for the 'Jaga,' " *Cahiers d'Études Africaines*, 13 (1973): 121–149.

The Philosophes and the Might of the Pen

The Enlightenment was the predominant intellectual movement in the West in the eighteenth century. Its thinkers, who called themselves philosophes, vowed to defend and promote the true, the secular, and the reasonable, and their pens were as powerful as the swords of the fabled heroes of the romances. These knights of rationality strived to rid the world of prejudice and ignorance, as well as ghosts, miracles, saints, and superstitions. The idea of Amazons survived the shift in sensibility from classical heroism to Christian martyrdom, and even underwent a wide resurgence in early modern times and during the age of exploration. But the intellectual climate of the Enlightenment was hostile to myth. The philosophes considered this mode of thought to be at best a waste of time, and at worst a major stumbling block in the path of human progress. Yet the rational thinkers of the seventeenth and eighteenth centuries were able to discover in the Amazon myth much that was satisfying, much that was even useful.

Francis Bacon, one of the harbingers of the Age of Reason, had nothing but contempt for myth-makers and their fantasies. Yet he cited Amazons in his 1622 essay "Of a Holy War." He argued, "I demand, is not such a preposterous government, against the first order of nature, for women to rule over men, it itself void, and to be suppressed?" Of course, with Elizabeth barely cold in her grave, Bacon felt obliged to state that he was not opposed to all female rulers—his complaint was not against the reign of a queen, "for that is supplied by counsel, and subordinate magistrates masculine." The nation he could not abide was one "where the regiment of state, justice, families, is all managed by women." He was more certain about his opposition to Amazons than he was on whether they actually ever existed. He cites them first as a "feigned case," but immediately adds that "antiquity makes it doubtful whether it were fiction or history."[1]

Similarly, Thomas Hobbes, who by his own admission did not believe in God, was not prepared to deny Amazons. They were too serviceable for his argument against divine right monarchy to toss out. Hobbes was trying to prove that the state is formed neither by nature nor by God, but by conscious and deliberate human agreement. The political community, he argued, has its origin in a social contract. As this contract was designed to meet particular human needs within a specific community, it could take any number of forms, including in some instances a female, or nonpatriarchal state. Even dominion within a family may be arranged by contract: "We find in History that the *Amazons* Contracted with the Men of neighboring Countries, to whom they had recourse for issue, that the issue Male should be sent back, but the Females remain with themselves: so that the dominion of the Females was in the Mother."[2]

For Hobbes, Amazons were useful, if only for rhetorical purposes. Another approach to Amazons was not to draft them directly into the armies of reason, but to submit them to a rigorous "basic training"; to reconcile, streamline, order, and arrange all the various and often conflicting classical accounts of their adventures, discarding elements that appeared fantastic, improbable, or out of joint. The motive for this undertaking was perfectly modern—the creation of a critical and rational history, yet the method employed appeared, at first glance, to be centuries old. Just like medieval scholars, the authors who undertook this venture scrambled for all possible "authorities" on their topic, correlating and reconciling the various sources of information. Pierre Petit in his 1687 *De Amazonibus dissertatio* and the Abbé Claude Marie Guyon in his 1748 *Histoire des Amazones* create veritable *Summae Amazonae* in the tradition of the Middle Ages. Like this earlier group of authors, Petit and Guyon sometimes mistook logical consistency for factual veracity.

Frontispieces from Pierre Petit's *De Amazonibus dissertatio* (Amsterdam, 1687) and *Traité historique sur les Amazones* (Leide, Marchand, 1718). (*Courtesy Rare Books and Manuscripts Division, The New York Public Library, Astor, Lenox and Tilden Foundations*)

But upon closer examination, the resemblance between medieval treatises and these histories of Amazons is superficial. For the Enlightenment historians discovered, almost in spite of themselves, that they could not make sense of their materials without creating and developing new methods, and raising questions that ultimately led to the birth of new fields of knowledge and forms of inquiry.

Petit's *De Amazonibus* is a modest and now uncelebrated work that incorporates some theoretical groundwork for the extraordinary achievements in the social sciences in the two centuries after him. In his assessment of the Amazon sagas springing from antiquity, he comes close to Jacob Bachofen's mid-nineteenth-century theory on the origin of myth and legend—that the accounts related of bygone times, even those which obviously contain elements of the fabulous, are heavily veiled cultural memories of concrete historical experiences. Given the sheer volume of the Amazon tales, Petit argued that it was far more rational to credit them with a degree of veracity than to discard them. Petit's argument in favor of the existence of Amazons hinged on two points. The first was his observation that the most prominent doubter among the ancients, Strabo, relied on nothing more solid than his own sexual bias, on a conviction that only men can lead armies and build cities, and, in general, perform the art and work of civilization. Petit's second argument was his own assertion that human character and behavior owe more to environmental factors than to any fixed biological program. In the case of Amazons, their excellence was due to the character of their homeland, especially the climate in which they lived. Following the example of Herodotus, Petit placed the Amazon motherland in the region of the Caucasus, around the Don. Petit contended that in cold climates there is less difference between male and female manners and inclinations than there is in more temperate climes. He believed that it was not the extreme cold alone that shaped Amazon character: their ability to equal, and even surpass men was also the result of their diet, education, and physical training. But though he was convinced that feminine weakness did not

One-breasted Amazons from Petit's *De Amazonibus dissertatio.* (*Courtesy Rare Books and Manuscripts Division, The New York Public Library, Astor, Lenox and Tilden Foundations*)

have its origin in nature, Petit was not prepared to have all females be Amazons, nor to suggest that the inequality of the sexes be ended:

> it is important not only for peace and domestic tranquility, but also for a serene and pleasant quality of life, that women, following the order of nature, be more gentle in spirit and weaker in body than men; for a man delights in someone shapely and agreeable, even if she is flighty and frivolous. Surely wise men would scorn women, along with all the bitterness of life and annoyances of the married state, if he did not receive very real and concrete advantages as a remedy and consolation.[3]

His praise of the submissive wife does not contradict his discussion of the potential of the female sex. Petit argued that every law has its exception: though men customarily or "naturally" rule over women, the opposite arrangement is not impossible.

It was also Petit's contention that Amazons won and maintained their superiority over men by interfering with the course of nature. He believed that these women most likely used some kind of drug to atrophy the right breast. As a physician, he was convinced that an actual surgical removal of the breast would have been far too dangerous an undertaking, more likely to result, if the patient survived at all, in the production of an invalid than an Amazon. Hippocrates and Galen, the great physicians of antiquity, were not correct, Petit argued, when they stated that the major effect of the removal or suppression of the right breast was the strengthening of the right shoulder. Such an effect, he argued, would hardly be worth the effort and sacrifice of so drastic a cause. It was Petit's belief that the procedure must lead to the strengthening not just of the shoulder, but of the entire body. To prove his argument on the necessity of removing a breast to make a woman an Amazon, Petit included in his book about two dozen engravings of coins and medals from his own collection and from other prominent collectors. He claimed that these drawings were of authentic artifacts of classical antiquity. The majority of these depict one-breasted women, and are, for this and other reasons, of dubious authenticity.[4] The uni-breasted physique was a major component in Petit's vision of Amazons, and both the 1687 Latin edition of his work as well as the 1717 French translation contain, in addition to his "artifacts," extraordinary frontispiece engravings with rather Rubenesque but clearly uni-mammalied Amazon queens standing in the foreground, with Rubens's burning and embattled bridge of Themiscyra in the background.

Petit also devoted a few pages to the discussion of Amazon sexuality. He (incorrectly) cited Hippocrates as an authority on the Amazon custom of crippling their male children, and ventures the suggestion that the Amazon motivation for such an unnatural act may not have been simply the precaution of disabling potential male warriors. Petit cites two proverbs, which he claimed were of Greek origin: "Cripples can very well conduct the labors a man performs for a woman" and "Cripples make passionate lovers." Thus Petit's Amazons never had to worry if men found them lovable, "because the Amazons not only used the boys they crippled as workers and craftsmen, they also employed them for the procreation of children."[5]

For the rest, Petit presented a rationalized synopsis of Amazon chronology and history, in which he divided their activity into three major wars, and cited the major sources for each "event." He placed the fall of Troy in the third millennium B.C. more than a thousand years too early, according to modern scholars. Petit argued that Amazons existed before the reign of Theseus, which he dated 2734 B.C.

Two generations later, mid-eighteenth century, the Abbé Claude Marie Guyon criticized Petit for hurling these shadowy "events" too far into the past. On other accounts, however, Guyon found in Petit a convenient and extremely useful authority. Indeed, Petit's supposedly ancient coins and medals depicting Amazons with a single breast provided Guyon with material he could not have found elsewhere.

The Abbé prefaced his *Histoire des Amazones* with a lengthy introduction detailing great queens and heroines and their great deeds, from biblical times to his own day. His main point was to demonstrate that women have never been totally excluded from history. Guyon agreed with Petit that the evidence for the existence of Amazons was too weighty to be dismissed: "there is no nation more celebrated, more remarkable, or better attested by the ancients than that of these illustrious female warriors. Temples, cities, counties, entire provinces, conserved the glory of their name long after their own day."[6] Guyon was the first to admit that the women of his own day were hardly Amazons. But he maintained that their frailty was clearly the result of their education and rearing, and that they had the potential to be quite otherwise: "there is no saying more common than 'it is men who are women and the women who are the men.' "

Like Petit, Guyon argued that the climate of Scythia had much to do with the production of Amazons. The frigid air of the Don gave them "the bravery, the passion, and the ferocity which terrified the peoples from the warmer climes." Guyon noted that the Greeks considered these regions to be uninhabitable. Although he did not believe a woman had to undergo a form of mastectomy in order to achieve Amazonian excellence, Guyon believed that the Amazons did suppress the right breast, and with the greatest rationality. It was his conviction that the women of his day were not as accomplished archers as were men, which proved to him that the presence of the right breast hinders drawing the bow: "the Amazons, determined to achieve a mastery in arms, willingly submitted to the pain and inconvenience of this mutilation in order to maintain the mode of life they embraced by choice and with honor."

Guyon, like all educated men of his time and social class, had a thorough knowledge of classical literature. He was struck by the popularity of the Amazon accounts, and the ever-present emphasis on the Amazon wars, "the valor with which they were fought, and the laurels the Amazons gained, even from the heroes themselves." He argued that the Greeks and Romans saw the Amazons not as ordinary enemies, but as representatives of a form of excellence, or a greater-than-life challenge. He undoubtedly had the Emperor Commodus in mind when he wrote that the Romans "were so full of marvelous esteem for them, that they knew no eulogy more flattering to a Prince than to compare him with these [women-warriors]."

The Abbé was convinced that Amazons could not have been just a popular tale that captured the fancy of the ancients. He freely admitted that the stories of the poets of old could not always be accepted as literally true. But he insisted that most accounts of Amazon activity contained at least a core of veracity. A major point in Guyon's argument was his distinction between what he called fable and the fabulous, or between fable and myth. He defined fable as conscious make-believe, an intellectual amusement "for the purpose of teaching the heart moral lessons and sentiments." But myth represents a simple fact of history, "which the narrator, seeking to embellish a worthy subject, has decorated with episodes and circumstances which, though their falsity is evident and obvious, do not destroy the truth. No reasonable mind would dismiss the entire tract as pure fiction; one must distinguish between what is reality and what is not. That is all that one may conclude from the fashion in which the poets have recounted the battles of the Amazons." The idea that myths may contain valuable historical information represents a leap in the social sciences, but there were none to follow in Guyon's footsteps. In general, Enlightenment thinkers saw their task as the elimination of the fabulous and the supernatural, and they were blind to the possible application of myth and legend as historical source materials.

But Guyon used his methodological insight freely, and following in the tradition of Petit, he culled from the classical accounts a single story line. He selected and retained all the incidents which fit his structure, and discarded those which did not. For example, along with Petit, he rejected Diodorus of Sicily's account of an early race of African Amazons who flourished one or two millennia before the events of the Trojan War as a poetic fiction.

Guyon rejected Petit's opinion that the Amazons used the boys they crippled for their sexual needs. He argued that the

Amazon women sacrificed their personal sexual fulfillment
for the benefit of their community, and that they maintained
"a type of celibacy." They made this celibacy manifest by their
continued wearing of the girdle, which was among the ancients "a symbol of feminine purity and chastity." Guyon
asserted that Amazons always wore this garment, and this
was proof enough to his mind that they had no sexual interest
in their crippled male slaves. The most zealous Amazon women,
he believed, never surrendered the girdle, and always adorned
themselves with this belt of virginity. Those Amazons who
bore children for the purpose of assuring the continuity of
their state renounced any further commerce with men the
moment they knew that they had conceived, and thereafter
returned to their celibate existence. Guyon was fascinated by
the Amazon attitude toward sex, which he found at once
both elevated and savage; the men were "unknown to them,
mere strangers that chance happened to bring to certain
designated places; and they retained for them neither the
sentiment nor the memory that one observes in beasts." The
attitude that any sexual partner will do because sex is only
to serve one's own needs is typically associated with masculine
boasting and swagger. It is therefore not surprising that Guyon
found this Amazonian role reversal refreshing and exciting,
and perhaps titillating. Petit's assumption that Amazons kept
crippled males to satisfy their sexual needs similarly confirmed all the erotic and sensual dreams the concept of
the Amazon has carried since earliest times.

Enlightenment Amazons did more than simply serve as
the inspiration of sexual fantasies. Some thinkers used the
women as raw data for the new field of comparative anthropology. Father Joseph Francois Lafitau's *Moeurs des sauvages
amériquains, comparées aux moeurs des premiers temps* (Customs
of the American Indians Compared with the Customs of Primitive Times) placed what appeared to be a seal of scientific
verification on the conviction of earlier writers and explorers
that there were Amazons in the New World.

Lafitau was a French Jesuit who spent five years (1712–
17) in the Iroquois mission of Sault Saint Louis, now Caugh-
nawaga, where he had direct contact with that tribe as well

as with Jesuit colleagues in New France who had made studies of the Huron. The knowledge he gained of the Iroquois and Huron served as the foundation for the theories and speculations he expressed in his *Moeurs*.

Lafitau was not the first thinker to draw parallels between Indian cultures and the various peoples of antiquity.[7] Such assumptions would naturally arise within the context of the Christian belief in a single creation for all the earth's peoples. But it was Lafitau's contribution to this theory of common origin to forego any reliance on false genealogies tracing the sons of Adam, or creation of Trojan princes like the medieval Francus and Brutus, and to make a direct systematic study of the Indian tribal life. To use his own words, "I have sought in these practices and customs vestiges of the most remote antiquity." This striking statement is the core to Lafitau's thinking. He added, "If the ancient authors have given me information on which to base happy conjectures about the Indians, the customs of the Indians have given me information on the basis of which I can understand more easily and explain more readily many things in the ancient authors." Here Lafitau comes very close to the formulation of the great American anthropologist, Lewis Henry Morgan, that contemporary "primitive" societies reflect the stages of social organization that are the common experience of all humanity. But Lafitau was not interested in presenting a general theory of human development. His basic argument was that in general, the customs of the Americans resemble those of the ancients in general, to such a degree that "one can infer from it that they all stem from the same stock." Lafitau explained his theory "that the largest number of the American peoples came originally from those barbarians who occupied the continent and islands of Greece, whence, having for many centuries sent out colonies in every direction. . . . These barbarians although confused in histories by a multitude of names . . . are, nevertheless almost universally included under the generic names of Pelesgians and Hellenians." But in the case of the Iroquois and Huron peoples, Lafitau believed he could make "reasonable probable conjectures" on their specific origin. He contended that these tribes descended from Thracian and Lycian migrations to America. As proof, he leaned heavily on the slender but sturdy shoulders of the Amazons.

Lafitau was convinced that the Amazon influence on America was beyond dispute, since "the customs of the Amazons are too individual and characteristic for us to be able to mistake them." After citing Diodorus of Sicily and Herodotus as sources on the earliest history of the Amazons, Lafitau remarks,

> perhaps we should regard them as a myth as Strabo did, if we had not been assured that, in our day, there are still found on the banks of the Marañon or Amazon River, some of those warrior women who glory in the works of Mars, live apart from men, practice continually at drawing the bow, keep only the girls with them, either killing the boys or returning them to their fathers at stated times when they seek their company. Father Lamberti of the order of the regular Clerics and Missionaries of the Colchidians says that there are still Amazons among the barbarous nations inhabiting the Caucasus.

Here we see an ironic instance of Lafitau using his newly developed methodology. It is perfectly true that the accounts of his contemporary Amazons were illuminated by, and shed light upon, the Amazons of antiquity. The old informs the new, and the new the old, but neither the past of the ancients nor the present of the conquerors has the power to confer veracity on the other.

In all fairness to Lafitau, he did not claim to have firsthand experience of warrior-women who lived apart from men. What he did claim to discover were certain characteristics of Iroquois and Huron societies which he believed to be unmistakable vestiges of the practices of the most ancient Amazons. Lafitau summed these traits up in a single, somewhat unpronounceable word: *gynecocracy*. By this he meant to signify feminine rule, such as existed among the ancient Lycians of Herodotus's description. He pointed to the matrilocal residence of the Iroquois family, the use of matrilineal descent and transmission of property, and what he perceived as the matriarchal power structure in both the Huron and the Iroquois tribes to verify the close parallel to the Lycians. He futable proof derived from philology: the Greek word for Lycian means wolf, and the wolf family is one of the three major divisions in the Iroquois and Huron tribes.

Lafitau used the three-family division to make yet another link between the Amazons of old and the New World Indians: in his third century B.C. *Argonautica,* Apollonius of Rhodes described the Amazon women whom his hero Jason only narrowly managed to avoid as being divided into three tribes. One of these, the Lycastians, Lafitau held, "corresponds exactly with the Wolf Clan of the Iroquois and Huron."

Lafitau cited the authority of several classical authors to establish the gynecocracy of the Lycians. But it was his own speculation that this form of social and political organization

> may possibly even have come from the Amazons whose empire is so vast in extent. It is likely enough that these women, some of whom settled in Lycia . . . tired at last of being always at war, and seeing their decadence and ruin at hand, finally compromised with their enemies, that they received them into the cities which they had built, keeping on one hand the domain which they already had whether that of the fields which they were cultivating or the children which they were bringing up, and, on the other hand, they did honour to the men by combining some of the latters' customs with theirs and leaving them the care of affairs in such a way that the men could have only the honour and they themselves all the responsibility.

Lafitau's conjectures would make the status of modern women among most of the world's peoples the result of the noblesse and generosity of these ancient Amazons who opted to do all the work and give the men all the credit and rewards.

In his discussion of gynecocracy, Lafitau is a precursor of J.J. Bachofen, whose 1861 *Mother Right* postulated an aboriginal Amazon state as the common experience of all humankind. But here again Lafitau avoided making any theoretical pronouncements about culture in general. He limited his remarks on gynecocracy to the statement that it was the basis of the Lycian government, and that "it might have been common formerly to almost all the primitive peoples of Greece, since it is quite widespread, as I have shown in speaking of the Cantabrians, the people of Spain and those in speaking of the Cantabrians, the people of Spain and those of Asia Minor. It is found among almost all the people who migrated from there."

Lafitau did not believe that all peoples have Amazons among their ancestors. This allowed him to rule out some of them, in particular the Hebrews, as possible founders of native American cultures. In his view the Lost Tribes never found their way to the American continent. For although "there were some practices to all men which the Jews must have had like other primitive peoples," the particular customs of America, "such as the gynecocracy of several tribes, the order of succession, of genealogies, of inheritances, etc . . . are quite the opposite of those essential to the Israelite government." Lafitau identified the Hebrew tribes as overwhelmingly patriarchal in character, and could not conceive of a Jewish Amazon.

Although Lafitau's *Moeurs* enjoyed a measure of success in the eighteenth century, he smarted under the barbs of Voltaire's cruel and pointed wit. In the privacy of the title page of his own copy of the *Moeurs,* Voltaire penned under Lafitau's name, "ignorant blockhead without any sense who wants to play the scholar." [8]

In his 1756 *Essai sur les moeurs,* penned in part as a satire of Lafitau, Voltaire wrote, "If one is unsurprised to find flies in America, it is stupidity to be astonished that men are also present there."[9] His dry and not exactly balanced summation of Lafitau's ideas made the poor father appear utterly ridiculous: "Finally, Lafitau has the Americans descend from the ancient Greeks, and here are his reasons—The Greeks have fables, some Americans have them too. The first Greeks went hunting, the Americans also go. The first Greeks had oracles, Americans have diviners. The Greeks used to dance at their festivals, they dance in America. One has to admit, these are convincing reasons."[10] Voltaire was particularly hostile to the Christian idea of the unity of creation: "In effect, since the blacks of Africa do not take their origin from our white peoples, why should the red, olive, and brown-skinned peoples of America come from our countries?"[11]

If Voltaire omitted Amazons from his bill of particulars against Lafitau, it was not because he considered this argument, a key point in Lafitau, beyond dispute. In his *Philosophical Dictionary* of 1764, Voltaire wrote in the essay "Amazons": "there is hardly any nation which does not boast of having produced such heroines; the number of these however, is not great; nature seems to have designed women for other purposes. . . . In short, every people have had their female warriors; but the Kingdom of the Amazons, on the banks of the Thermodon, is, like most other ancient stories, nothing more than a poetic fiction."[12] It was Lafitau's comparative method, and especially the way he applied it in the *Customs*, that Voltaire found lacking in rigor and food only for satire. According to Fenton, Voltaire's attack gave the *"coup de grace* to Lafitau's standing as a scholar."[13]

Although he made Lafitau look foolish, in his own *Essai sur les moeurs* Voltaire proved himself to be clearly inferior to Lafitau in knowledge of America, and to possess more than his share of absurd ideas about that continent:

> in general, the New World does not contain anything near the number of people it could hold. There are certain natural causes for this: first, the excessive cold, which in America, at the same latitude as Paris and Vienna, is as piercing as at the artic circle. Secondly, American rivers are, for the most part, at least twenty, or thirty times wider than ours. The frequent floods are bound to bring sterility, and consequently, mortality, in immense regions. The mountains, being very much higher, are also more uninhabitable than ours; the strong and violent poisons which cover the American soil make the slightest scratch of an arrow that has been dipped in them, fatal.[14]

Voltaire had denied Lafitau and his American Amazons without having any firsthand experience of the New World, and it is interesting that at least one Enlightenment explorer who did see America did not agree with him. The highly regarded scientist and philosophe Claude Marie de la Condamine thought it likely that there were in his own day, or there had been in the not too distant past, Amazons in America. La Condamine's *Relation abrégée d'un voyage fait dans l'interieur de l'Amérique Méridionale* (A Succinct Abridgement of a Voyage within the Island Parts of South America) (1745) was an account of his trip down the Amazon River that he made at the request of the *Académie Royale des Sciences*. His mission was part of a project the *Académie* was conducting to settle once and for all time the question of the shape of the earth: is it elongated at the poles, as the faulty (but popular in official French Catholic circles) physics of Descartes decreed, or was the earth, as Newton argued, slightly flattened at the poles and elevated at the equator?

While measuring the length of the first three degrees of the meridian at the equator, La Condamine also made many observations of the terrain and its natives. He even included a report on American Amazons because, he wrote, "I thought it might reasonably be expected of me."[15] Indeed, who cares about the figure of the earth if one can gain firsthand knowledge of the Amazons? And the Amazon question was one that needed to be settled with the seal of scientific authority. Even though the Académie did not ask La Condamine to investigate Amazons, he knew that any man of science sent to this part of the world would be expected to do so.

La Condamine went about his work in a systematic way, questioning Indians of all the various tribes whose nations he traversed. He met not a single native who would claim a direct encounter with an Amazon. But when he questioned the natives about these women, "they all told us that they had been informed of the same by their parents, adding thereto a thousand other particulars, too long to be repeated, but which all of them served to confirm that there has been, in this continent, a commonwealth of females, who lived by themselves, without having any males amongst them; and that they have retired to the north, far up within the inland countries."

When La Condamine and his party pursued an Indian whose *father* had actually seen the Amazons, he found they were too late—the man was deceased. But his surviving seventy-year-old son "assured us that his grandfather had actually seen these females. . . . He added his grandfather has spoken with four of them, one of which had a child at her breast, and told us the names of each of them."

In hot pursuit of the elusive women, the French scientific expedition came upon the Topayas tribe, where the most highly valued jewels were certain green stones. These the men inherited from their fathers, who in turn had received them as gifts from the "women without husbands." The same sources placed the women at a point beyond where the river becomes unnavigable because of falls, and thence many days' journey on foot through a jungle and then over high mountains. An old man La Condamine questioned claimed that in 1726 he had journeyed inland from the river and came upon a tribe of long-eared men. The latter presented many green stones to their wives and daughters and said they received them from the Amazons who were still a few weeks' journey away. According to La Condamine, the various accounts he gathered seemed to concur in placing the Amazons "at the mountains at the heart of Guiana, a region whither neither the Portuguese of Para, nor the French of Cayenne have yet penetrated." He admitted the possibility that "this ambulatory nation may again have changed its abode."

His favorite theory, however, was that the American woman-warriors no longer maintained an exclusively female community, "that they had now laid aside their ancient customs; whether they have been subdued by any other nation, or, whether their daughters, being weary of their solitude, have at last forgot the aversion their mothers had to mankind: wherefore, though, at present, no actual traces of this female republick should remain, this would not be sufficient for us to affirm there never was any such."

La Condamine added the reflection that many of the characteristics ascribed to the Amazons in the various Indian accounts may have originated with the questions raised by their European interrogators, who were "prepossessed with the manners attributed to the ancient *Amazons* of *Asia.*" The enthusiastic European reception to stories about woman-warriors and their customs "may have indirectly induced the *Indians* to adopt it into their accounts." These considerations led La Condamine to argue that the question of Amazons in America should be approached as a separate question, entirely independent of ancient accounts of the Amazons of Asia, or modern accounts of African warrior-women, "because what we read thereof, either in the ancient or modern historians, is at least intermingled with many fables, and liable to be disputed."

It was La Condamine's conviction that the evidence for

Amazons in America was more weighty than any theory that placed the women elsewhere. "If ever there could be any *Amazons* in the world," he reasoned, "it must be in *America*." He could understand Amazon society only as a deliberate rebellion on the part of women whom men forced into unsuitable, unfair, and onerous labor. In America

> the vagabond lives of the women, who often follow their husbands to the wars, and are not a lot happier when at home with their families, might naturally put it into their minds, and at the same time afford them frequent opportunities to escape from the hard yoke of their tyrants, by endeavoring to provide themselves a settlement, where they might live independently, and at least, not be reduced to the wretched condition of slaves, and beasts of burden.

Hence, there have surely been Amazons in America. Not that a philosophe could trust the natives' stories, for "all, or the most part, of the *Indians* of *South America,* are liars, credulous, and fond of anything surprizing." But, La Condamine argued, it was unthinkable that South American Indians read Diodorus Siculus or Justin on the Amazons. Yet, "nevertheless, a report of such a nation had obtained *footing* amongst the *Indians* in the center of *America* before the *Spaniards* had penetrated thither; and mention has been made of them since, among many peoples who had never seen Europeans." La Condamine believed that these stories from so many diverse native peoples must be based on some concrete historical reality. For reasons entirely other than Lafitau's supposed Thracian and Lycian migrations, he believed that there had been Amazons in America, and that perhaps, in some remote swamp or jungle or mountain retreat, they still thrived.

La Condamine drew other lessons from native Americans. These peoples whom he judged to be capable of spawning Amazons "pass their lives without thought, and grow old without having taken leave of infancy, all the failings of which they retain." He considered Indian cultures to be an example of human "degeneracy" and refused to join the ranks of those philosophes like Jean Jacques Rousseau who glorified "natural man," unspoiled by the artificiality and corruption of society. His experience in America had taught him quite otherwise: "one cannot observe, without being mortified, how little a man, when wholly left to the guidance of mere nature, differs from the brutes." The work of La Condamine established the germ of an idea that was to be pursued by scholars of the next generations: societies that produce or contain Amazons represent the basest and most primitive level of culture, which is barely recognizable as human. Therefore, the art and work of civilization can only be accomplished by opposition and overcoming these warrior-women. Men must continue war against the Amazons, not for personal glory, but to build and maintain an avenue for human progress.

In the multivolume collective intellectual production of midcentury, the *Encyclopédie, où dictionnaire raisonné des sciences, des arts, et des métiers* (1751–65), there appear several articles relating to "Amazone." They show that many of the philosophes had neither Voltaire's conviction that Amazons are make-believe, nor La Condamine's assurance in their reality. The Abbé Mallet's article "Amazone" takes no position whatsoever on the warrior-women. A second article, "Amazones, rivière des Amazones" by the better-known editor of the *Encyclopédie,* Jean le Rond d'Alembert, presents the story of the naming of the river, and praises La Condamine's map of the same. D'Alembert also cites La Condamine's testimony that he saw "neither Amazons nor anything like them" on his journey, but that on the basis of the testimony he gathered, "he believed it probable enough that there has been *Amazons* in America, that is, a society of women who live without having regular contact with men."[16] By ascribing this belief to La Condamine, D'Alembert guards himself against the accusation that he is vouching for the existence of these women.

Perhaps the best summary of the philosophes' attitude toward Amazons is a remark of the historian Edward Gibbon in his *Decline and Fall of the Roman Empire* (1776). He notes that the Emperor Aurelian paraded the female Goths he captured under a banner marked "Amazons." He footnotes this with the comment, "Among barbarous nations women have often combated by the side of their husbands. But it is *almost* impossible that a society of Amazons should ever have

existed in the old or new world"[17]—a statement which incorporates both the cautious doubt, as well as the often subtle
but nonetheless evident misogyny of most Enlightenment
thinkers.

The contempt for women is particularly apparent in the
popular chapbook, *The History of Hector, Prince of Troy.* This
volume, slender in size and in literary value, was one of the
eighteenth-century forerunners of the modern-day comic.
book. However, the Penthesilea of this Troy story has little
in common with the twentieth-century Wonder Woman. The
chapbook appears to be a hastily executed admixture of the
Amazon as a Renaissance courtly lady, and the medieval misogynistic portrayal of the woman-out-of-line. Honor, dignity,
and a loyal following are Penthesilea's, but she gets butchered
like a beast on the field:

> Penthesilea, the Amazon Queen, hearing of Hector's fame,
> came about this time to the aid of the Trojans; but finding that
> prince dead, she vowed revenge, and accordingly in a battle
> issued forth with her train of near a thousand ladies, and made
> the Grecian host to fly before them. Pyrus the Grecian chief
> in the room of Achilles, enraged that a woman should eclipse
> his honour, engaged her, but she bore him to the ground,
> giving him a great wound; but he remounted, and running
> upon her, broke her helmet, which falling off, cut her body
> in twain, which was afterwards honourably buried. The ladies
> revenged the death of their queen by putting the Greeks en-
> tirely to rout.[18]

This popular image of Amazons writhing in their own
gore, even if they are eventually buried "honorably," should
have been sufficient to deter serious writers, especially women
writers, from dealing with the Amazon legends. But the dismembered warrior-women of the chapbook did not prevent
the composition of a five-act drama in verse, the *Tragedie des
Amazones.* Its author was one of the few prominent women
of eighteenth-century French literature, Marie Anne Fiquet
du Boccage. Although the eighteenth century was not an age
of female emancipation, and even less a time of liberated
women,[19] Madame du Boccage was one of the few upper-
class women whose education was full enough to permit them

to participate in the intellectual and artistic life of her age.

She was born Marie Anne Le Page in 1710, the daughter of a wealthy bourgeois family of Rouen. In addition to her own intellectual gifts, the Le Page daughter had the advantage of money and a good deal of social mobility. After an education at an exclusive Parisian convent, she returned home at seventeen to marry Joseph Fiquet du Boccage, himself a published poet and translator, who shared her literary endeavors. Until his death in 1767, he was her constant friend and companion. Madame du Boccage enjoyed the company of many outstanding men as well as a tiny circle of intellectually gifted and active women in Rouen. After 1733, she and her husband spent eight months a year in Paris, where one evening a week their home became a literary salon attended by some of the most outstanding people of the century—French, British, American, and Italian. Her salon had a more sober and serious tone than the drawing rooms of her rivals; Marmontel, the famous chronicler of that milieu, complained that he found the salon of Madame du Boccage "boring." But the evidence bears witness that Madame du Boccage tried very hard to amuse and please Marmontel, and for that matter, everyone else.

It must have been a very special triumph for her when she received the prize for poetry from the Academy of Rouen in 1746. Voltaire himself dubbed her "la Sapho du Normandie."[20] Now that her reputation as a poet seemed secure, du Boccage proceeded to write her great tragedy, in verse, *Amazones*. In July and August of 1749, the *Comédiens Ordinaire du Roi* presented the drama eleven times—it was neither a roaring success nor a conspicuous failure.

Far more remarkable than the fact of the play's production and reception was the viewpoint of its author. The play, like the work of Christine de Pisan almost four hundred years earlier, is striking evidence that the single most important factor in determining an author's approach to the treatment of Amazon themes is the gender of that author. Women never write about Amazons to glorify men. Just as Christine de Pisan's tastes and sensibilities belonged to the late medieval world, the interests and concerns of Marie Anne du Boccage were those of her own Age of Reason. Yet both authors' works are pervaded by a demand for fair play for women, and by a conscious effort to oppose male misogyny.

The closest precedents in time that du Boccage had for her play were a series of seventeenth-century English dramas about Amazon societies. The earliest, best known, and most typical was John Fletcher's 1622 *The Sea Voyage*. In this drama the Amazon queen and her warrior-women all happily sur- render their freedom for the love and protection of a man— in this case, a long-lost husband. The theme of Amazon so- cieties dissolving because their warriors prefer the marriage bed to the tossing of javelins also characterized Edward How- ard's *The Woman's Conquest* (1670) and *The Six Days Adventure; or, The New Utopia* (1671), Thomas D'Urfey's *A Commonwealth of Women* (1685), and others.[21]

However, unlike these precedents, Madame du Boccage's work does not end with the dissolution of an Amazon state; it closes with a strong and viable female community. Her play has a moral, but that moral is not the superiority of male- dominated domestic arrangements or societies. Madame du Boccage's Amazons are capable and competent rulers and warriors. Unlike Edward Gibbon, she had no difficulty en- visioning societies in which women ruled.

The play opens after a significant Amazon victory against Greek attackers at the Amazon capital of Themiscyra. Con- trary to the Greek and Roman legends, Madame du Boccage's Amazons have *defeated* Theseus, king of Athens. He and his companion Idas are prisoners of the women.

The theme of the play is the conflict between love and duty, and it was a typical example of the Enlightenment sen- sibility. What was unique to Madame du Boccage's work was her selection of the fabled Amazon nation as a vehicle for expressing the conviction that a rational, dignified, and well- ordered life precludes any extravagant displays of emotion. Her play does have some unrequited love, and even a suicide, but Queen Orithe kills herself not so much because Theseus loves her sister, but because she violated Amazonian law by allowing herself to fall in love in the first place. The emotions of the protagonists in the play are all very controlled—there is neither dark brooding nor deep loathing, none of the *sturm und drang* that would characterize nineteenth-century plays on the same theme. Nor does Madame du Boccage portray love as a particularly feminine weakness; the hero Theseus also falls in love, but not with Orithe, the queen who loves him.

The story line is thin and sequential almost to a fault. It has no flashbacks, no secondary plots. But Madame du Boccage interspersed the action with discussions between Theseus and the Amazon Menalippe, who tries to explain Amazon training and values to the captured king:

> Since earliest infancy our destiny is to bear arms.
> Our eyes are hard and severe, devoid of tears,
> We ignore the art of the flatterer, designed to charm,
> We inspire fear, not the desire to love.
> Our hands ignore the arts of adornment
> In order to work with iron and forge our armor.
> Far from disciplining our feet to musical cadences,
> They get their training at running and wrestling.[22]

Like the Spartan citizens of classical antiquity, the Amazons' devotion to their community was complete. Each Amazon considered the good of her community to be of greater importance than her own romantic adventures.

> And the son of Venus is wasting his charms
> On the daughters of Mars, his arrows are to no avail.
> If we submit to the laws of nature,
> It is only to participate in the future race,
> And to repopulate these fields with women whose
>   arms
> Are free, generous, and formidable in combat.
> May they always be faithful to our virtues.
> And see tyrants destroyed, and our laws reign
>   immortal.

Theseus, in reply, attempts to hold before her the prospect of ruling by feminine wile in lieu of military weapons:

> In other climes you would rule by your charms,
> That sweeter empire is scarcely known here.

Menalippe is quick to answer that Amazons would lose
their freedom in this "sweeter empire":

> Liberty, Theseus, is the sovereign good.
> Discord, envy, and the vain lust for gold,
> Germinate and thrive in the bosom of pleasure.
> Amongst us work and frugality,
> Maintain virtue, peace, and truth.

She scolds him both for the degree to which men, in "the
empire of kings," allow young beauties to rule them through
coquetry, and for the male contempt and disdain of the same
women when time fades their beauty:

> Far from being dreaded here, time brings us a prize,
> Here, a wrinkled brow signifies authority.

She concludes her speech with the hope that the Amazon
priestess will order his immediate death.

It is clear that discussion can never unite the Amazon and
the Athenian. Madame du Boccage resorts to action. Idas
escapes and returns to the camp with a rallied and battle-
ready band of Athenians. Menalippe gleefully kills someone
she believes is Theseus and is disappointed when she learns
it was Idas fighting in his armor. Victory belongs to the Greeks.
Theseus makes a gallant gesture to leave Orithe on the throne,
but she kills herself and passes the Amazon rule to Menalippe, whose unswerving devotion to Amazonian ideals makes
her truly worthy of the throne. Theseus embarks on the long
journey to Athens with Antiope as his bride, content to leave
behind Menalippe at the head of a strong, viable and com-
fortably remote Amazonian state.

Not all admirers of the *Amazones* were willing to believe
that Madame du Boccage actually wrote the play, since com-
posing tragedies has never been a traditionally feminine endeavor. Some argued that a certain Monsieur Linaut was the
real author, while others insisted that her good friend, the
Abbé du Resnel, had been the one to wield the pen.[23] A play
too good for a woman to write was undoubtedly considered
not at all bad.

Shortly after the production of *Amazones* came the death
of Voltaire's cherished mistress, friend, and intellectual com-

panion, Emilie Bretueil du Châtelet. The grieving Voltaire wrote du Boccage, "Alas, Madame, it was only four days ago that we reread your tragedy together." Du Châtelet had been an excellent physicist, and Voltaire wrote in the same letter, "she was, like you, the glory of her sex and of the French nation. She was to natural philosophy what you are to poetry."[24]

Although the *Amazones* was translated into Italian in 1756 and German in 1762, Madame du Boccage seems to have dropped tragedy as a genre. Only a year after the production of her play, she wrote an epic poem on the discovery of America, *La Colombiade*. The work displays much erudition about the New World, which is not surprising in the light of the fact that for many years La Condamine was a regular guest at her salon. The poem is a highly imaginative work. In keeping with epic tradition, the whims and wiles of the gods have some role in human fate. Madame du Boccage uses native American deities to wear the wings and carry the thunderbolts of the gods of Olympus. But although du Boccage calls the powerful Indian queen whose love Columbus spurns, and whose forces he battles, "a mighty Amazon" who is "more ferocious than Sermiramis and Penthesilea,"[25] the poem is not *Amazones* transported to the New World. The stage belongs to Columbus, to his courage and his victory.

In spite of the fact that Madame du Boccage used the Amazon image freely as a source of strength for women, the two best known feminist theorists of her day seemed reluctant to call upon Amazons, ancient or modern, real or imagined, in their arguments for female equality. In his *Sur l'Admission des femmes au droit de Cité* (1789) the Marquis de Condorcet argued that citizenship should not be dependent upon physical strength. He pointed out that some women are as strong as some men. This seemed obvious enough to Condorcet without invoking Amazons. Similarly, Mary Wollstonecraft in her *Vindication of the Rights of Women* (1792) did not mention Amazons, because she envisioned an informed and liberated woman who could achieve autonomy without assuming total domination over men.

But during the French Revolution, when many women

found themselves in a situation where they had to grab weapons or at least contemplate the possibility of doing so, the Amazon became the role model for the woman-at-arms. Women of action welcomed the "examples" the Amazons stories provided them. These women-at-arms came from a great variety of political groups. They were for and against the king, the Jacobins, the Girondins, the Revolution and the Counter-Revolution.[26] Aside from scattered saints and martyrs, to whom else in history or in legend could fighting women turn for example and emulation than the Amazons? Perhaps not all French women had the swagger of the anonymous author of *Mère Duchêne* (1791): "I offer my services to the nation as a warrior. I am naturally inclined to fist fighting, and I am used to boxing with my dear husband. At the first drumbeat I take up arms, I raise a squadron of Amazons, I put myself at their head, I thrust into the enemy battalions as if they were butter."[27]

But even if a few eighteenth-century women dreamed of slicing through enemy male battalions, and if Madame du Boccage took the idea of a successful viable community of Amazon warriors seriously, the fact remains that the Amazon image in the eighteenth century was shaped predominantly by men for their purposes. In a scientific age, Amazons were co-opted into the struggle for rationality: they became the raw data for the new scientific social sciences. Petit and Guyon had employed Amazons to show that with proper scrutiny, seemingly legendary material could be of use as historical sources. Lafitau used the assumption of a remote Amazonian origin to account for some of the matriarchal or matrilineal customs of the Iroquois and Huron tribes of native Americans. While most of the more prominent Enlightenment thinkers like Voltaire, D'Alembert, and Gibbon contented themselves with the reassuring and misogynist statement that Amazons *probably* never existed, La Condamine was certain there were, or had been in the recent past, Amazons in the jungles of South America. He sowed the seeds for what became an elaborate theory in the next century: the existence of Amazons in America, or anyplace else, was a testimony to the extremely primitive and barbarous character of the societies in which they lived, as well as a reminder of the vast superiority of societies dominated by European men. The philosophes demonstrated that the pen, when dipped deep into the well of wit, sarcasm, and contempt, could indeed be mightier than the sword. Like every age before it, the Enlightenment left for posterity its heap of dead and wounded Amazons. In an age of reason, whose thinkers were pledged to the elimination of all make-believe, the Amazon was a myth that survived—and even flourished.

Notes

1. In *The Works of Francis Bacon*, ed. Basil Montagu, vol. II (Philadelphia: M. Murphy, 1876), p. 442.
2. Thomas Hobbes, *The Leviathan*, ed. Francis B. Randall (New York: Washington Square Press, 1964), pp. 140–41.
3. Pierre Petit, *Traité historique des Amazons* (Leiden: Marchand, 1718), p. 175.
4. The engravings of artifacts that are known today (like the famous Amazon coin of Commodus) differ visibly from the originals and it is hard to escape the conclusion that many of Petit's examples reflect antiquity as he and his sources believed it to be, and not as the ancients themselves portrayed it.
5. Petit, *Traité historique*, pp. 265–66. Petit cites Erasmus, Chilide II, Century IX, who in turn cited Athenaeus and Aristotle as the sources of these proverbs.
6. Claude Marie Guyon, *Histoire des Amazones*, 2 vols. (Amsterdam, 1748), vol. 1, pp. 7–8. All citations are from vol. I, pp. 4, 15, 83, 86 and vol. II, pp. 25–26, 95–96 of this edition.
7. See Father Joseph Francois Lafitau, *Customs of the American Indians Compared with the Customs of Primitive Times*, ed. and trans. William N. Fenton and Elizabeth Moore, vols. XLVIII and XLIX of Publications of the Champlain Society (Toronto: Champlain Society, 1974–1977), I: XXIX-CXIX. All citations are from vol. I, pp. 26, 37, 56–57, 72, 79–80, 261, 285 of this edition.
8. Cited by Theodore Besterman in *Oeuvres Completes de Voltaire*, vol. 3. (Danbury, Oxfordshire: Voltaire Foundation, 1975), p. 109, n. 3.

9. Voltaire, *Essai sur les moeurs*, ed. René Pomeau, 2 vols. (Paris: Garnier Frères, 1963), II: 340.

10. Ibid., I: 30.

11. Ibid., II: 340.

12. Voltaire, *Oeuvres Completes*, XVII: 130.

13. Lafitau, *Customs*, p. cviii.

14. Voltaire, *Essai sur les moeurs*, II: 346.

15. *A Succinct Abridgement of a Voyage Made within the Island Parts of South America by Mons. de la Condamine*, trans. anon. (London: Withers and Goodfall, 1747), p. 10. All citations from La Condamine are from pp. 26–27, 51–52, 54–56 of this edition.

16. *Encyclopédie, où Dictionnaire raisonné des sciences, des arts et des métiers*, ed. Denis Diderot and Jean le Rond d'Alembert, vol. 1 (Paris: Briasson, David, LeBreton & Durand, 1751), p. 318.

17. Edward Gibbon, *The Decline and Fall of the Roman Empire*. 6 vols. (London: W. Strahan & T. Cadwell, 1776–1788), v.1. p. 315, n. 78, p. xlvi.

18. *The History of Hector, Prince of Troy* (London, ca. 1750); p. 22. Copies of this chapbook exist in New York at the Morgan-Pierpont Library as well as the New York Public Library.

19. See A. Kleinbaum, "Women in the Age of Light," in Renata Bridenthal and Claudia Koonz, eds., *Becoming Visible* (Boston: Houghton Mifflin, 1977), pp. 217–35.

20. Grace Gill-Mark, *Anne-Marie du Boccage, Une Femme de Lettres au XVIIIᵉ Siècle* (Paris: Librairie Ancien Honoré Champion, 1927), p. 26.

21. See Jean Elisabeth Gagen, *The New Woman, Her Emergence in English Drama 1600–1730* (New York: Twayne Publishers, 1954), pp. 161–77, for a full discussion of these English "Amazon" plays.

22. *Amazones, Tragédie en Cinq Actes par Madame du Boccage...* (Paris: Meriget, 1749), pp. 21–23. The citations are from Act II, Scene V of this edition.

23. Gill-Mark, *Ann-Marie du Boccage*, p. 152.

24. Voltaire to Madame du Boccage, 12 October 1749, *Les Oeuvres Complètes de Voltaire*, ed. Theodore Besterman, vol. XCV (Geneva: Institut et Musée Voltaire, 1970), pp. 176–77.

25. Madame du Boccage, *La Colombiade* (Paris: Desaint & Saillant, 1756). These citations are from the eighth and ninth songs.

26. There is much information on this subject in Baron Marc de Villiers, *Histoire des Clubs de Femmes et des Légions d'Amazones, 1793–1848–1871* (Paris: Plon, 1910). Unfortunately, many of

the author's references are incomplete, and he does not always distinguish between women who simply armed themselves and women who armed themselves and saw themselves as Amazons.

27. *A Letter from Mère Duchêne*, Fall 1791, in *Women in Revolutionary Paris*, eds. D. Levy, H. Applewhite, and M. Johnson (Urbana: University of Illinois Press, 1979), pp. 98–99.

The Agony and the Exorcism: The Nineteenth-Century Battle

As in the instance of every profession, every title, every
honor, by the time women get it, either it is no longer worth
very much, or its value and meaning have changed considerably. Such was the case with *nature*. Had Enlightenment
thinkers identified women with nature, then females would
have been hailed as the embodiment of order and reason.
But it was not the philosophes, but the Romantic thinkers of
the first half of the nineteenth century and those who were
later influenced by Romantic thought, who equated woman
and nature. For them, nature was not a realm of decorum
and rationality; it was a condition to be overcome and controlled—the very antithesis of civilization.[1] Armed with new
insights from the biological sciences; incipient notions about
evolution and the struggle for existence; knowledge of geology and its altered perspective of historical time; political
experience involving the violence and disorder of revolution,
class conflict, struggles for national unification and independence; and raising fundamental questions about the function of the state, distribution of property, and the possibility
of human happiness and progress, the Romantics challenged
every assumption of the Enlightenment. Nature, which the
philosophes saw as tranquil and orderly, became the symbol
of the irrational, bestial, and untamed wildness—that is, for
the feminine. Since men had already been at war against the
Amazon for two thousand years, she was the perfect vehicle
for equation of woman and this new vision of nature in nineteenth-century art and letters, and "science."

One of the earliest works in this new tradition was the

drama *Penthesilea* by the German playwright Heinrich von Kleist. He composed the play in 1808, the same year in which his close friend Goethe completed *Faust*. It was a unique moment in time and in sensibility. Both works would have been considered by Enlightenment thinkers of only a generation or two earlier to be absurd and barbarous. Theirs had been an age of rationalism, and Enlightenment thinkers discarded myth and feeling as so much debris opposing rationality and human betterment. Writers like Kleist, Goethe, and Schiller were at the center of the movement, which was, at least in part, a reaction against the judgments of the eighteenth century. Emotion, imagination, religion, and tradition, the Romantics argued, were the major components of our humanity. Like the Enlightenment, the Romantic age was international in scope, but the German Romantics left their special mark on the movement. Kleist and his circle were creators of *sturm und drang*, (storm and stress), an absolute rejection of the classical and Enlightenment notion of the mean. For moderation and measure these thinkers opposed unrelenting trial and striving. The mean to them was dull, insipid, unenticing: they wanted to reach the heights of pure joy or know the agony of the depths of despair.

Heinrich von Kleist's strength lay in his ability to go beyond limits. He was unafraid and unashamed to peer into the abyss of human passion and to name clearly what he saw and what he found. If the action of Kleist's plays seems preposterous and dreamlike, it is because reality is impoverished. Kleist knew that in real life, in the ordinary order of events, one never gets enough glory, enough fame, enough love, enough sex. Humans are never sated, and in the midst of life's blessings they scan the horizon for a sign of something better, something more. The hero and the Amazon were perfect symbols of this seeking after transcendence, for this all-too-human hunger and thirst.

From its very first telling, the love story of Achilles and Penthesilea had a rather perverse, offbeat, indeed necrophiliac element. It was not the Amazon, but the corpse of the Amazon, that inspired Achilles' love. And Achilles himself had created that corpse. The story dated from almost three

From a mid-1950s production of *Penthesilea,* starring Maria Wimmer and Heinz Baumann.

millennia before his time, but Kleist was the first to develop its full erotic and sensual potential.

The dreamlike mood of *Penthesilea* is reinforced by its hazy geography. The action takes place before the walls of Troy, where Greeks and Trojans are thick in battle. Kleist moved the bridge on which Rubens's seventeenth-century Amazons had battled (see dustjacket) from the Amazon homeland of Themiscyra to Troy, and it is a major prop in several of the scenes. But it is less of a problem to figure out what the bridge is doing at Troy than it is to understand why Kleist's Amazons are there.

When the Greeks first sight them, the women are attacking the Trojans, but it quickly becomes obvious that they have not come to fight for the Greeks. They are like raw and blind energy, which from the very beginning has a very sexual tone. Kleist makes extensive use of language that equates eating and lovemaking. The love of Penthesilea and Achilles is fated to be devouring and all-consuming. Diomede describes the virgin Amazon queen as a "rav'ning she-wolf" who pursues her prey with "gaunt, hungry eye" (Sc. 1).[2] Odysseus is concerned about Achilles, who is like a hound unleashed against a giant stag with "teeth firm closed in the shaggy throat" (Sc. 1) who will not abandon his deadly prey.

Kleist's Penthesilea is a ferocious and bestial warrior and a gorgeous desirable woman all at once. Hot in the pursuit of Achilles,

> We see her quickly press her tiny hands,
> . . . to her forehead,
> O'er which all disarrayed her long locks fall.
>
> (Sc. 2)

But as she continues to rage against him, another Greek remarks that she is "A foaming-jawed hyena! 'Tis no woman!" (Sc. 2).

By Scene 4, Kleist's Achilles and Penthesilea love and hate each other beyond measure. Achilles announces that he is willing to woo Penthesilea "many long months through—Ay, years." But he also declares that after

> I first have my sport with her,
> And then, her brow adorned with bleeding gashes,
> Shall drag her by her feet behind my car.
>
> (Sc. 4)

This is, of course, the terrible fate Achilles has already dealt to the corpse of Hector.

Early in the play, Penthesilea can see her vendetta against Achilles as a purely military struggle:

> Into the battle will I fling myself;
> There with his haughty smile he waits me, there
> I'll see him at my feet or no more live.
>
> (Sc. 5)

But four scenes later she knows she is doomed; she sees that her unrelenting hunt for Achilles is proof of her own passion out of control:

> What is it I long for when I strike at him?
> Is it to send him headlong to the shades?
> I long—ye gods above! I only long—
> To this warm breast I long to draw him close!
>
> (Sc. 9)

Like the troops of her women, Penthesilea is bound by Amazon law. She cannot mate except with a man she has captured. When some of the Greek prisoners spy young Amazon girls weaving wreaths of roses, gathered with great difficulty along the dusty plains of Troy, they cry out against the inhumanity of the women who "would lead us decked with flowers like bulls of sacrifice to our death." A stunned Amazon girl replies that the men are going to Diana's temple, "Where sweet orgies without constraint or measure" (Sc. 7) await them. They can hardly believe their fortune, and the prisoners whisper among themselves, "Was ever dream so crazed as this reality?"

But the course of love does not run smoothly, and the Greeks are never to have the promised orgies. The tide of battle changes several times, with Greek captive of Amazon and Amazon captive of Greek. In the end they will go home quite alone, with Achilles dead and Penthesilea a suicide, his blood and gore still dripping from her lips.

There is one marvelous scene of wooing, where a wounded yet still victorious Penthesilea explains her Amazon creed and the customs of her people to an adoring, amazed, and incredulous Achilles. He asks, what has led her, "Full of insensate rage, most like a Fury,/ To fall thus headlong on the tribes of Argos?" (Sc. 15). Her response identifies her action as more of a rite of puberty than a plan of battle: "not for me the common arts of gentler womanhood." She cannot choose her love, "With shy downward eyes, or with bright wanton nosegay." No, she must find him "on the bloody field of war" and with "harsh arms of brass" draw near the man "whom rather I would press to this soft breast." She adds, "this ban was laid by word of our first mothers."

But how did such a horrible custom come into being? Achilles begs her to "speak plainer." Her explanation is a remarkable case of geographical confusion, as well as nineteenth-century fantasies of race and sex. Some fierce Ethiopians captured the men of a Scythian tribe, and tried to force its women to be wives. The raging women hated their "loathsome" beds, and on the eve of the marriage of their queen Tanais and the Ethiopian chief Vexoris, they followed their queen's example and drove their blades right through the hearts of their unwanted lovers. Thus began the Amazon nation, for

> Now in open folk-moot was decreed;
> Free as the wind that sweeps the unsheltered fallow
> Are women who have wrought so great a deed
> And to the male no more subservient.
>
> (Sc. 15)

But as Queen Tanais was about to grasp "the mighty, golden bow of the Scythian realm," Penthesilea continues, the terrible stern voice of Mars (whom Kleist makes the Scythian deity) is heard warning,

> Never can weak women, hampered still
> By the full swelling bosom, learn to use
> The taut bow's deadly swiftness, as can men!
>
> (Sc. 15)

Kleist was influenced by some of the Roman as well as the medieval versions of the Amazon myths, and fascinated by the grotesque mutilation they depicted. His queen "tore away her own right breast, baptising thus/all these women who would wield the bow."

Kleist portrays his "hero" Achilles lost in admiration for the primordial Amazon:

> Why then, by God! She had no need of breasts!
> She could have been as well a queen of men,
> And from my heart I bow in reverence to her.
>
> (Sc. 15)

But then he has to confront the horrible thought that perhaps this is still the Amazon way. He cannot believe that "all these lovely forms" which surround him, "in youthful bloom, the pride of womanhood, are barbarously, inhumanely, deformed—?" It is now for Penthesilea to assure Achilles that he will find nothing lacking in her, that "all youth's tendrest, sweetest feelings . . ." remain, and "in this left breast they have taken refuge." Kleist even manages to suggest an advantage in love with a one-breasted woman. Penthesilea explains that the concentration of all her feelings in her left breast has made them "by that much, nearer to my heart." Her words imply that Achilles, too, can share this proximity. Love with an Amazon is not going to be a mundane, ordinary experience. It is no old and well-rehearsed dance of familiar steps. Achilles is so thrilled by Penthesilea's discourse he can hardly force himself to listen to her every word. He keeps lapsing into his own reverie, and smiling with intense, personal joy. When she chides him for his grin, he replies,

> For thy beauty,
> My thoughts had strayed. Forgive me. I was wond'ring
> If thou wert not come down to me from the moon.
>
> (Sc. 15)

With this she pauses and explains that she will shortly lead him to Themiscyra, where, at the Temple of Diana they will attend together "The Feast of the Flowering Virgins," or "The Feast of Roses," which will end in a long-awaited orgy.

Shortly after their mutual declaration of love, the Greeks

win a clear victory over the Amazon force. Achilles is now, inconveniently for Penthesilea's plans, free. It is a situation that he himself plans to remedy. Achilles challenges the wounded and half-crazed Penthesilea to a single combat. His intention is to allow her to defeat him—he is willing to go, as her captive, to the Temple of Diana. He believes that she will understand that he really loves her and does not seek a knock-down, drag-out combat. He also believes Penthesilea loves him too much to hurt him. He explains to Diomede:

> She will not harm me, I tell you! Sooner far
> Would her mailed arm mangle her own fair bosom
> And cry: "Triumph!" when her heart's blood spurts
>   forth
> Then it would rage against me! A month, no more
> I will do service to her hot desires. . . .
>
> (Sc. 21)

After this token service, he reasons, Penthesilea would be ready to come to his own Pythia with him as his bride. But his companions Odysseus and Diomede can only wonder, "Is this man driving mad . . . ?" The scene is ominous, and the stage directions call for clashes of thunder. And then comes the terrible message:

> HERALD: Ay, she will fight: already she comes on.
> But 'tis with dogs and elephants she comes
> And a whole savage host on horseback: what
> Their part is in this single combat is yet dark.
>   ACHILLES: This is her tribute paid to custom. Come!
> Oh, she is full of tricks, by all the gods!
> —You say, with dogs?
>   HERALD: Yes.
>   ACHILLES: And with elephants?
>
> (Sc. 21)

With the introduction of the dogs and elephants, Kleist's play loses any semblance of realism it might have had earlier. But it was not reality, but the realm of nightmare that Kleist sought to portray. His hero is as mad as his Amazon. He remains in his delusion that neither Penthesilea nor her animals intend him harm:

ACHILLES (*to himself*):
Sure they will feed from your hand. Come, follow me!
Oh! They are tame as she.

(Sc. 21)

The Amazons know the doom and horror of nightmare
are upon them when their mad queen has trampled the three
Amazons attempting to restrain her from battle. No medieval
or Renaissance Amazon queen, aided by scores of unicorns
or griffons, was ever reported to turn on her own warriors.
Her own high priestess condemns Penthesilea as a "lewd she-
dog." Penthesilea runs "With maniac tread among her hounds,"
"With foam-flecked lips she goes and calls them sisters,/who
howl and howl. . . ." (Sc. 22). The priestess begs the "daughters of Ares" to stop the queen, but it is too late. Achilles,
who "half-playfully is armed but with a spear and thinks no
danger," has advanced into battle, and realizes too late his
fatal error. He is attempting to flee when she shoots an arrow
through his neck, and he is still alive when Penthesilea sum-
mons her hounds:

And flings herself—herself with the whole pack!—
Upon him and by his helmet's plume, a bitch
In the company of dogs—one grips his breast,
Another's jaws close on his neck—drags him
To earth, that far around the ground re-echoes.
He, writhing in a pool of his own gore,
Touches her delicate cheek and calls to her:
"Penthesilea! What dost thou? My belovèd
Is this the Feast of Roses thou didst promise?"

(Sc. 23)

In spite of this ludicrous declaration of unswerving love, it
is apparent that this is not an ordinary lovers' quarrel where
all hurt can be mended. Kleist made the demise of Achilles
as horrendous as his love would have been sublime. In the
territory of dream there is no measure, no middle. Kleist
knew that a passion of the intensity of the hero's and the
Amazon's had no relation to the classical ideal of moderation.
The Amazon Meroë describes the terrible scene:

> She strikes, first tearing his armour from his limbs,
> Strikes deep her teeth into his snowy breast,
> She and the dogs in ghastly rivalry . . .
> . . . as I appeared,
> Black blood was dripping from her mouth and hands.
>
> (Sc. 23)

By far the silliest line in the play belongs to Penthesilea, who
Kleist portrays as unable to comprehend her deed. Unbe-
lieving, she asks her women, "I did kiss him to death?" (Sc.
24). But she later explains to her women that she is guilty of
no more than a lover's error:

> So—it was a mistake, Kissing—biting—
> Where is the difference? When we truly love
> It's easy to do one when we mean the other.
>
> (Sc. 24)

She whispers into the ear of the mangled corpse,

> Poor man, of all men poorest, you forgive me?
> It was a slip—believe me!—the wrong word—
> I must control my too impetuous lips.
> But now I tell you clearly what I meant:
> This, my belovèd, this—and nothing more.
> (*She kisses him.*)
>
> (Sc. 24)

When her women try to remove Penthesilea from Achilles'
mangled corpse, she again attempts to plead her case. Many
a woman, she argues, will tell a man "that she loves him so/
Beyond words she would eat him up for love," yet how many
women have followed their words? Penthesilea did not fail
Achilles, she simply carried out the promised deed: "I did it
word for word; It was no pretending/I was not quite as mad
as they would have it" (Sc. 24). Her last act, after releasing
her women from the Amazon law, is to sink a dagger deep
into her own breast, steeped through with "the hot, biting
venom of remorse."

In his image of Penthesilea "kissing" Achilles to death,
Kleist saw something that Freud attempted to give "scientific"
expression almost a century later. In his *Interpretation of Dreams*[3]
Freud specifically cited Kleist's *Penthesilea* as an example of

Maria Wimmer as Penthesilea.

the impulse of cruelty in human love relationships. Freud's contemporary, the British poet Laurence Binyon arrived at the same place from another direction. His 1905 poem *Penthesilea* stressed the love in loathing: "Hate, hope, fear, longing, 'tis all one, 'tis love/Betwixt a man and a woman. . . ."[4] But Binyon's insight was no longer startling, and in spite of his equation of hate and love between the sexes, his poem is a conventional rendering of the Troy story. It seems to be galaxies away from the intensity of Kleist's obsession with the Amazon as the quintessential romantic challenge as well as the embodiment of the forces of untamed nature.

The most explicit identification of women as Amazon and Amazon as nature came two generations after Kleist, with the Swiss philosopher and social theorist Johan Jakob Bachofen. What Kleist had suggested as poetry and feeling, Bachofen attempted to state as "scientific" fact, turning from a poetic obsession with Amazons to a virtual exorcism of them. On the wings of his own contributions to modern social science, touching at once the fields of history, anthropology, psychology, sociology, and philosophy, he constructed a theory of human society that assumed that all of humanity shared an Amazonian past: "*Amazonism is a universal phenomenon. It is not based on the special or historical circumstances of any particular people, but on conditions that are characteristic of all human existence.*"[5]

Bachofen did not intend to ennoble women by his thesis of a universally shared Amazon experience. His theory positing the power of women at the dawn of human development is so fundamentally misogynistic that it offers little to any useful reconstruction of the human past. Bachofen's Amazon is universal, and hence natural. The glory of human civilization has been in overcoming and conquering nature. At the height of human achievement, the Amazon can be nothing more than a skeleton in the closet.

Bachofen flourished in an intellectual climate favorable to the discussion of universal human experiences. The Enlightenment thinker Lafitau, in his *Customs of the American Indians* had stopped short of speaking of common stages of human development. The science of his day gave him no model to

Currier and Ives, "Queen of the Amazons Attacked by a Lion." (Courtesy The Harry T. Peters Collection, Museum of the City of New York)

suggest stages of shared development in the organic world. Nor was there any dynamic of change or process in the human sphere. The Enlightenment, fixing on the model of mathematical physics, found with Newton's help that all motion on heaven and earth could be reduced to a few simple mathematical laws. Enlightenment thinkers made some tentative efforts to see if politics, economics, and history might also exhibit a similar lawfulness, but it was not until W. F. Hegel's posthumous "Lectures on the Philosophy of History" (1837) that there existed a logic of change in the arena of human events. Rather than seeing the past as static, or as a cycle ever recurring of the same level, Hegel saw human history as the stage of constant struggle and process. Bachofen was very much influenced by Hegel's "dialectical idealism," as well as by Karl Marx's recasting of that leap in philosophy in the form of dialectical materialism. Bachofen's theories of social change place great emphasis on the material, or economic aspects of every stage of human development.

Equally if not more important for Bachofen were Charles Darwin's *On the Origin of Species* (1859) and *The Descent of Man* (1871). These works created the structure in which human social evolution became imaginable. It was only when talk of the development of new and higher species, the struggle for existence, the survival of the fittest, and the extinction of lower and unfit forms became part of the vocabulary of biological science, that the physical biological world became a model for the moral one. Bachofen without Darwin would be unthinkable.

Implicit in the theory of evolution was the notion of progress. Although Darwin had emphasized that the divergence of species and natural selection does not always favor the development of higher forms of life, and that some species have survived through the millennia because they remained primitive and unspecialized in their requirements for existence, he himself spoke of higher and lower stages of human life. In *The Descent of Man* Darwin stated that he

> would just as soon be descended from that heroic little monkey, who braved his dreaded enemy in order to save the life of his keeper . . . as from a savage who delights to torture his enemies, offers up bloody sacrifices, practises infanticide without

remorse, and treats his wives like slaves, knows no decency, and is haunted by the grossest superstitions.

Man may be excused for feeling some pride at having risen . . . to the very summit of the organic scale.[6]

The difference between his own cultivated and refined society and the culture of barbarians is proof enough, he argued, that we have emerged from "lower" levels of human society, which in turn shared a biological link with other mammals. It was Darwin himself who opened the way for the application of the terms "higher" and "lower" to the human sphere.

Another major contribution of nineteenth-century science to social theory in general, and to the discussion of Amazons in particular, was the expanded notion of time that it brought. The new sciences of geology and archaeology made it clear that the earth has been here and hosted human inhabitants many millennia prior to the earliest written historical records. Now it was apparent that written history was only a minute portion of a greatly extended story.

Yet for all this expansion of the notion of how long men and women have peopled the earth, for most social scientists the classical stories and legends about the Amazons seemed to fit the description of myth or poetry. Here is where the revolutionary character of Bachofen's work makes itself apparent. He insisted that this material should not be ignored and tossed away. Although the eighteenth-century Abbé Claude Marie Guyon had made some tentative suggestions in this direction, Bachofen was the first to state the "principle" that "the mythical tradition may be taken as a faithful reflection of the life of those times in which historical antiquity is rooted. It is a manifestation of primordial thinking, an immediate historical revelation, and consequently a highly reliable historical source." Bachofen insited that "myth must form the starting point for any serious investigation of ancient history." For him, there is no point in distinguishing between myth and history, unless we wish to refer to different modes of expression. But this distinction "has neither meaning nor justification when it creates a hiatus in the continuity of human development."

Bachofen's study of what he believed were the appropriate

materials of ancient history led him to assert that "the stories
of the Amazons and [the hero] Bellerophon are real and not
poetic." He argued that as difficult or even impossible as some
of these tales may seem, they are nonetheless true. "History
has risen to even greater heights than the creative imagination." It was the poverty of modern scholarship, Bachofen
said, to have "denied what it should have sought to understand." Hence, our learning leaves us ignorant and despair-
ing, wracked with "skepticism, confusion, and hopeless
nihilism." Bachofen freely admitted that "it is impossible to
prove the existence of Amazonian states." But he was little
troubled by this impossibility. He insisted that the problem
is "implicit in the very nature of history." He went on to
contend that "no single historical tradition has ever been
proved. We harken only to rumor. To deny traditions of this
kind is . . . to battle with the millennia."

Bachofen justified his assumptions about the historical reality
of Amazons on the grounds that it would be impossible to
construct, on the basis of evidence from history, myth, and
legend, a coherent picture of human development without
admitting the authenticity of such a stage. It is when Bachofen starts to unfold his vision of the nature of this human
development, however, that his ideas about these warrior-
women, and indeed, about women in general, become
clear.

In the beginning, says Bachofen, there was little to distinguish man from the animals. Sexual life was "promiscuous
and public." Men formed "no lasting bond with any particular
woman," but shared the "common enjoyment of women."
Presumably women also had sexual freedom at such a stage,
though Bachofen does not speak of women "keeping" men
in common. At any rate, this was a stage of existence that
preceded human culture. Here there is no ordered tilling of
the earth, only "natural generation" and "swamp vegetation."

It is women who create the first stage of a truly human
culture by introducing marriage, thereby breaking the bonds
of "crudely sensual animal life." But, Bachofen argues, in its
early stages matriarchy does not immediately assume the
peaceful and pastoral character it possessed in its heyday.

For the first stage of feminine power is Amazonism, born of "acts of bloody vengeance against the male sex." It is the sense of degradation and despair that causes women to rise, "exalting her to that warlike grandeur which, though it seems to exceed the bonds of womanhood, is rooted simply in her need for higher life." It takes not a little good faith to follow Bachofen down the tortuous path of the male fantasy he presented as profound dialectical reasoning: "Amazonism, despite its savage degeneration, signifies an appreciable rise in human culture." Amazon existence is "a regression and perversion" in later stages of human culture. But the first of the Amazons took a "step forward toward a purer form of life," because Amazonism contained "the first germ of matriarchy which founded the political civilization of peoples." Although regulated matriarchy had the capability to, and did in some cases, "degenerate" into "Amazonian severity and Amazonian customs," Amazon life generally preceded "conjugal matriarchy" and was in fact "a preparation for it."

Bachofen insists that Amazonism is an "unnatural degeneration of feminine existence." He notes that in the legends it was the god Dionysus who summoned women in their "maternal vocation of motherhood" by evoking their recognition of "the glorious superiority of his own male-phallic nature." Though the Amazons of the most ancient legends attempted to oppose Dionysus, soon their resistance to the new god "shifted to an equally resolute devotion" and we hear of the warrior-women "fighting at his side." And so the bloody Amazon rebellion against the degradation of hetaerism led to the start of human culture. It was the Amazons who led the way to settled life:

> from the banks of the Nile to the shores of the Black Sea, from Central Asia to Italy, Amazonian names and deeds are interwoven with the history of the founding of cities which later become famous.... Countless ancient traditions support this same historical fact: women put an end to nomadic life by burning the ships; women gave cities their names, and, as in Rome or in Elis, women inaugurated the first apportionment of the land. In bringing about fixed settlement, womanhood fulfills its natural vocation.

Of course, this first step of human culture is far from reflecting the full glory and destiny of the human race. It is but the infancy of man: "matriarchy is necessary to the education of mankind and particularly of men. Just as the child is first disciplined by his mother, so the races of men are first disciplined by women. The male must serve before he can govern." And while the male was serving, Bachofen admits, the matriarchal world was perfumed by "an air of tender humanity." There was peace, a sense of brotherhood and cooperation, and harmony with nature: "the matriarchal period is indeed the poetry of history." Men took their inspiration from women whose "unblemished beauty, whose chastity and high-mindedness could awaken love even in the immortals."

Yet for all Bachofen's nostalgic longing for the women of old who inspired "high deeds" among the men they ruled, he ultimately found the charms of the maternal world cloying and debilitating. Those "noble actions" were not so much in consequence of matriarchy, but in opposition to it. The matriarchal world implies "acceptance of nature," "material confinement," and finally, "perpetual rest, peaceful enjoyment, and eternal childhood in an aging body." Thus the "poetry of history" turns out to be, on closer examination, a bitter song. Though charming, lovely, and seductive, its real nature is a saga of restriction and imprisonment and, ultimately, decay. Along with his contemporary, Friedrich Nietzsche, Bachofen shared a contempt for peace, repose, and for all that was feminine. He worried about our modern "cultivated but enfeebled times," and argued that "when the power to perform high deeds flags, the flight of the spirit falters also."

Although matriarchy represents, in Bachofen's schema, the first step in human culture, it offers nothing to separate men from the beasts. Like the women who rule within it, matriarchy is hopelessly material and earthbound, a journey without a destination, movement without development: "maternity pertains to the physical side of man, the only thing he shares with the animals." But through struggle, man finds the route to transcendence. Gradually "he becomes aware of his paternal nature, in battle he raises himself above the maternity to which he had wholly belonged, in battle he strives upward to his own divinity." And finally "the triumph of paternity brings with it the liberation of the spirit from the manifestations of nature." Man thus "becomes conscious of his higher calling," by grasping the "paternal-spiritual principle which belongs to him alone."

The act of reproduction, according to Bachofen, is not at all the same experience for the man as it is for the woman. In reading Bachofen's description of the sexual act, one could easily lose sight of the fact that both partners are in the same place at the same time. Actually, they are doing very different things: "triumphant paternity partakes of the heavenly light, while childbearing motherhood is bound up in the earth that bears all things." While the woman is flailing in the mud, the male is soaring above her and all creation in a blaze of divine, transcendent light.

Small wonder, then, that the progress of civilization begins with the overthrow of mother right: "the progress of civilization is not favorable to woman. She is at her best in the so-called barbaric periods; later epochs destroy her hegemony." Thus Bachofen picks up from where La Condamine had left off a century earlier by making the extent of masculine dominion a measure of civilization: "the more primordial the people, the more the feminine nature principle will dominate religious life and the higher women's social position will be."

Though Bachofen enjoyed the friendship of many of the extraordinary minds of his day, like Nietzsche, and he married the daughter of his admirer Jakob Burckhardt, his contemporaries' rejection of his printed works was brutal. The recognition he sought came later in his life when his work was hailed by scholars of the newest social science, anthropology. John F. McLennan's *Primitive Marriage* (1865), and Lewis Henry Morgan's *Ancient Society* (1877) both acknowledged a debt to Bachofen, and it was through Morgan's work that Bachofen's ideas came to influence Friedrich Engels. In particular, Engels's *The Origin of the Family, Private Property, and the State* (1884) accepted, though not without criticism, most of Bachofen's ideas.

To Friedrich Engels, there was no question about Bach-

ofen's significance as a major thinker in the history of the
social sciences. In his *Preface to the fourth edition* of his *Origin
of the Family* Engels stated, "The study of the history of the
family dates from 1861, from the publication of Bachofen's
Mütterrecht." Engels then listed what he considered the four
critical propositions in Bachofen's work, and proceeded to
discuss each of these systematically in his *Origin.* Though
Engels admired Bachofen, he wryly noted that "it is . . . a
tough and by no means always a grateful task to plow through
Bachofen's solid tome." His main criticism of Bachofen is
that he looked at "not the development of men's actual conditions of life, but the religious reflection of these conditions
inside their heads" to account for "the historical changes in
the social position of the sexes in relation to each other." The
problem with Bachofen's work is that any conception "which
makes religion [i.e., myth] the lever of world history, must
finally end in pure mysticism."[7]

Engels probably considered Bachofen's discussion of Amazons as part of the blunder that thinker made in treating
myth too literally. But Engels did accept the idea that matriarchy was the original human condition. A long line of
other scholars, beginning with Edward Westermarck (*The
History of Human Marriage*, 1891), have questioned whether
an authentic matriarchal condition ever existed among any
historical peoples. But Bachofen's use of the terms "backward," "primitive," and "regressive" to describe female power
has been widely accepted, along with his assertion that western European civilization has as its only true beginning the
patriarchal legal and social structure of classical Rome. His
belief that the patriarchal form of the family is its highest
form has also been widely accepted. The man who was rejected by the historians of his own day might well be beside
himself with joy if he could see the extent to which some of
his ideas, at least, still dominate the Western civilization textbooks of the late twentieth century.

The notion that female power in any form denotes a lower
stage of culture is also present in Sir Richard Burton's *A
Mission to Gelele, King of Dahome* (1865). Burton was the British
consul at Dahomey from 1861 through 1865, and he described the customs of that African state (modern-day Benin)

in great detail and with great distaste. He was, at heart, an explorer and a man of action, and he hated the lengthy and elaborate ceremonies at Gelele's court. Gelele returned the compliment by refusing to negotiate with him on what Queen Victoria considered to be critical issues: the ending of the slave trade and the termination of human sacrifice. Burton was remarkably matter-of-fact in his description of the several thousand strong Amazon guard that surrounded the king and served as the most formidable part of the Dahomian army. He notes that the woman-warriors went at least as far back as the reign of Gezo, Gelele's father, and that earlier observers had reported the presence of these Amazons even in the eighteenth century. But Burton was not interested in any historical explanation of their origins, and even though he described their costume as including a strip of crocodile hide, he refused to make the connection which at least one author later suggested,[8] between these women and the Amazons of very ancient Africa, who Diodorus Siculus had described as having bedecked themselves in snakeskins. Burton's explanation for the Amazons of Dahomey was rooted entirely in the present he observed. He noted his impression that in many of the African races he had himself seen, there was little difference between the sexes. The women seemed to exhibit the same physical strength as the men, and in the case of Dahomey, the females appeared stronger and larger than the males. Since he saw the men as puny, it seemed to him that nature selected the women to bear the major burden of military service.

Burton explained the ferocity of the female regiments by the sexual abstinence the king forced upon them. Gelele examined every women of marriageable age, and apparently his throne gave him the right to choose as many of them as he pleased for his domestic harem and to place many of the others into military service. He considered all the women to be royal brides, and he demanded strict fidelity, punishing all adulteresses with death. According to Burton, a woman with an unpleasant disposition was sure to end up doing military service: "the Xanthippes, who make men's eyes yellow, are very properly put into the army."[9]

Burton described the female army as having right and left

wings, and being divided into companies carrying five different kinds of arms: there were blunderbuss women, elephant hunters, razor women, archeresses (complete with
poisoned arrows), and infantry-carrying muskets. Yet, on the
whole, Burton appears to have been very disappointed by
the Dahomian Amazons: "I expected to see Penthesileas,
Thalestrices, Dianas—lovely names! I saw old, ugly, and square-
built frows." These women had none of the allure that classical legend ascribed to the Amazons of old. The only passion
they aroused in Burton was revulsion. For him, the female
troops were remarkable only "for a stupendous stratopyga
[buttocks] and for a development of adipose [fat] tissue which
suggested anything but unwed virginity."[10]

Burton's account was read eagerly by his proper and cultivated Victorian readers because it confirmed much of what
they already knew. By the late nineteenth century, the di-
chotomy between the natural and the civilized was well established, and female power was associated with the former:
"male dominance was now bound up with decency, the re-
finement and control of the passions, private property, and
natural selection."[11]

Agnes Strickland, the Victorian biographer and author of
the lengthy series *Lives of the Queens of England,* gives an
example of this moral self-righteousness in her life of Eleanor
of Aquitaine. She eagerly seized upon stories fabricated long
after the death of that great medieval queen. These tales told
of Eleanor playing the role of the Amazon when she took
the cross for the Second Crusade. Eleanor is said to have
adorned a brilliantly colored Amazonian costume, and to
have thundered over the hills of Vézelay astride a white stal-
lion, and to have led a band of women similarly mounted
and attired. They are said to have tossed their abandoned
spindles and distaffs into the hands of faint-hearted (or perhaps sensible) knights who did not take the cross.[12] For Strickland, to be an Amazon was to be improper and perhaps even
immoral. Eleanor had been a "foolish woman," and her
"Amazonian exercises" were only part of "a thousand follies"
she and her court performed in public.[13] To Agnes Strickland
and her readers the image of Amazonian exercises conjured

up visions of bared breasts and naked thighs, of a rudeness and barbarism they had learned to transcend in the name of civilization. If left in the hands of women like Eleanor, England could well lapse into a Dahomey.

The Amazon was a popular image, but rarely a positive one in the nineteenth century. As Nina Auerbach notes in her *Communities of Women*, the Amazon was a favorite image in Victorian literature. She was usually invoked to characterize a woman who is autonomous: the heroine of Louisa May Alcott's *Work: A Story of Experience* (1875) is a strong-willed woman who tries to be self-supporting. For a while, she earns her living as an actress playing the role of an Amazon queen. The women of Elizabeth Gaskill's novel *Cranford* (1851–53) are dubbed Amazons because in their world of teas, social visits, and gossip, the men are truly peripheral. But the images in these works are, by and large, superficial, and as Auerbach notes, "the Amazons bob up repeatedly in Victorian writing, usually to be vanished as soon as evoked."[14]

In nineteenth-century France the fascination with the Amazon was more deep-rooted. From early modern times, the French word *amazone* meant an elegant woman who rides on horseback. It was a title to which any skilled female equestrian could aspire. The term also referred to a particular style of riding—to sit sidesaddle was to ride *à l'amazone*. Perhaps this posture suggested to the French public the Scythian (and, presumably ancient Amazonian) habit of twisting around in the saddle in order to fire arrows in retreat. Although the origin of the term *à l'amazone* is not clear, it is evident that the *amazone* was a very elegant woman. During the Second Empire, the empress Eugenie, who was an accomplished horsewoman, wore a special white piqué riding habit while inspecting her husband's troops. Although many elegant French women imitated Eugenie's white costume, the *amazone* portrayed by French painters like Manet, Constantin Guys, Daumier, and Renoir was typically attired in black, in an outfit that included a tall, narrow, and rather masculine top hat, and a slim almost tubular black skirt. Many of these elegant French horsewomen were described as *lionnes* or *amazones* by their contemporaries. They carried riding whips and wore

some garments traditionally associated with male attire. Many
seemed to move with impunity back and forth across the thin
line that divided the fashionable woman from the prostitute.[15]
A recent dictionary of French colloquialisms still defines the
amazone as a fashionable harlot.[16]

But neither the skill of the horsewomen who rode in the
Bois de Boulogne nor the courage of the heroines of Victorian fiction could rescue the Amazon from disgrace and
disapproval. Perhaps more than any other time in history,
the task of overcoming Amazons captured the imagination
of the nineteenth century, and conquering the Amazon was
not merely an act of physical and martial bravado, it was a
moral duty on the behalf of civilization.

Notes

1. See Elizabeth Fee, "The Sexual Politics of Victorian Social Anthropology," in Mary Hartman and Lois Banner, eds., *Clio's
   Consciousness Raised* (New York: Harper & Row, 1974), pp. 86–
   102.
2. Throughout this chapter I have used the excellent English
   translation by Humphrey Trevelyan, in Eric Bentley, ed., *The
   Classic Theatre Vol. II: Five German Plays* (New York: Doubleday,
   1959), pp. 213–419. The play is a single act divided into 24
   scenes.
3. Volume IV of *The Complete Psychological Works of Freud*, ed. and
   trans. James Strachey (London: Hogarth Press, 1900), p. 291,
   n. 2.
4. Laurence Binyon, *Penthesilea* (London: Constable & Co., 1905),
   p. 30.
5. J. J. Bachofen, *Mother Right*, in *Myth, Religion, and Mother Right,
   Selected Writings of J. J. Bachofen*, trans. Ralph Manheim
   (Princeton: Princeton University Press, 1967), p. 105. All citations from Bachofen are from pp. 73–75, 81, 83–84, 100,
   105–107, 109–111, 134, 143–144, 151, 154, 170–171 of this
   translation.
6. Charles Darwin, *The Descent of Man* (New York: Appleton, 1872),
   Vol. II, p. 386.
7. Friedrich Engels, *The Origin of the Family, Private Property and*

the State, ed. Eleanor Burke Leacock (New York: International Publishers, 1975), pp. 75-77.

8. See Guy Cadogen Rothery, *The Amazons in Antiquity and Modern Times* (London: Francis Griffiths, 1910), p. 112.

9. Sir Richard Burton, *A Mission to Gelele, King of Dahome* (London: Routledge and Kegan Paul, 1966), p. 257.

10. Ibid., p. 262.

11. Fee, "Sexual Politics," p. 101.

12. One of the earliest sources for these stories is Isaac de Larrey, *Histoire d'Éléanor de Guyenne, Duchess d'Aquitaine* (London, and Paris: Cussac, 1788), p. 59.

13. Agnes Strickland, *Lives of the Queens of England*, vol. I (London: Bell and Daldy, 1873), pp. 168–69.

14. Nina Auerbach, *Communities of Women* (Cambridge, Massachusetts: Harvard University Press, 1978), p. 79.

15. Patricia Mainardi discusses this phenomenon in "Edouard Manet's 'View of the Universal Esposition of 1867,' " *Arts Magazine*, vol. 54, no. 5 (January 1980), pp. 105–15; see especially p. 115, n. 45 and 46.

16. Joseph Marks et al., *The New French-English Dictionary of Slang and Colloquialisms* (New York: E.P. Dutton, 1971), p. 13.

Understanding Them/
Joining Them

Along with rapid technological developments, fast food, mass production and mass warfare, and all the other mixed and pure blessings of modern times, the West has experienced an enormous increase in the number of people who have the ability and leisure to read, watch television and films, visit museums, attend the theater, and in general participate in some form of cultural activity. This democratization of culture has created a demand for information and discussion of many issues and ideas that are geared to a general reading public, rather than serving a small circle of professional scholars.

During the opening decades of the twentieth century there were a handful of thinkers who tried to serve this vastly expanded reading public by trying to answer once and forever the question, did Amazons exist, and if so, when and where? They ignored the fact that the idea of Amazons had itself become part of history and they searched for that primordial Amazon with a seriousness of purpose and intensity of dedication that rivaled religious zeal. To some extent, these great and grave thinkers shared a common assumption— Amazons per se could not possibly have existed. The Greeks were stupid/nearsighted/afraid of their wives and mothers/ or all of the above. What the Greeks called "Amazons" were really something else, but they did not concur on what or who this something else was.

The most thorough of the early twentieth-century works was Guy Cadogen Rothery's *The Amazons in Antiquity and Modern Times*. Rothery presents a carefully researched and

fairly complete account of all the various Amazon legends
and stories. But he wrote from the point of view of a male
scholar who shared Bachofen's conviction that the Amazon
condition was an unnatural one, and one that women would
sustain only with the greatest difficulty. In the manner of a
true follower of Bachofen, he did not make a strong distinction between myth and history. He called the Amazon
stories "myths," but these myths were not the result of flights
of fancy: "they must be looked upon as symbolical exagger-
ations of certain ancient facts."[1] Having posited a basis in
reality for the Amazons, Rothery goes on to weave the various
stories into a chronological, historical presentation, frequently using adjectives like "hardpressed," "desperate," and
"stubborn" to describe the women. In fact, he believed the
stories told something of the eternal feminine: "under stress,
human nature is very much today what it was yesterday and
will be tomorrow; and woman, being woman, under stress is
very apt to exaggerate human passions."

As Rothery saw it, the Greek Amazon legends had two
entirely different stages. The earliest stories emphasized the
deadly nature of the women: "we are told of a turbulent,
bloodthirsty race, cannibalistic, addicted to human sacrifice
in their religious observances, sworn to repudiate the natural
order of society, living only to make war on their neighbors,
implacable in their hatreds." This version, Rothery argued,
carried a message, "to a people struggling toward a higher
civilization to beware of barbarians and their ways." This
same theory saw the Amazons as a poetic representation of
the Persians, who were the actual barbarians whom the Greeks
did, in fact, defeat in the late sixth and early fifth centuries
B.C.

Rothery argued that what he felt were the original stories,
all emphasizing the danger and ferocity of the women, were
altered by what he claimed to be the characteristically Greek
"humanizing spirit." The fear and horror of the old tales
"was softened to an attitude of admiration before physical
beauty and courage, and a tender pity for woman, fomentor
of strife though she might be." Hence, it is only because of
Greek magnanimity that Amazons become wonderful, beau-

tiful, and sexually desirable—all titles that Rothery claimed they did not really deserve.

In his conclusions, Rothery rejected the possibility that there ever was "a long-sustained woman's state." He argued that the stories made sense only if one accepted "the fighting Amazons as religious, or regal-religious bodies." He believed that the foundation of the legends lay in the female attendants of a deity "who at all events, in the degenerate days of her cult in Asia Minor, represented lust *in exelsis*. And here, it is likely enough, the myth was founded on solid fact." Although the stories do not agree on the exact nature of Amazon religion, "it is well-nigh certain that the savage horde from Scythia paid homage to some prototype of Astarte," a goddess known for her cruelty and link with blood and mutilation. Rothery reasoned that thousands of warrior-priestesses, guarding the person and domains of a male semidivine king, could well be mistaken by outside observers as a nation of Amazons.

Rothery's final page contains a memorial of a practice that has quite fallen into disuse, if not disfavor. It was common for historians of the early twentieth century to close their works with some remarks on the general shape of history as they perceived it from the vantage of their study. Rothery concluded that the general picture of the human condition "happily points to immense strides accomplished in the march of progress." But along with the "aspirations to higher things," the general human saga has also displayed "the tendency to fall into error and distort half-truths and to degenerate so far as to seemingly sanction ghastly practices." Amazons would, of course, fall into this latter tendency. They are part of "the disconcerting phenomena of reflux eddies," in the general picture of "onrushing waves."

The most startling modern theory was the one enunciated by Walther Leonhard in his *Hetticher und Amazonen* (1911). As the ancient historian Palaephatus had proposed, the Amazons were indeed warriors, but they were not women. Palaephatus had suggested in antiquity that his own forefathers were perhaps a bit nearsighted. In fighting beardless but long-haired male opponents, they fell under the mistaken

illusion that they were battling females. Leonhard's theory
was an update of that idea, with the addition that these beardless, long-haired warriors were now positively identified as
the Hittites. The latter were one of several warlike Indo-
European peoples who invaded the ancient Near East early
in the second millennium B.C. Between 1450 and 1200 as
ample documentation shows, the Hittites dominated Syria
and constituted a gnawing thorn in the side of the Egyptian
Empire. Their power collapsed around 1200 B.C., crushed
under a wave of new Semitic invaders. The Hittites left in
their wake the influence of their own culture (writing, religion, art, political institutions, literature), as well as a series
of cities they founded around their stronghold in Anatolia.
Many scholars believe, for example, that the Hittites are the
true founders of the ancient city of Ephesus.

Leonhard, in an amazing sleight of armchair scholarship,
came up with a series of arguments pointing to the identity
of Amazons and Hittites. The places that were supposedly
Amazon strongholds, like Themiscyra and the Thermodon
River of the Greek stories, were in Hittite territory. The
period of the greatest Amazon "activity" coincides with the
heyday of the Hittite Empire. Both "peoples" used iron weapons and rode horses. Both worshipped a hostile goddess, and
some Hittite religious ceremonies display a certain "herma-
phroditic" element—their kings dressed in feminine attire
while worshipping the goddess. The Hittites had "matriarchal tendencies"—their queens were powerful. And finally,
the Greeks were mysteriously silent about their Hittite neighbors, but they told many stories about Amazons. Maybe the
Amazons were, in fact, Hittites.

This assumption solves so many problems. No matter that
the Amazons left posterity no writings, no literature, no law
codes, no treaties, and not a single building or monument
even in ruins. All the artifacts of an entire civilization, and
one of unquestioned historical authenticity, was now theirs.
The ancients weren't lying, they were just a bit confused, and
European men could reassure themselves that an autonomous community of warrior-women never existed. Leonhard
was, of course, violently attacked with the honed and razor-

sharpened words that only academicians thrust at each other. The sharpest wounds were inflicted by Adolphe Reinache, in his lengthy article, "L'origine des Amazones."[2] Reinache argued that Leonhard's work was totally derivative, to put it bluntly, copied from any number of earlier sources discussing the Hittite versus the Amazon warrior question. Even more serious was Reinache's simple statement that Leonhard was wrong—not because he identified Amazons with a historical nation, but because he chose the wrong nation. He argued that the geographical coincidence claimed by Leonhard for Hittite and Amazon strongholds does not stand up to close scrutiny. The Hittites, Reinache claimed, were only part of the picture. The Thracians (Phrygians) and Cimmerians also served as models for the Amazons. He argued that the legends "were enriched by the contacts the Greeks sustained with all the warring nations of the North and the Levant." The Amazons themselves are in fact "résumés," a kind of alphabet soup summation of centuries of Greek historical experience.

The great Russian scholar Michael Rostovtzeff, in his *Iranians and Greeks in South Russia*, did not attempt to verify every detail of the Greek stories, but he did speak of the "semi-historical legend of the Amazons." Herodotus had spoken of a group of Amazon women who landed on a Scythian shore. After an intense struggle with the male inhabitants, whose language they did not understand, they married them and created the foundation of the new Sauromatian people. Rostovtzeff believed that story bore witness to a real event, "to a fierce struggle between the Maeotian and Scythian conquerors, terminating not in a complete Scythian victory but in compromise and intermarriage; to the co-existence of two racial elements on the shore of the Sea of Azov, and to the strong Scythian influence on the Sauromatians."[3] The Amazons themselves, he thought, were undoubtedly the warrior-priestesses of the mother-goddess who was widely worshipped throughout Asia Minor in historical times.

Other scholars had focused on the rather Amazonian nature of the Sauromatian wives themselves. As early as 1875, Adolf Klügman, in *Die Amazonen in der Attischen Literatur und*

Kunst, contented himself with saying that it was the hunting and fighting Sauromatian wives of the Don region who served as the prototypes of the Amazons and inspired all the Greek stories. That such wives existed, and that they participated in "manlike" activities, cannot be denied. Modern Soviet archaeologists have discovered that fully 20 percent of female Sauromatian burials of the sixth and fifth centuries B.C. are with weapons—presumably so the mistresses of these deadly tools could avail themselves of them in the next world as well.[4] These same Sauromatian graves also give evidence of cannibalism, another gruesome practice that pops up in the Greek Amazon stories.

The most recent word on this issue, though almost certainly not the last word, was uttered by Pierre Samuel in his *Amazones, Guerrières et Gaillardes* (Amazons, Female Warriors, and Playgirls) (1975). The work contains a detailed examination and classification ("psychological," "allegorical," "pure realist," "transported realist") of much of the literature which would account for Amazons. Samuel's presentation of the various theories is barbed, to the point, and very witty, but he does not seem to see any inconsistency in his own abandonment of the safety and broad vision of his broad view to leap into the fire alongside of John Garstang (*The Hittite Empire* [1909]). Samuel argues that Garstang's long-neglected work contains the first important step toward revealing the true identity of the Amazons of the Greek stories. Garstang, a specialist on Hittite civilization, pointed to evidence that has led some scholars to speculate that the Hittite Empire was on the verge of collapse around 1200 B.C. Hittite difficulties at this time came both from internal rebellions as well as outside attacks on their empire by Achaeans and Phrygians. His theory was simply that small bands of armed priestesses attempted to defend the holy places and their own persons during the turmoil, and that the belligerent sacred women still live as the Amazons of the Greek legends. This theory, Samuel argues, needs only slight modification to be viable. The Hittite priestesses were, in effect, numerous, as well as respected, and most likely "recruited from the more dynamic elements of the feminine population." And the story of Penthesilea is really true, "right to the letter." We need only assume "a temporary alliance of a group of Hittite women with the Trojans."[5]

But how can wives be Amazons? If the Amazons were wives, why didn't the Greeks talk about their husbands? If the Amazons were effeminate, or quasihermaphroditic Hittite men, why didn't the Greeks say so? Why did they glory in fighting strong, fierce, and powerful *women*? And if the Amazons were Hittite women, as Samuel argues, or some of the Hittite women, why don't the extant remains and relics of Hittite culture talk about them and display their influence? Why do Hittite law codes vest all authority in the male as the head of the family?

It is neither possible nor profitable to name all the voices in the late nineteenth- and early twentieth-century scholarly discussion of these issues. All these men arrived at the same discovery: Amazons were grounded in a real phenomenon, but not precisely in real Amazons. They were ready to accept the seven dwarfs, but not Snow White, who, like an autonomous female community, could not possibly have existed. Most people cared little if Amazons were Hittites; Sauromatians; beardless somewhat effeminate men; bloodthirsty, heartless priestesses; or, for that matter, angry Carmelite nuns. The elaborate structures and speculations of the scholars had little to do with the Amazons of Everyman's dreams.

The Amazon has become an important ingredient in one of the best-loved formulas of the twentieth century. The historian of popular culture, John Cawelti, defined formulas as "principles for the selection of certain plots, characters and settings, which possess in addition to their basic narrative structures the dimensions of collective ritual, game and dream."[6] Let the scholars scrutinize east European female burials and seek Amazons' remains in the moldy ruins of four-wheel and six-wheel Scythian wagons. What everyone wants to hear is the story of that splendid Amazon queen whose hatred of and opposition to men melted away before the superior military and sexual prowess of a true hero. She is the Amazon who became the star of stage, screen, and television. She served to reassure men that even if women attempted to undertake activities usually reserved for men, the traditional gender system will always prevail in the end.

The first of the Broadway Amazons appeared in Julian Thompson's 1931 play, *The Warrior's Husband*. Thompson used the theme of Hercules' and Theseus's attack on the Amazon homeland (Pontus, in the play) as the basis for a comedy on sex-role reversal. The play has no message other than to capitalize on the idea that men and women can look. pretty silly when they switch traditional roles, and its greatest glory was to have been the vehicle for the first major Broadway role of a young and virtually unknown actress, Katharine Hepburn (in the role of the Amazon princess Antiope.) The critics unanimously acclaimed her in their reviews of the March 11, 1932 opening, citing her "alluring silhouette and tomboy manners" (The Brooklyn *Eagle*), and "her boyish, steel-spring-like figure, woman in spite herself" (New York *Herald Tribune*.) A decade later, they still recalled *The Warrior's Husband* as the play in which "Katharine Hepburn first bared her lovely legs" (*Morning Telegram*, March 5, 1942). Hepburn shared the critics' praise with Collin Keith-Johnson (Theseus), and especially with Romney Brent, who played the difficult role of Sapiens, husband to Queen Hippolyta. In order to get the most possible mileage from the theme of the world upside-down, Thompson's plot has Queen Hippolyta agree to marry the son of her crusty and corrupt munitions supplier, Pomposia. The marriage is entirely for reasons of state—Hippolyta does not have the cash to equip the five thousand women she needs to oppose the Greek invasion. Thus began the custom of elevating men to the status and protection of marriage in Pontus, when formerly their function had been strictly to amuse and entertain the female warriors (when they grew weary of fighting), and cook, spin, and weave and mend, mind the children, etcetera. Sapiens is a perfect example of masculine grace and beauty, and his long beard is styled into corkscrew curls.

In the opening scene at Hippolyta's palace, the sentries are bickering among themselves. One accuses the other of squandering an entire weeks' pay on her boyfriend. One of the women calls another a "daughter of a dog," which evokes

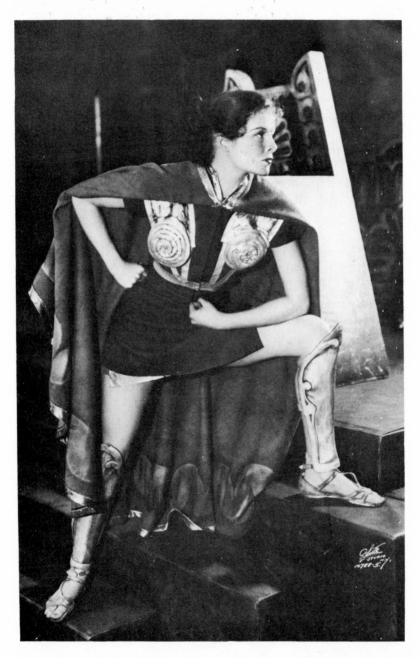

Katharine Hepburn as the Amazon princess Antiope, in *The War-rior's Husband*, 1932. (*Courtesy The New York Public Library*)

a fierce outcry from the Amazon whose "beautiful and pure" little father has been called a dog. And so on. The discussion shifts to Hippolyta's impending marriage with quips like: "What's a husband?—A man you can't get rid of," and, "I'd hate to think of living with the fathers of some of *my* children," and finally, "No civilization can live with a system like that." The marriage proceeds, and so does the invasion. Amazon sentries capture Theseus and the Greek war correspondent, Homer, and lead them to court. It was not until they frisked their captives that they learned of their sex—after all, with all their armor, "they were masquerading as women." Poor Sapiens discovers that his lot is to be a "war groom."

In the next act, Hercules, who after all, has led the Greeks to Pontus to get the sacred girdle of Diana from Hippolyta as one of his labors, challenges the queen to single combat. Thompson has a lot of fun with Greek mythology. In Act 3 the feisty Antiope, carried off to the Greek tents by Theseus, kicks Achilles in the heel. There is a lot of stage business about who is wearing the sacred girdle and where (Antiope and Hippolyta have changed garments to keep their symbol of authority out of Greek hands). Hercules makes off with the borrowed girdle Hippolyta wore for one day (on the basis of which Homer and Theseus declare his labor accomplished), Hippolyta reclaims the sacred one, and Antiope leaves for Greece with Theseus, asking, "isn't surrender sometimes sweeter than victory?" She leaves behind a furious Hippolyta, who promises to turn her hounds on the fallen Amazon princess if she ever again ventures near Pontus.

All this is precisely what Thompson saw as the point of his play:

> there are certain facts which we might as well make up our minds to accept with good graces as to fight grimly against, and one of these is the certainty that the majority of women will, until the end of time, consider the world well lost for love. There is nothing that can be done about it. Women are simply made that way.
>
> Causes of careers may have their appeal up to a certain point, but beyond that they cease to have any importance.[7]

Certainly an important sector of Thompson's audience agreed with him.

The play was enormously popular, perhaps because of its reassuring lesson in traditional values. Only fourteen months after the Broadway opening, a film version of the same title premiered at the New York Radio City Music Hall on May 11, 1933. Elissa Landi drew rave notices in what critics called the "Katharine Hepburn role," but Ernest Truex's Sapiens received mixed reviews. A musical comedy version was immediately slated, but for reasons not entirely clear, the Richard Rodgers and Lorenz Hart production *By Jupiter!* did not open at the Shubert Theatre until June 3 of 1942. It had an all-star cast (Ray Bolger as Sapiens, Constance Moore as Antiope, sets by Jo Mielziner, staging by Joshua Logan). The reviews were raves, and the show did well. The score was largely forgettable, except for that timeless ballad, "Wait Till You See Her," a tune most moderns can hum, without having the slightest idea that it was written for Theseus of Athens, attempting to describe Antiope, the Amazon who stole his heart, to the Greeks.

Of course, musicals are written to be viewed as performances, and not to be read as literature. Yet it is hard not to grin at stage directions that call for an entire company of Amazons to perform a drill dance, and even require a group of eight to slip away and return with toe shoes, swords, and shields to do a special dance in front of the other performers. And only on Broadway can one imagine a Greek army rallied, in the opening song "For Jupiter and Greece," with the cry, "Out of the trenches, and after the wenches!"* (Act I, Scene I). Rodgers and Hart followed Thompson's script of *The Warrior's Husband* with only minor modifications in the story line. The musical ran 427 performances, closing only when Ray Bolger had to fly to the South Seas to entertain American troops.[8] There was even a 1967 off-Broadway revival production, which was successful enough to merit an RCA Victor recording of the full score.

---

*Copyright © 1942 by Chappel & Co., Inc. Copyright renewed. International copyright secured. All Rights Reserved. Used by permission.

If the American G.I. returned home too late to catch *By Jupiter* on Broadway, he could resort to the adventure stories that cluttered men's magazines of the World War II era.[9] The formula was identical—a hero is captured and imprisoned by women of extraordinary beauty, incalculable strength, and immense wealth. Of course, the hero's sexual prowess is so great that the Amazons save him instead of slaughtering him as custom decreed, etcetera.

Amazon dreams don't die, and the formula is as viable as ever. The made-for-television film *Gold of the Amazon Women*, which the razor-tongued critic Katy Kelly dubbed the worst television film of 1979, nevertheless entertained countless viewers by relating the same old story. While some may have smiled with Katy Kelly at the spectacle of paunchy male adventurers locked in bamboo cages by absurdly attired (and equally paunchy) "Amazon" women, for others the film was an opportunity to do precisely the kind of collective dreaming John Cawelti identified as characteristic of the concept of the formula.

But the story of male conquest of the Amazon has not been the only twentieth-century formula. Americans especially have also enjoyed the fantasy of Wonder Woman. Making her debut in 1941, she was an Amazon princess, the daughter of Queen Hippolyta who left the female society of Paradise Island to help the United States of America fight the Nazis, just as Penthesilea had come to aid the Trojans so many years ago. Her creator knew that most of his readers would be blissfully unaware of the letter of the classical tradition, which made the Amazon assistance to the Trojans utterly useless. Like so many of the Amazons before her, Wonder Woman was a male creation, designed mainly to carry a message to men. Under the pen of the psychologist William Moulton Marston (using Charles Moulton as a pen name), Wonder Woman emerged with a heavy burden around her slender neck. She bore the mission of demonstrating the superiority of the feminine principle. But since one cannot be better than Superman, Marston had to settle for making her an equal—a superheroine who was a match for any superhero. This equality was an exciting idea for some of her admirers.

Wonder Woman had all the claptrap and paraphernalia of a magical pop-heroine: an invisible airplane, bullet-resistant bracelets, and a magic lasso. But in addition to these fantastic elements, she had real prowess and true grit. As Gloria Steinem, one of her first fans remarks, "she still had to get to the plane, throw the lasso with accuracy, and be agile enough to catch bullets on the steel-enclosed wrists."[10] And though she never really lost her prowess, with Marston's death in 1947 Wonder Woman lost her psychological message. She was no longer an example of the superiority of the eternal feminine, which in and of itself was no great loss. But worst of all, she became a superheroine who was only incidentally female, and there was hardly any further mention of her Amazonian origin. The 1974 film *Wonder Woman* starred Cathy Lee Crosby and Ricardo Montalban. It does open on an Amazon island, inhabited only by women, but it is mainly an adventure story that does not elaborate on the nature of the society on that distant island. As in the comic strip, Wonder Woman adopts the disguise of the mild-mannered secretary, Diana, who is clearly modeled on Superman's Clark Kent identity, equally as boring, and even more subservient. Also, Wonder Woman's recent metamorphosis as a TV series was primarily as a prime-time adventure story, with virtually no mention or use of the Amazon dream.

The Amazons who occasionally appear in episodes of the comic strips "Prince Valiant" and "Buck Rogers" are, as in the case of Wonder Woman, virtuous and virtually sexless do-gooders. They add variety but little spice to the formula of the superhero.

In the hands of male authors, the Amazon image is an extremely vulnerable one. It is always on the verge of breeding out, or fading away. Sometimes the woman is turned into a "serviceable" wife, sometimes she is killed. But dead or alive in the end, the Amazon in her never survives. The Amazons in male adventures are finished the moment the hero of the story shows his true character. Only from women's pens do stories of Amazon success emerge.

Yet Charlotte Perkins Gilman's *Herland* (1915), the most Amazonian work, perhaps, of early twentieth-century literature, never once mentions the word *Amazon*. Perhaps that celebrated American feminist saw the term as being too loaded with both male hostility and desire. The women of Herland, Gilman's utopia, are neither lesbians nor courtesans—they are not particularly "sexy." For more than two thousand years after the last male among them died, none of the women has expressed her sexuality or been the object of masculine or feminine sexual desire. It is not that the women of Herland are man-hating, it is only that there is hardly any memory among them of what a man is.

Theirs is truly an Amazonian community, a self-sustaining female nation. Like the Amazons of Greek legend (whom Gilman undoubtedly had in mind), once they had to take up arms to defend their society. Once they were the desperate widows of a tribe of slain male warriors, left to their own resources to defend their formerly proud nation. But unlike the women of the Greek stories, they never declared a truce with neighboring tribes in order to procreate with local men. Gilman eliminates an annual mating season as an option for these women, for she has their country sealed off from the world by a disastrous earthquake, leaving the women to die off behind the unscalable walls of a newly created cliff. Hemmed in by nature, they saw their last two male infants die, and they waited with sorrow and resignation for the extinction of their entire race. But Gilman has a miracle occur—one woman gives birth to a daughter, then another daughter, then another, until she bears five in all. And each of these daughters bears five daughters, and so on, until an entire race of women existed who had borne each other through parthenogenesis, each of them able to trace her origin back to this great First Mother. Since Herland women do not produce males, they never had to follow the Amazonian practice of killing or maiming male offspring.

In a brilliant narrative device, Gilman unfolds the story of Herland through the experiences of three American men, three old friends whose common tie since school days was their keen interest "in science." Terry Nicholson is independently wealthy, extremely handsome and "masculine," and very popular and sought after by the ladies back home.

Something is Missing On The Planet Of The Amazon Women. Men.

8:00PM

Buck Rogers

The place, the city of Zantia. Where women are gorgeous. And men are...rare. Buck discovers he is auctioned off to the highest bidder—as he uncovers a dangerous political plot!
Gil Gerard, Ann Dusenberry, Anne Jefferys.

(Courtesy MCA Publishing and Leisure Concepts Inc.)

Jeff Margrave is a medical doctor with the inclination of a poet, and the actual narrator, Vandyke Jennings, is a sociologist who finds great comfort in his jargon and classifications. The men deliberately seek out Herland to confirm a legend conveyed by "natives" they met on one of their many ventures.

The three hero-adventurers no sooner land their chopper but they blunder into the captivity of the calm, somewhat amused, extremely strong, and obviously intelligent women. They soon discover that during their imprisonment they would be expected not only to learn the language of Herland but also to teach their own to the women.

The heroes are, of course, struck by the absence of men; by the plenty and variety of fruits and nuts they are offered as nourishment; by the beauty and the obviously intelligent design and planning of the cities, the streets, and the structures they see.

Having conjured up Herland, Gilman is free to thrust out into any number of avenues of social criticism and satire, and she does. Witness the following dialogue on women and work between the heroes and their student-tutors:

> "Tell us—what is the work of the world, that men do—which we have not here?"
>
> "Oh, everything," Terry said grandly. "The men do everything with us." He squared his broad shoulders and lifted his chest. "We do not allow our women to work. Women are loved—idolized—honored—kept in the home to care for the children."
>
> "What is 'the home'?" asked Somel a little wistfully.
>
> But Zava begged: "Tell me first, do *no* women work, really?"
>
> "Why, yes," Terry admitted. "Some have to, of the poorer sort."
>
> "About how many—in your country?"
>
> "About seven or eight million," said Jeff, as mischievous as ever.[11]

Gilman's main focus was on a critique of the sex relations of her own present time. This she does with humor and skill through her treatment of her hyper-male character, Terry.

Terry is a misfit in Herland. He marches to the rhythm of a drummer who expired in this part of the world centuries ago. His comportment either displeases, or positively offends, and his gestures and signals are those of a beached whale—without purpose or meaning in an alien environment.

It is Terry himself who points to his discomfort with his constant complaint that the women of Herland were not "feminine." The trinkets and glittering paste jewels that he initially presented to them they treated as curiosities and placed in a museum. Herland lacked the excitement of adventure and sexual encounter. As Terry said, "but I like Something Doing. Here it's all done." It is his hope that when the heroes are released from their instructors (who Terry dubbed "the Colonels") and are permitted at least to meet the "girls of Herland, he will find that sexual tension which has been so sadly missing from his life during his period of captivity. At last the Colonels invite the captives to address classes of the younger women. The men are beside themselves with excitement: they carefully primp and groom and select the most colorful and attractive garments they can locate in their new wardrobes. The men soon "were surprised to find, on meeting large audiences, that we were the most highly decorated, especially Terry."

The Colonels ask the heroes to present a sort of synopsis of the world history from which Herland had been so fortuitously detached, and then to meet with their audience in smaller groups. Terry jumped in among the girls, "somewhat as a glad swimmer takes to the sea." Jeff, always the product of high breeding and imbued with a deep sense of chivalry, "approached as to a sacrament." Van, who entered the experience calmly and with goodwill, finds that his circle is the largest. The girls were puzzled by Jeff's reverence, and irritated by Terry's "suave and masterful approach" and his "too-intimate glances." Somel, a Colonel, explains to Van, "we like you the best . . . because you seem more like us." Van is quite insulted, until he recalls "how little like 'women' in our derogatory sense they were."

For Terry, the long-awaited encounter was a most bitter disappointment. He later insisted, when he was back safely in the company of his buddies, that Herland had no girls. All he met were, "boys! Nothing but boys, most of 'em. A standoffish, disagreeable lot at that. Critical, impertinent youngsters. No girls at all."

The experience confirmed for Terry that everything was amiss in Herland. His plaint led Van to reflect: "as to Terry's criticism, it was true. These women, whose essential distinction of motherhood was the dominant note of their whole culture, were strikingly deficient in what we call 'feminity.' This led me very promptly to the conviction that those 'feminine charms' we are so fond of are not feminine at all, but mere reflected masculinity—developed to please us because they had to please us, and in no way essential to the real fulfillment of their great process." Terry, of course, can never come to terms with Herland. He does, like Van and Jeff, come to love deeply the particular woman he first encountered when their helicopter landed. But he is unable to rid himself of the notion that women delight in men who use a show of physical force while courting, and he is eventually expelled from Herland as incorrigible.

Gilman uses the men's bickering over whether or not Herland females are "womanly" to develop a theme which, for feminists, is of vital interest—namely, the nature of motherhood. Her interest was not in motherhood as it has existed, but in motherhood as it may have once or might someday prevail—unmolded, untinted, undirected by partriarchy, which is of course the theme of Adrienne Rich's recent *Of Woman Born*.[12] As Van explains, in Herland there is a complete absence of "the possessiveness, and privatization of motherhood, that the men had observed back home, where each mother was interested only in her own pink bundle of fascinating babyhood, and taking but the faintest theoretical interest in anyone else's bundle, to say nothing of the common needs of *all* the bundles." Motherhood in Herland was "the highest social service—a sacrament really"—undertaken by most of the population once in a lifetime. Gilman's women were in complete mastery of their fecundity—their pregnancies resulted from a protracted period of an intense longing for a child, a longing that the women could, without great difficulty, control and regulate for the good of the entire community. Every baby received the welcome and love of all, and while every woman had ample opportunity to participate in the nurturing of her own child, most of the childrearing was done communally by specially trained experts. Each child had only one name, her own. The women of Herland saw no reason to give a child a tag so that everyone would know which daughter came from which mother. All of this led Van to reflect on "the difference between the purely maternal and the paternal attitude of mind. The element of personal pride seemed strangely lacking." When Terry accused the women of showing no pride in their daughters by their refusal to pass on to them their own name, the women insisted that it was only because "the finished product is not a private one." Herland has no private households of a mother and her children. The women could not understand what it meant to be a "housewife" in the world outside. As Van explained, "they had no exact analogue for our word *home*, any more than for our Roman-based *family*." Nor did the women of Herland have any feeling precisely comparable to patriotism, with its pride and combativeness. The social bond in Herland was made of a different stuff, Van explains: "all the surrendering devotion our women have put into their private families, these women put into their country and race. All the loyalty and service men expect of their wives, they gave, not singly to men, but collectively to one another." And, as it was with the Amazons of old, motherhood in Herland was undertaken not so much for personal fulfillment, but out of a strong sense of devotion and commitment to the community: "and the mother instinct, with us so painfully intense, so thwarted by conditions, so concentrated in personal devotion to a few, so bitterly hurt by death, disease, or barrenness, and even by the mere growth of the children, leaving the mother alone in her empty nest—all this feeling with them flowed out in a strong, wide current, unbroken through the generations, deepening and widening through the years, including every child in all the land."

Although the women of Gilman's Herland have sacrificed their own sexuality, they are not adverse to the possibility of sexual union with men. Jeff and his pregnant wife Celis remain behind, as everyone anxiously awaits this "new kind of

birth." Here Gilman's irony is especially brilliant. Her readers
know very well that it was not the pregnancy that was extraordinary, but the relationship between the male and the
female which produced it. Only by creating the utopia of
Herland, which discarded the traditional male-female gender
and power divisions, could the author envision heterosexual
pairing based on love, mutuality, friendship and trust. Gilman's narrator, Van, leaves Herland with Ellador, Gilman's
new woman, to carry the lessons of that society to the world
outside.

While Gilman had shied away from the word Amazon even
in a work of fiction, her work was followed fifteen years later
by Helen Diner's *Mothers and Amazons* (1930), which claimed
the Amazon as a historical actuality.[13] Diner, a German feminist of two generations ago, adopted a startling and often
fruitful vantage point. She saw herself as writing the "first
feminine history of culture," and to reach her goal she es-
chewed even the pretense of adherence to the historian's
pious shibboleth of impartiality. It did not embarrass her to
note that her work "endeavors to remain as one-sided as
possible." Diner argued that a feminine bias was justifiable
in view of the fact that all existing histories had been penned
from a male point of view. Whenever the historian attempts
to exercise her/his craft, "the male stage remains the darling
object of historical contemplation."

Diner was determined to tell the woman's story. But her
driving interest was not in what women were doing in male-
dominated societies, but in what the world is like "in those
areas where it is arranged by the woman, according to her
nature, to the exclusion of the male as a personality." In other
words, her concern was to investigate the nature of matriarchy, and her focus would necessarily fall mainly on what the
period scholars call "prehistory." Diner argued that this period was an immensely vast span of time: she was ready to
grant the ancient Egyptian claim that their dynasties could
be traced back twenty-eight thousand years before the (probably legendary) first pharaoh, Menes, and she thought the
Sumerian claim to sixty-four thousand years of uninter-
rupted history was well within the realm of possibility. Thus
her vision of prehistory was one of humanity flourishing

century after century under the mild and benign rule of the Great Mothers. It is a lovely and reassuring vision, a candle to light the gloom of mortality and the ephemeral nature of all human endeavor. But as John Lundin, her translator, noted, modern scientific techniques like radioactive carbon dating have tended to "reduce rather than increase the life-spans of the more ancient kingdoms." So this marvelous space, this world enough and time for matriarchy that formed so important a part of Diner's consciousness turns out to be no longer available, already rented to precultural, and probably prehuman occupants.

Of course, Diner did not rest her entire argument on this romanticized vision of a matriarchal past. Like Bachofen (to whom, along with Briffault she acknowledged a debt), she scanned the available historical evidence for Egypt, Crete, Lycia, Caria, Babylon, and other ancient places. She also culled the more recent past of the Celts, the Teutons, India, China, and North and South America for cultural groups exhibiting matriarchal characteristics. She examined the anthropology of her day, citing especially the status of women among the Assam tribes of India, the eastern European Kamchatka, and the apparent total male-female role reversal amongst the Dyak of North Borneo. But ultimately Diner's main interest lay in the question of origins.

One only has to view the title of her first chapter, "Parthenogenesis," to see that Diner is venturing into areas where few had dared to tread. She begins with a paraphrase of Saint John, "In the beginning, there was woman." Contrary to the account in Genesis, Diner made the male secondary, derivative, an afterthought: "the original female in the animal species not only reproduces herself but also is the sole creatress of the male; the male never is anything without the female." Diner argued that the idea of parthenogenesis, in which the female actively creates, was transformed with patriarchy and Christianity into the notion of immaculate conception, wherein the female is passive, receiving rather than creating. The Christian version of the story, Diner argued, obscured and distorted the true primacy of the female.

In general, Diner's book abounds in giant intellectual leaps, and insight after insight ranging from the sublime to the absurd. Her ideas are drawn from analogy with the sciences, from history, from myth and legend, from religion, and from any number of sources she carried with her to her grave. Perhaps it was part of her rebellion against a society in which men made all the rules, perhaps because she herself lacked formal academic training, but her *Mothers* violates all the norms of a serious academic study. It has no footnotes, no bibliography, and, except for occasional catalogues of a group of classical authors, no sources. Even feminists who sympathize with Diner's basic perceptions cannot read the book without a sense of frustration, a frustration that is only exacerbated, for example, when Diner makes the statement that the cult image of Artemis of Ephesus is "ringed with beads of rubies and chains of sacrificed Amazon breasts" and gives no source for this information.

Diner was, of course, condemned by the scholarly world and pretty much ignored by the general public. Like many feminists before her, as well as countless lesbian women, Diner could not envision true female autonomy and a complete blossoming of all womanly potential without discarding sexual relations between women and men. Diner's and Gilman's vision of parthenogenesis would eliminate the need for male participation in reproduction. It is, perhaps, an interesting and ironic footnote to their vision to note that modern attempts at "cloning," whether factual or fraudulent, are designed so that men can produce sons without the use of any genetic material from the female.[14]

The first woman to claim Amazon glory as well as her own lesbian sexuality was the beautiful, wealthy, American horsewoman, Natalie Clifford Barney. She was the woman who inspired Remy de Gourmont's famous *Lettres à l'Amazone*, essays which appeared in the Mecure de France in 1912–13, as well as "l'Amazone" of Romaine Brooks's 1920 painting. Her most recent biographer, Jean Chalon, remarks that Natalie Barney was "the Amazon who engendered hosts of Amazons who continue to flourish today."[15] The "hosts of Amazons" he is referring to are the modern lesbian women who choose to wear the labyris, the double-headed axe historians and poets have always associated with the Amazon. They are staking their claim to an image and role model which the circumstances of patriarchy have otherwise denied to these women, and indeed to all women.

For Natalie Barney, the name Amazon had nothing to do with male derision or desire. It was an expression of her own excellence and transcendence of the ordinary, the humdrum, and the mediocre. Barney's Amazon was a symbol of glory, and in this sense the women of the modern lesbian-feminist movement have shown themselves to be her daughters.

One of the most important works of the modern movement is Monique Wittig's *Les Guérillères*. It is a book about a female society, which is an important counterpart to Gilman's *Herland*, because Wittig's women are in full possession of all the anger and all the sexuality that were missing in Gilman's utopia. Wittig's fantasy is not one of women separated from men by a series of natural disasters, but of women banding together to fight a long war against the forces of male domination, with hand-to-hand, spear-to-spear, and javelin-to-javelin combat. No atomic nuclear bombardment, no plastic explosives, machine guns, helicopters, or tanks mar this vision of suffering and struggle within the boundaries of human comprehension. Wittig's image is of an archaic war, of meaningful personal struggle and personal death.

Wittig's women lay down the burden that has shoved women out of the mainstream and onto the pedestal for ages—that of purity and moral superiority. They are real warriors: they bleed and die, and they also maim and kill.

Monique Wittig's book is only one of the many fantasies of feminine futures that blossomed in recent decades, especially in lesbian literature. These works are eloquent testimony to the fact that men have lost their monopoly on Amazon dreams, and that when women get to tell the story, the Amazons win.

In an age of Broadway Amazons, comic book and television Amazons, of drugstore Trojans, Amazon perfume, Wonder Woman swimsuits and underwear, the Amazon has finally come of age. And while men attempt to account for her, and dream of conquering her and possessing her, modern women in pursuit of self-definition and autonomy have opted to join her.

Notes

1. Guy Cadogen Rothery, *The Amazons in Antiquity and Modern Times* (London: Francis Griffiths, 1910), p. 84. All citations are from pp. 1–2, 11–12, 213 from this edition.
2. Adolphe Reinache, "L'origine des Amazones," *Revue de l'Histoire des Religions*, 67(1913): 277–307.
3. Michael Rostovtzeff, *Iranians and Greeks in South Russia* (Oxford: Clarendon Press, 1922), p. 33.
4. See T. Sulimirski, *The Sarmatians* (New York: Praeger, 1970), p. 48.
5. Pierre Samuel, *Amazones, Guerrières et Gaillardes* (Grenoble: Presses Universitaires de Grenoble, 1975), pp. 71–72.
6. John G. Cawelti, "The Concept of Formula in the Study of Popular Literature," *Journal of Popular Culture*, vol. 3, no. 3 (Winter 1969): 381–90.
7. Julian Thompson, *The Warrior's Husband* (New York: Samuel French, 1931), p. 19. Used by permission of Samuel French, Inc.
8. The script of the production of *By Jupiter* is in the collection of the New York Public Library Theatre Divison at Lincoln Center.
9. Samuel, *Amazones*, p. 17 discusses some of these stories.
10. Gloria Steinem and Phyllis Chesler, *Wonder Woman* (New York: Bonanza Books, 1972), unpaged introduction by Steinem.
11. Charlotte Perkins Gilman, *Herland*, ed. Ann J. Lane (New York: Pantheon, 1979), pp. 60–61. All citations are from pp. 58–59, 69, 75–76, 84–87, 89, 94–95, 99 from this edition.
12. Adrienne Rich, *Of Woman Born* (New York: W. W. Norton, 1976). See especially chapters 4 and 5.
13. Helen Diner, *Mothers and Amazons*, ed. and trans. John Philip Lundin (New York: Anchor Books, 1973), p. xix. All citations are from pp. 1, 22–23, 99 of this edition.
14. See the reputedly accurate account of a millionaire reproducing himself in David Rorvik, *In His Image* (New York: Lippincott, 1978).
15. Jean Chalon, *Portrait of a Seductress, the World of Natalie Barney*, trans. Carol Barke (New York: Crown, 1979), p. 2.

Postscript: The Amazon and the Feminist

As one would expect from a hand-me-down garment, the Amazon image is not a perfect fit for the feminist. The woman who wears it finds that some parts are too narrow and confining, while others are too loose, baggy, and exaggerated. Yet it would be silly for the feminist to discard the Amazon image. It has been through centuries of very hard service, yet it is neither shabby nor worn.

When men first created the image, they gave the Amazons the task of certifying the military strength and the virility of their heroes. Dionysus, Theseus, Heracles, Achilles, and Alexander all had an encounter, either hostile or amorous or both, with an Amazon. At the height of the Athenian civilization, the story of how their ancestors had long ago withstood and triumphed over an Amazon siege of that city-state was a source of patriotic fervor and civic pride.

The Romans, who claimed to descend from the very Trojans who had (unsuccessfully) fought the Greeks, chose not to glory in the legend that Amazons battled alongside them. Instead they continued to develop the Greek theme of conquest of Amazons and they considered such a struggle to be evidence of an almost supernatural ability of power on the part of those who dared to attempt it. The Roman use of Amazon figures on sarcophagi and other funerary monuments clearly established the connection between Amazons and transcendence, even of death. Neither in the Greek nor the Roman classical culture did the Amazon image serve to glorify women. It was used by male authors, artists, and political leaders to enhance their own perception of themselves as historically significant.

In the Middle Ages, the general shift to a Christian sensibility meant that the conquest of Amazons was no longer a feat that men dreamed about, or even considered particularly admirable. As the early church father Lactantius stated, the task of the true Christian was to conquer anger and lust, rather than fierce beasts and various strange ferocious beings. The idea of Amazons nonetheless persisted, chiefly because of the long tradition associating this myth with the legends of Troy. Medieval culture abounds in Troy stories, but in most of them Amazons were victims rather than heroines. Often, they were literally slaughtered in the field by heroes whom medieval authors represented as restoring God's order.

There are two notable exceptions to the typical medieval Troy story. Benoît de Sainte-More's *Roman de Troie* was greatly influenced by the twelfth-century doctrine of romantic love. Benoît's Amazons are great courtly ladies exhibiting all the virtues of the code of chivalry. His work illustrates how much the brief flowering of the cult of courtly love influenced attitudes toward women, even toward mythical women.

The second departure is the many stories of the woman-warriors that appear in the works of Christine de Pisan, whom Joan Kelly, the prominent theorist of women's history called "the first modern woman."[1] Christine's stories are pervaded by a strong sense of fair play, as well as a thoroughly feminist pride in the power and strength of the Amazons and in their civilizing work.

During the Renaissance, the assertion of the strength and competence of the individual, and the possibility of performing great deeds and noble actions reemerged as an ideal, alongside of—and almost in spite of—Christian asceticism. The age was characterized by a marvelous, almost dizzying geographical confusion and by a sense of confidence that all new worlds that European man encountered would easily yield to his comprehension and control. Authors indulged in Amazon dreams, fashioning from the Amazon image a promise of adventure, sexual fulfillment, and unspeakable wealth. The idea of the Amazons' incredible wealth began with Benoît, who had bestowed riches upon his Amazons, along with the other virtues of chivalry. By the time of the Renaissance romances, the Amazon became a marker, a signpost for the explorer of a new land. She is where the gold is.

The Amazon image was important for the Europeans' attempt to understand and give meaning to their new experiences. The legends helped them to comprehend (albeit incorrectly) customs and forms of social organization which otherwise might have been unintelligible to them. It was Columbus, or rather Peter Martyr's account of the voyages of Columbus, who first placed warrior-women in America, thereby creating the New World Amazon, at the same time that his geographic confusion yielded for all posterity the New World Indian.

Just as the Amazon image survived its lengthy service in the glorification of classical heroes, and endured the scorn and moral outrage of Christian authors as well as the boldness and the greed of the conquistadors, it went on to flourish in the Enlightenment. This in spite of the fact that the eighteenth-century philosophes declared themselves to be enemies of myth. Many philosophes were reluctant to dismiss the idea of Amazons. They used what they thought was the possibility, or probability, of an actual Amazon state to construct political and social theories. The Jesuit father Joseph Lafitau could comprehend the seemingly matriarchal customs of the American Huron and Iroquois peoples only by assuming that these, tribes descended from a stock of people that included an authentic Amazon ancestry. The scientist La Condamine considered Amazonism among native American women to be a natural consequence of the brutal treatment they received at the hands of their savage male companions.

The tendency to construct "scientific" theories of culture around an assumption of Amazons as a concrete historical reality reached its culmination in the work of J. J. Bachofen, who developed a theory of cultural stages common to all of humanity. Bachofen's "Amazonian" stage was one he considered only slightly higher or more advanced than pure animal existence. All the art and work of civilization, he claimed, could be accomplished only by overthrowing this extremely

primitive Amazonian level. Just like the Greeks and Romans
of old, Bachofen placed his interest in struggling against and
overcoming Amazons—only this time it was perceived as a
rational struggle in the interest of science and of civilization.

Bachofen may have been inspired in part by Heinrich von
Kleist's *Penthesilea*, written earlier in the century. In this play
Kleist fully exploited the perverse and heroic nature of the
Achilles-Penthesilea tale. His Amazon carried the message
that the impulse to harm and hate is part of intense love.
After biting, indeed chewing the hero Achilles until he was
lifeless, Penthesilea ruefully explained that her act was a mere
"slip of the tongue"; she accidentally "kissed" Achilles to death.
For Kleist and Bachofen the Amazon image stood for raw
sexual energy which was the very antithesis of civilization.

After initial twentieth-century attempts to rationalize the
myth, the Amazon image has by and large slipped from favor
as a vehicle for social theory. But it has lost none of its ability
to remain a vital impulse in the products of popular culture.
Just a scant half century ago, Katharine Hepburn was making
her Broadway debut as an Amazon princess. The 1940s saw
Amazons toe-dancing on Broadway, as well as the birth of
the comic strip "Wonder Woman." Today, Amazons are all
over science fiction literature, especially space fantasies, television programs, and serials, and Madison Avenue adver-
tising copy.

For almost three millennia, the Amazon image had been
shaped by men and molded to tell their dreams. Understand-
ably, some women have come to regard the image as tainted
with male desire and contempt. The Amazon image is not a
garment of their own design, and it requires some modifications to be truly becoming. Yet the fabric of the Amazon
image is still gorgeous, and it promises many more centuries
of serviceable use. The reasons for keeping the image alive
for the feminist go far beyond any considerations of thrift.
The bother of alterations and mending of the image is easily
offset by the glamor, the excitement, and the glory of simply
wearing it. Since the fifteenth century, feminist theorists have
found the Amazon image, in spite of its slight imperfections,
to be one of their most cherished possessions.

Opposition to misogyny—male hatred and disdain of women—has had a long continuous tradition, if only among a tiny handful of women. If misogyny has changed little since Christine de Pisan's day, there has also been little change in the tactics feminists have used against it. As recently as 1946, the eminent historian Mary Beard, in *Woman as Force in History*, drew exactly the same lessons of strength from the Amazon image as had Christine de Pisan five hundred years earlier.

Beard pointed to archaeological evidence of armed female burials as reinforcing "the Greek contention that fighting women, the Amazons, were real women, not creatures of the imagination." She went on to argue that in the fights and wars of early civilization, "women were active in those conflicts in every way that men were, on some scale." Citing Plutarch, Tacitus, Dio Cassius, and other Roman historians, Beard concluded that "women of antiquity not only went to war with marauding war bands or in defense of themselves and their people; they often initiated or inspired great military enterprises undertaken for the conquest and subjugation of others."[2] The point here, however, is not whether Amazons did or did not exist, but that the Amazon stories, for Christine de Pisan as well as Mary Beard, in combination with real historical experience or memories of women who did actually rule and use arms, helped to create an image of women as makers of civilization and culture. As long as civilization continues to be gauged in terms of arms and rule, of political and military leadership, the Amazon image will remain critical for women, even if an Amazon state never receives the sanction and certification of being an indisputable historical fact. It is enough that the legends create a possibility, a foot in the door, a vantage point from which women can see themselves and be seen as movers and shapers of the historical process. Otherwise women are forever doomed to being defined by others and being left out of historical records and accounts.

There is another glory in the Amazon image that is closely related to the opportunity to shape history: the autonomy of the Amazon. She can leave her mark on the shape of events

because she is free to act without having to depend on men.
Here, too, the Amazon image helps to provide a role model.
The warrior-women of classical legends governed and sustained their own communities. They met men unarmed only
for the purpose of mating, and they reared their female
offspring to excel in arms and to make their primary purpose
service to the Amazon community. In the fifteenth century
Christine de Pisan had expressed her love and greatest tribute to her own mother by calling her "strong and free,/ and
more worthy than Penthesilee." Even Madame du Boccage's
very conventional eighteenth-century tragedy has Princess
Menalippe respond to Theseus's remark "in other climes you
would rule with your charms," with the insistence "liberty,
Theseus, is the sovereign good."

More recently, Maxine Hong Kingston wrote in *The Woman
Warrior*, "nobody supports me at the expense of his own
adventure,"[3] while Monique Wittig, in *Les Guérillères*, sees
autonomy not in terms of escaping the onus and guilt of
dependence, but in freeing oneself from oppression: "Has
he not written, power and possession of women, leisure and
enjoyment of women?. . . Better for you to see your guts in
the sun and utter the death-rattle than to live a life that
anyone can appropriate."[4]

A vision of political power, of military prowess, and a role
model of autonomy and hence dignity—these are the treasures embroidered on the Amazon image. The feminist finds
that the garment requires just a few slight alterations. Especially snug and constraining is that part of the image which
depicts the Amazon warrior as motivated by blind and unrelenting hatred of all men. In the oldest Greek legends as
well as the modern formula-stories, the Amazon deals death
to hundreds before she is halted by the extraordinary sword
or lovemaking of the hero to whom she surrenders. But from
the earliest inception of feminist theory, feminism has never
been a program to exterminate, or even to hate men. The
feminist opposes the social relations of male domination and
the misogyny that springs from and helps to perpetuate these
relations. She struggles not against men, but against their
unjust aversion and disdain.

Even feminists who dream of fighting men are uncomfortable dressed in the traditional Amazon image. They feel too confined in the myth of unceasing and undirected warfare. A prominent theme in Kingston's *The Woman Warrior* is the fantasy of being trained to be, and becoming, a female-avenger. She dresses as a male warrior, raises an army of thousands and sets off on her campaigns. Although her focus is on a traditionally male activity, she experiences everything as a wife and mother: "I inspired my army, and I fed them."[5] Even more remarkable than her nurturing, is her dream that her husband comes to fight at her side. She has only to alter her armor from "young thin warrior" to "fat warrior" to accommodate her pregnancy and later the nursing of her infant son. Kingston insists that "marriage and childbirth strengthen the swordswoman, who is not a maid like Joan of Arc."[6] Her woman-warrior suggests that the Amazon image, which permits women to try on masculine roles, can be tight and scanty. It does not cover that part of human nature which has traditionally been considered "female" and which contemporary feminists have claimed with great pride.

But Kingston's book also points to a section of the Amazon image that is too large and exaggerated. Her woman-warrior is secure in her affirmation of female sexuality. The Amazon of the male stories is less happily adjusted. She is a woman whose hypersexuality can satisfy the most virile hero, but she has problems achieving her own sexual satisfaction. According to Diodorus Siculus and Quintus Curtius, Alexander the Great was unable to meet the sexual demands of the Amazon queen Thalestris: an amusing detail, but overblown and frivolous for the feminist who does not define her liberation in terms of driving men to distraction, wearing them out, and keeping them as love slaves.

Equally exaggerated are the late medieval and Renaissance versions of the Amazon myth that depicted the women as virgins. It has occasionally been evoked to answer the misogynist charge that women are unsatiably carnal. But neither in the Amazon stories of Christine de Pisan nor in the work of Maxine Hong Kingston and other moderns, is there any evidence that women are willing to surrender their sexuality for the prize of respectability.

The contemporary emergence of the Amazon-as-lesbian

is a significant development. It is a thoroughly female-defined image. The women of the modern lesbian-feminist movement are insisting that women do not have to renounce love to be free of male authority. They have found love, nurture, and support as women loving women. For women who are not erotically oriented toward other women, however, the lesbian-Amazon image, even though it was created by women, is the wrong fit.

In addition to being here too wide and there too narrow, the Amazon image offers the feminist nothing original or exclusive. Cheap copies and imitations, more or less well executed, abound in all the media. The Amazon formula-story is part of popular comedy and drama, cinema and television, and all manner of literature from culture high and low.

And finally, the feminist is forced to realize that there can be a pain associated with the wearing of the Amazon dream. Its golden threads scratch and wound a thin and delicate skin. The men who created the epitome of the female for purposes of their own never intended to glorify women, and they feel free to use the term Amazon as an insult as readily as they might use it for praise. The image can itch and feel like a hair shirt on the woman who is an Amazon because she is, from a male point of view, oversized, aggressive, competitive, or gay.

Yet as every woman knows, if a garment itches, you simply wear a petticoat underneath it. A woman's wardrobe contains many images from which she can choose: she is the Smiths' daughter, John's wife, or Billy and Susie's mother. But in the Amazon image she can be herself, and the property of no one else: in this dream, she can fly.

Notes

1. Joan Kelly, "Early Feminism and the *Querelle des Femmes*, 1400–1789," *Signs* 8, 1(Fall 1982).Kelly argued that Christine de Pisan represents the first modern female sensibility, in the same way that Petrarch embodies the male one.

2. Mary Beard, *Woman as Force in History* (New York: Macmillan, 1946), pp. 288, 291.
3. Maxine Hong Kingston, *The Woman Warrior* (New York: Knopf, 1976), p. 48.
4. Monique Wittig, *Les Guérillères*, trans. David Le Vay (New York: Avon Books, 1969), p. 116.
5. Kingston, *Woman Warrior*, p. 37.
6. Ibid., p. 48.

Additional Works
Consulted

The notes at the end of each chapter contain complete bibliographical data for all works cited in the text.

Abensour, Leon. 1923 *La femme et le féminisme avant la révolution.* Paris: E. Leroux

Bacon, Helen H. 1961. *Barbarians in Greek tragedy.* New Haven: Yale Univ. Press.

Bayle, Pierre. 1820. *Dictionnaire historique et critique.* Nouvelle édition, vol. 1, "Achilléa," pp. 167–170. Paris: Desoer.

Bell, Susan. 1976. Christine de Pisan (1364–1430). *Feminist Studies* 3:173–184.

Bennett, Florence Mary. 1967. *Religious cults associated with the amazons.* New York: Alms Press.

Bernheimer, Richard. 1952. *Wild men in the Middle Ages.* Cambridge: Harvard Univ. Press.

Boemus, Joannes. 1611. *The manner, lawes, and customes of all nations.* Trans. Edward Aston. London: G. Eld & Francis Burton.

Bush, Douglas. 1932. *Mythology and the renaissance tradition in English poetry.* Minneapolis: Univ. of Minnesota Press.

Cawelti, John G. 1976. *Adventure, mystery, and romance, formula stories as art and popular culture.* Chicago: Univ. of Chicago Press.

Chambers, Frank McMinn. 1941. Some legends concerning Eleanor of Aquitaine. *Speculum* 16:459–468.

Chinard, Gilbert. 1911. *L'Exotisme Américain dans la littérature Française au XVIᵉ siecle.* Paris: Hachette.

Curtius, Ernst Robert. 1953. *European literature in the Latin Middle Ages.* Trans. Willard R. Trask. Bollingen Series, no. 36. New York: Pantheon Books.

Del Real, Carlos Alonso. 1967. *Realidad y leyenda de las amazonas.* Madrid: Espasa Calpe.

Elwood, Louise Butler. 1940. *Queen Califia's land, an historical sketch of California*. San Francisco: Grabhorn Press.

Glover, T. R. 1924. *Herodotus*. Sather Classical Lectures, no. 3. Berkeley: Univ. of California Press.

Gourmont, Remy de. 1929. *Lettres à l'amazone*. Paris: Mecure de France.

Guinot, Eugene. 1840. La lionne. *Les Français paints par eux-mêmes*. vol. 2. Paris: L. Curmier.

Hayn, Hugo. 1905. *Vier neue curiositäten-bibliographieen*. Jena: H. W. Schmidt's Verlagsbuchhandlung, Gustav Tauscher. Reprinted by Zentral-Antiquariat der Deutschen Demokratischen Republic, Leipzig, 1967.

Helbling, Robert. 1975. *The major works of Heinrich von Kleist*. New York: New Directions.

Hennig, Richard. 1957. *Les grandes enigmes de l'universe*. Paris: Robert Laffont.

Herskovits, Melville J. 1938. *Dahomey, an ancient West African kingdom*. New York: J. J. Augustin.

Highet, Gilbert. 1967. *The Classical Tradition*. Corrected ed. Oxford: Oxford Univ. Press.

Hodgen, Margaret T. 1964. *Early anthropology in the sixteenth and seventeenth centuries*. Philadelphia: Univ. of Pennsylvania Press.

Hulsius, Levinus, comp. 1598–1663. [*Voyages*] 6 pts. in 74 vols. Nürnberg: Oppenheym, Hanaw.

Hyginus. 1960. *The myths of Hyginus*. Trans. Mary Grant. Humanistic Studies, no. 34. Lawrence: Univ. of Kansas Publications.

Jones, Howard Mumford. 1964. *O strange new world*. New York: Viking Press.

Kelly, Amy. 1950. *Eleanor of Aquitaine and the four kings*. Cambridge: Harvard Univ. Press.

Klein, Hans. 1919. *Die Antiken Amazonensagen in der deutschen Literatur*. Leipzig: Radelli & Hill.

Kunzle, David. 1973. *The early comic strip*. Berkeley: Univ. of California Press.

Labande, Edmont-René. 1952. Pour une image véridique d'Aléinor d'Aquitaine. *Bullétin de la Société des Antiquaires de l' Oeust*. 2:195–234.

Leonhard, Walter. 1911. *Hetticher und amazonen*. Leipzig: B.G. Teubner.

Lopez, Duart. 1598. *Warhaffte und Eigentliche Bescreibung des Königreichs Congo in Africa*. Trans. Augustinum Cassidorum. Illus. Israel von Bry. Frankfurt: Johan Saur.

(Lydgate, John). 1555. *The ancient historie and onely trewe and sincere cronicle of the warres betwixte the Grecians and the Trojans . . . written by Daretus a Trojan and Dictus a Grecian . . . digested in Latin by Guido de Colompris & trans. into English by John Lydgate.*

Macrobius. 1969. *The saturnalia.* Trans. Percival Vaughan Davies. New York: Columbia Univ. Press.

Mansur, Melvin White. 1940. *The treatment of Homeric characters by Quintus of Smyrna.* Ph.D. dissertation, Columbia University.

Meade, Marion. 1977. *Eleanor of Aquitaine.* New York: Hawthorn Books.

Minns, Ellis H. 1913. *Scythians and Greeks, a survey of ancient history and archeology on the north coast of the Euxine from the Danube to the Caucasus.* 2 vols. Cambridge: Cambridge Univ. Press

Morison, Samuel Eliot. 1940. *Portuguese voyages to America in the fifteenth century.* Cambridge: Harvard Univ. Press.

Nery, F. J. de Santa-Anna. 1885. *Le pays des amazones.* Paris: L. Finzine.

Nicetas. 1685. Vol. 5. Histoire de l'empereur Jean Comene. *Histoire de Constantinople.* Trans. Paris: Cousin Damian Foucault.

O'Gorman, Edmundo. 1961. *The invention of America.* Bloomington: Indiana Univ. Press.

Olschki, Leonardo. 1941. Ponce de Léon's fountain of youth: history of a geographic myth. *Hispanic American Historical Review,* vol. 21, no. 3, pp. 361–385.

Orellana, Francisco de. 1859. The voyage of Francisco de Orellans down the river of the amazons, A.D. 1540–41. *Expeditions into the valley of the amazons, 1539, 1540, 1639.* Trans. and ed. Clements R. Markham. London: Hakluyt Society.

Paley, F. A. 1876. *On Quintus Smyrnaeus and the "Homer" of the tragic poets.* Cambridge, England: J. Palmer.

Phillips, James E., Jr. 1942. The woman ruler in Spenser's "Faerie Queene." *Huntington Library Quarterly. 5:211–234.*

Purchas, Samuel. 1617. *Purchas his pilgrimage, or relations of the world and the religions observed in all ages . . .* London: William Stansby.

Redlich, Roman. 1942. *Die Amazonensarkophage des 2 & 3 iahrhunderts n. Christ.* Schriften zur kunst des altertums, Archeologischen Institut des Deutschen Reiches, Band 4. Berlin.

Reinach, Salomon. 1909. *Repertoire de reliefs Grecs et Romains.* 2 vols. Paris: Ernest Leroux.

Rice, Tamara Talbot. 1961. *The Scythians.* New York: Praeger.

Richardson, Joanna. 1967. *The courtesans, the demi-monde in 19th century France.* Cleveland: World.

————. 1971. *La vie Parisienne, 1852–1870*. London: Hamish Hamilton.

Roscher, W. H. 1884–1856. Amazonen. *Lexikon der Greichischen und römischen mythologie*. Leipzig: B. G. Teubner.

Rosenberg, Melrich V. 1937. *Eleanor of Aquitaine*. Boston: Houghton Mifflin.

Tarbell, F. B. 1920. Centauomachy and amazonomachy in Greek art: the reasons for their popularity. *American Journal of Archeology*. 24:226–231.

Thévet, André. 1575. *La cosmographie universelle*. 2 vols. Paris: Pierre.

Toepffer. 1894. Amazones-mythologisch in A. Pauly, G. Wissowa, and W. Kroll, *Real-Encyclopädie d. Klassischen Altertumswissenschaft*. vol. 1, pt. 2. Stuttgart: Alfred Druckenmüller.

Tuve, Rosemund. 1940. Spenser and some pictorial conventions with particular reference to illuminated manuscripts. *Studies in philology*. 37:149–176.

William, Archbishop of Tyre. 1943. *A history of deeds done beyond the sea*. vol. 2. Trans. Emily Atwater Babcock and A. C. Krey. New York: Columbia Univ. Press.

Withington, Robert. 1918–1920. *English pageantry*. 2 vols. Cambridge: Harvard Univ. Press.

Wolff, Hans M. 1938. Kleist's Amazonenstaat im Lichte Rousseaus. *Modern Language Association of America publications*. 53:189–206.

Wright, Celeste Turner. 1940. The Amazons in Elizabethan literature. *Studies in Philology*. 37:433–456.

Wulfing, Ernst, ed. 1902, 1903. *The laud Troy book*. Early English Text Society, original ser. nos. 121, 122. London: Kegan Paul, Trench, Trübner.

INDEX

[Page numbers in *italics* refer to illustrations.]

233